FLORIDA STATE
UNIVERSITY LIBRARIES

JUN 12 1997

TALLAHASSEE, FLORIDA

Olive Branch and Sword

Olive Branch and Sword

The United States and Mexico, 1845–1848

by DEAN B. MAHIN

McFarland & Company, Inc., Publishers
Jefferson, North Carolina, and London

To Ursula

British Library Cataloguing-in-Publication data are available

Library of Congress Cataloguing-in-Publication Data

Mahin, Dean B., 1925–
 Olive branch and sword : the United States and Mexico, 1845–1848 / by Dean B. Mahin.
  p. cm.
 Includes index.
 ISBN 0-7864-0258-X (library binding : 50# alkaline paper) ∞
 1. Mexican War, 1846–1848. 2. United States — Foreign relations — Mexico. 3. Mexico — Foreign relations — United States. 4. Mexican War, 1846–1848 — Peace. 5. United States — Foreign relations —1845–1849. 6. Polk, James K. (James Knox), 1795–1849. 7. Trist, Nicholas Philip, 1800–1874. I. Title.
E408.M34 1997
973.6'22 — dc21   96-29655
                                                                CIP

©1997 Dean B. Mahin. All rights reserved

No part of this book, specifically including the index, may be reproduced or transmitted in any form or by any means, electronic or mechanical, including photocopying or recording, or by any information storage and retrieval system, without permission in writing from the publisher.

Manufactured in the United States of America

McFarland & Company, Inc., Publishers
 Box 611, Jefferson, North Carolina 28640

Contents

Preface		1
Prologue:	*Talents, Integrity, and Honor*	5
ONE	Our Flag Is Insulted	17
TWO	A Common Destiny	30
THREE	The Cup of Forbearance	47
FOUR	Hostilities May Be Considered as Commenced	62
FIVE	A Peace Must Be Conquered	77
SIX	Bread Upon the Waters	91
SEVEN	Too Much Blood Has Been Shed	108
EIGHT	The Painful Necessity	116
NINE	Mr. Trist Is Recalled	125
TEN	I Will Make a Treaty	137
ELEVEN	An Exceedingly Laborious Negotiation	151
TWELVE	A Solemn Duty	164
THIRTEEN	A Firm and Universal Peace	174
FOURTEEN	A Bold and Firm Course	182
Epilogue:	*A Friend of Peace*	187
Notes		201
Index		227

Maps
(by Richard Brome)

Disputed Area Between Nueces and Rio Grande Rivers   38

Central Mexico   92

Vicinity of Mexico City   109

U.S.–Mexican Border Between Rio Grande and Colorado Rivers   154

Preface

On May 14, 1846, two days after the U.S. Congress declared that the United States was at war with Mexico, Secretary of State James Buchanan brought President James K. Polk a draft circular to U.S. ministers abroad. It included a statement that the United States had not gone to war to obtain territory from Mexico. Since Polk had gone to war to acquire California, he wrote a new paragraph: "We go to war with Mexico solely for the purpose of conquering an honorable and permanent peace... We shall bear the olive branch in one hand, the sword in the other."

For three years Polk carried the olive branch in one hand and the sword in the other, giving priority first to one and then the other. The present book is mainly the story of these fluctuating but consistent policies toward Mexico and of the unique role of a little-known diplomat — Nicholas P. Trist — in bringing the war to an early conclusion that saved the United States from becoming caught in a quagmire in Mexico.

In the United States, the war with Mexico from 1846 to 1848 is regarded as a relatively minor incident in a century of westward expansion. American historians have tended to view the war as an episode in the internal development of the United States and have paid relatively little attention to the diplomatic history of the Mexican War era or to the international ramifications of the war. In Mexico the war remains a bitter memory and a dark shadow over U.S.-Mexican relations.

Many factors contributed to tensions between the United States and Mexico in the quarter century after Mexican independence from Spain. These included the very different cultures of the two societies, the extreme nationalism of two new nations, deep-seated racial antipathies, grossly inadequate and extremely slow international communications, ineffective diplomatic representation, the misjudgments of political leaders in both countries, and, especially, conflicting territorial interests in western North America. Responsibility for the beginning of the war is shared by both countries. The United

States provoked the war by sending an army into an area the Mexicans regarded as their national territory; Mexico began the war by attacking the U.S. Army in the disputed area.

The 150th anniversary of the war with Mexico offers an opportunity for a new look at its beginning and the process by which it was ended. Although the story of U.S.-Mexican relations prior to the war is intertwined with the stories of the independence of Texas from Mexico and of the later U.S. annexation of Texas, general readers — for whom this book is primarily written — easily lose their way among the twists and turns of these complex stories. The broad survey in Chapter One of U.S.-Mexican and Texas-Mexican relations prior to 1845 provides the general reader with essential background but is not intended as a comprehensive account of U.S.-Mexican relations or of Texas history prior to annexation.

Two other caveats are necessary. First, this book is not a military history of the war with Mexico. That history has been reviewed in some detail in at least eighteen books published in the United States, nine of which appeared since 1950. Some of these books can be found at most public libraries. This book provides only essential minimum information on military events that influenced the process toward peace.

Second, this book is concerned primarily with the story of U.S. diplomacy in the Mexican War period. It focuses on Polk's and Trist's perceptions of developments and intentions in Mexico, rather than on detailed analysis of the policies and politics of the five Mexican governments between 1845 and 1848. The condensed quotes from Polk's diary and messages and from Trist's dispatches and letters convey their perceptions and attitudes much more clearly than any summaries I might write.

No other book in print provides as comprehensive an analysis of James K. Polk's policies toward Mexico. Although my highly critical assessment of Polk will not please those in the United States who consider him one of our great presidents, it will be thought much too charitable by most Mexican scholars and by those in the United States who have absorbed Mexican viewpoints on the war.

The book contains the first detailed account of Trist's peace mission in Mexico and of Polk's reactions to the mission. Although few Americans have ever heard of him, Nicholas Trist was the only man who single-handedly ended a major American war. The treaties ending other such wars were negotiated by large delegations. Trist was the sole American negotiator of the treaty that ended America's first foreign war and increased U.S. territory by about one-third. Moreover, he negotiated the treaty in spite of orders from the president to abandon his peace mission in Mexico.

Trist was sent to Mexico in the spring of 1847, following American victories in northern and central Mexico, to deliver Polk's peace terms. The Mexican president, Santa Anna, refused to negotiate until the American army won two more battles near the Mexican capital in August. Initial negotiations ended when Santa Anna rejected the peace terms delivered by Trist. Polk, angered by the rejection of his peace terms and unaware of subsequent military and political events in Mexico, ordered Trist to abandon his mission. By the time Trist received the recall order in mid–November, however, the Mexican capital had been captured by the American army, Santa Anna had been deposed, and Trist was about to open new peace negotiations with a new civilian government.

Fearful of the dire consequences if this chance for peace were lost, Trist decided to ignore the recall order and to proceed with negotiations in accordance with his original instructions. Polk was furious with Trist for his insubordination, but the peace treaty Trist signed on February 2, 1848, contained almost everything Polk had hoped for. He sent it to the Senate, which approved it on March 10, 1848, but the ungrateful president refused to pay Trist for his services performed after he received the recall order.

For nearly a century and half, Trist's role has remained in the shadows because of the secrecy surrounding his mission, his inability to write a history of the mission, the nation's subsequent preoccupation with the Civil War, and the inclination of later generations to regard the extension of the nation to the Pacific as the nation's inevitable destiny.

The present book examines the very real danger — until Trist decided to ignore the recall order — that James K. Polk's stubborn policies in Mexico would result in a disastrous long-term military occupation in Mexico or an equally dangerous effort to annex additional Mexican territory below the Rio Grande. It examines and rejects the thesis that Trist prevented the annexation of all of Mexico by the United States. Finally, it concludes that the unexpected prompt end of the war limited the scope of the growing controversy over slavery in territories acquired from Mexico and provided essential prerequisites for the Great Compromise that avoided civil war in the United States in the 1850s.

Prologue: Talents, Integrity, and Honor

Prior to his mission in Mexico, Nicholas Philip Trist was closely associated with five of the men who served as president of the United States in the first half of the nineteenth century — Thomas Jefferson, James Madison, Andrew Jackson, Martin Van Buren, and James Buchanan.

Trist's association with Jefferson was the result of a friendship between his grandmother and Jefferson which began as the Revolution was ending in 1783. That year Jefferson lived for ten weeks at a Philadelphia boardinghouse run by a Mrs. House and her daughter, Mrs. Eliza Trist. In 1775, Eliza House had married a British army doctor, Lieutenant Nicholas Trist. By 1783, Dr. Trist had been released from British service and had gone to a settlement of former British officers near Natchez. Eliza planned to join him in the spring with their 8-year-old son, Hore Browse Trist.

Jefferson arrived in Philadelphia only a few months after the death of his wife. The lonely widower enjoyed the sympathetic friendship of Eliza Trist, a kind and sensitive woman, and found in her "a rare pattern of goodness, prudence, and good sense."[1] During these weeks in 1783, Jefferson established a friendship with her that lasted as long as they both lived.

When Eliza arrived in Natchez the following year, she learned that her husband had died of yellow fever. She returned to the boardinghouse in Philadelphia and continued the role of landlady to the Founding Fathers during the drafting of the Constitution in 1787 and during sessions of the new Congress of the United States held in Philadelphia during the 1790s.[2] In 1798, Eliza Trist, her 23-year-old son, and his new wife, Mary Brown Trist, settled in Charlottesville, Virginia, near Vice President Jefferson's home at Monticello. Eliza's first grandchild, Nicholas Philip Trist, was born there on June 2, 1800. The next spring Eliza's former boarder was sworn in as third president of the United States at the new capital in Washington

City. That summer President Jefferson also had a new grandchild; Virginia Jefferson Randolph, who would become Mrs. Nicholas P. Trist, was born at Monticello on August 22, 1801.

In 1802, President Jefferson appointed Hore Browse Trist collector of customs at Natchez; after the Louisiana Purchase in 1803, he was named collector at New Orleans. The following year Hore Browse Trist died of yellow fever, as had his father. Nicholas' mother married a New Orleans lawyer and, after he died in 1810, a Creole cotton and sugar planter. Nicholas and his brother, another Hore Browse Trist, attended school in New Orleans, and the teenage boys were there or close when General Andrew Jackson repelled a British army at nearby Chalmette in 1815.

Eliza Trist returned to Virginia in 1817 and told ex-president Jefferson of her concern for the education of her teenage grandsons. His response was to invite the boys to live for a while at Monticello. The large family of Jefferson's daughter, Martha Jefferson Randolph, lived with him. During the eight months he spent at Monticello in 1818-19, young Nicholas Trist formed a strong attachment for the Jefferson granddaughter nearest his own age, Virginia Jefferson Randolph.

In 1819, Trist received an appointment to the U.S. Military Academy, perhaps from Jefferson's neighbor, President James Monroe. There he developed a friendship with Andrew Jackson Donelson, nephew of the hero of New Orleans. Trist left West Point after his third year, without graduating. His decision was influenced by a frail constitution that was ill-suited to life in the frontier army, an independent nature that resisted army discipline, and the impossibility of supporting a wife on a lieutenant's pay.

For the next three years, Nicholas assisted his brother with the development of a plantation near Donaldsonville, 60 miles up the Mississippi from New Orleans. In his spare time he studied law, using a small collection of law books assembled with Jefferson's assistance. In the summer of 1824, Nicholas returned to Virginia, and he was married to Virginia Jefferson Randolph in the parlor at Monticello on September 11, 1824. They remained at Monticello for four years, two before and two after Jefferson's death.

Nicholas was the only other adult male in the large family at Monticello. Jefferson's son-in-law, Thomas Mann Randolph, was estranged from his wife and lived elsewhere. The oldest grandson, Thomas Jefferson Randolph, managed his father's nearby estate, and the other Randolph boys were still young. The new grandson-in-law often joined Jefferson on his morning rides and participated actively in the drawing room conversation after dinner. Trist wrote that his relationship with Jefferson grew into "an intimacy as close, a familiarity as unreserved, as was permitted by the disparity of years."[3] This statement is supported by comments by James Madison that

Jefferson "thought highly" of Trist[4] and by a Virginia congressman that Trist "possessed in the highest degree the confidence and affection of Mr. Jefferson."[5]

During Trist's first year at Monticello, Jefferson was still in good health, and there were many interesting visitors, including Congressman Daniel Webster of Massachusetts, Senator Thomas Hart Benton of Missouri, and Jefferson's ally during the Revolution, the Marquis de Lafayette. Trist resumed his study of law under Jefferson's general supervision, but his reading soon wandered far afield. Jefferson had sold his extensive library to the U.S. government after the British burned the infant Library of Congress in 1814, but he had accumulated about 1,000 more books by 1824. Trist had studied mathematics, engineering, and military science at West Point and had read law for three years in Louisiana. Now his education was broadened by a wide exposure to political science and public affairs. Given the library, the resident sage, and the visiting statesmen, Monticello in 1824 and 1825 was an ideal place to acquire a liberal education. After the University of Virginia opened its doors nearby on March 7, 1825, the professors were frequent dinner guests at Monticello.

Trist's second year as a member of Jefferson's family was overshadowed by the failing health of the Sage of Monticello. When Lafayette returned to Monticello in August 1825 after his triumphal tour of America, Jefferson was immobilized on his couch in a painful condition. By the beginning of 1826, it was obvious that he would not live much longer and that his creditors would begin hounding the family as soon as Jefferson was dead. The only happy event of that gloomy spring was the birth of the Trists' first child, a girl. She was named Martha Jefferson Trist after her grandmother and was the last child born at Monticello during Jefferson's lifetime.

Trist helped to nurse Jefferson as he held on to life until the nation's 50th Fourth of July. That morning Trist wrote his sister-in-law that Jefferson "has been to the last the same calm, clear-minded, amiable philosopher."[6] Jeff Randolph and Nicholas Trist were with the author of the Declaration of Independence when he died at midday on July 4, 1826.

Nicholas and Virginia Trist remained at Monticello for two very difficult years after Jefferson's death. To them fell the heartbreaking task of dismantling Jefferson's estate to meet some of his debts. The plantation slaves were sold, except for a few given their freedom pursuant to Jefferson's will. Most of the household furnishings were sold in an auction in January 1827. The Trists and some of the older Randolphs existed for nearly two years in the "bare castle" with scarcely a spare bed or chair.

During 1827 and 1828, Trist searched for suitable employment, while living on his share of the profits of the plantation at Donaldsonville. Although he considered a law practice, he feared he was not suited for a legal career. He bought a share in a small Charlottesville newspaper but quarreled with his associates and never played an active editorial role.

The only positive development in this dreary period was the beginning of a close association with ex-president James Madison. Together Madison and Trist carried on the labor of love of Jefferson's last decade, the development of the University of Virginia. Madison succeeded Jefferson as rector, and Trist was appointed secretary of the university's Board of Visitors. Their efforts on behalf of the fledgling university created a bond between the aging Madison and young Trist which persisted during the remaining decade of Madison's life. During those years Madison wrote Trist 65 letters, entertained him from time to time at Montpelier, and enlisted him as a defender of the Constitution against the insidious doctrine of "nullification." Trist became a true disciple of the Father of the Constitution. He wrote in 1831 that Madison's mind was "replete with the honey of history, fully stored with digested truth and practical wisdom."[7]

In the fall of 1828, Secretary of State Henry Clay offered Trist a clerkship in the State Department. Although the Whig statesman had been no political friend of Jefferson, he had been appalled by the destitute situation of Jefferson's family after his death. Clay wrote Trist that he hoped the appointment would "contribute to the personal comfort of your mother-in-law, Mrs. Randolph."[8] Trist delayed his departure for Washington until the birth of his second child in mid–November. The boy, Thomas Jefferson Trist, was a deaf mute; he would later attend and then teach at a school for the deaf in Philadelphia.

By the time Trist arrived in Washington, President John Quincy Adams had been defeated by the hero of New Orleans, General Andrew Jackson. Trist worked in the State Department under Henry Clay in the last three months of the Adams administration and remained for the first four years of the Jackson administration. He kept his position in the new Democratic administration because of his relationship with Jefferson, founder of the Democratic party, and his friendship at West Point with Jackson's nephew, Andrew Jackson Donelson, who was now his uncle's secretary in the White House.

Jackson's secretary of state was Martin Van Buren, a former New York state official and legislator, U.S. senator, and governor. Trist established a solid friendship with Van Buren. A decade later, when Van Buren had succeeded Jackson in the White House, he kept Trist as consul in Havana despite strong charges against him by British officials and by American mariners.

Most of the diplomatic problems of Jackson's first term involved trade, boundaries, or claims by Americans against foreign governments. One of Trist's assignments was to deal with correspondence related to the American "spoliation" claims against France dating back to the Napoleonic wars and to claims by the French government arising from its interpretation of the Louisiana Purchase treaty of 1803.[5] These were logical assignments for a clerk who knew French and had grown up in Louisiana. He was also involved with other diplomatic problems of the period, including the dispute with England over the Maine boundary, the negotiation for the opening of English ports in the West Indies to American trade, and the American offer to purchase Texas from Mexico.

Trist's advancement in the Jackson administration resulted from the social and family crisis of Jackson's first term, the Eaton Affair. In the early 1820s, bachelor Senator John Eaton of Tennessee apparently had an affair in Washington with his innkeeper's daughter, Peggy O'Neal Timberlake, while her husband was at sea in the navy. Timberlake later died, Peggy married Eaton, and he became Jackson's secretary of war. The wives of Jackson's other cabinet members refused to mingle socially with Peggy Eaton. Since Jackson's wife had died just before he became president, his nephew's wife became the presiding lady at the White House. When Emily Donelson also refused to receive Peggy Eaton, Jackson sent the Donelsons back to Tennessee. The Eaton Affair was resolved by Eaton's resignation, but Jackson needed a temporary secretary until Donelson's return could be arranged. He chose Donelson's friend in the State Department, Nicholas P. Trist.

During the four months that Trist served as full-time secretary to the president, from mid–May to mid–September 1831, he earned Andrew Jackson's respect and affection. Several years later Jackson gave Trist a letter of reference: "Whenever you meet a friend of mine whose acquaintance may be desirable to you, I beg you to show him this letter as an evidence of the great confidence which I repose in your talents, integrity, and honor."[9]

Trist also became a great admirer of Old Hickory. He was in the cabinet room one day when the secretary of state commented that acceptance of a compromise line for the Maine border would raise a clamor in New England. "I care nothing for clamors, sir," Jackson retorted. "I do precisely what I think just and right!" The comment, recorded by Trist and used by several of Jackson's biographers, captures the essence of Trist's view of Jackson and, in large measure, of himself.[9]

When Donelson returned to Washington in the fall, Trist returned to the State Department. During the next several years, he was called back to the White House on several occasions, however, to take over for brief periods some or all of the duties of the secretary to the president. Van Buren had resigned as secretary of state in the spring of 1831, and his successor was a former Louisiana senator, Edward Livingston. Trist had known Livingston in Louisiana and may have had a family connection with him through his mother's second marriage to Philip Livingston Jones.

In the fall of 1831, Trist was guide and mentor in Washington to two young Frenchmen his brother-in-law had met in Boston. The purpose of their visit, Joseph Coolidge wrote, was "to see and judge from personal observation ... the nature and operation of our political institutions."[10] Trist was their indefatigable guide in Washington and helped them gather documents. One of the men, M. de Tocqueville, later sent Trist a copy of his book, *Democracy in America*, which has remained a classic.

Late in 1831, Virginia Trist gave birth to their third and last child, another Hore Browse Trist. He would become a doctor and serve as a medical officer in the U.S. Navy and in the Confederate army. Nicholas was the only breadwinner in the large family that lived with him in Washington in the early 1830s. There were nineteen persons in the eleven-room house, including five Trists, Virginia's mother, six of Virginia's brothers and sisters, two children of her dead sister, and servants. During the winter adults and children spent daytime hours together in a single room, because they couldn't afford firewood to heat the whole house.

For several years during Jackson's first term, Nicholas Trist was an active although anonymous participant in the national debate over the doctrine of "nullification," the alleged right of a state to nullify a law to which it strongly objected. The doctrine's premise was that the Constitution was a compact between sovereign states, each of which had the right to "nullify" any action of the Federal government which it deemed an infraction of the constitutional compact. This doctrine was formulated mainly by John C. Calhoun of South Carolina as a way to avoid the impact of tariff legislation that increased the cost of manufactured goods imported by Southern states.

James Madison was very upset that in justification of their doctrine, the nullifiers used resolutions drafted by Jefferson and adopted by the Virginia and Kentucky legislatures in 1798 to protest the oppressive Alien and Sedition Acts. Madison wrote Trist that the Virginians had issued only an abstract declaration calling for protests against the abuses, while the South Carolinians declared their right to actual resistance.[11]

Trist was in the Senate gallery when Senator Daniel Webster replied to the assertion of the nullification doctrine by South Carolina Senator Robert Hayne. Webster's oratory stimulated Trist to contribute letters to newspapers rebutting some of the principal arguments of the nullifiers. During the subsequent three years, Trist wrote at least eight long letters that were printed by newspapers in Washington or Richmond, as well as other cities.[12] The letters included constitutional arguments against the doctrine of nullification which were derived in part from Trist's extensive correspondence with the Father of the Constitution, James Madison. He encouraged Trist to use the arguments where they would do the most good without indicating their source. As was customary in that era, each letter was signed only with a slogan or vague identifier such as "A Virginian," and the author of the letter and the source of the arguments remained unknown to readers.

In November 1832 a popular convention convened by the South Carolina legislature adopted a Nullification Ordinance that prohibited state or Federal officials from collecting in South Carolina the customs duties required by the tariff acts adopted by the Congress earlier that year. President Jackson's response, the Nullification Proclamation, was one of the most important state papers of his presidency. There are various indications that Nicholas Trist contributed ideas and language used in the Nullification Proclamation. The opportunity to do so was provided by his close relationships with Jackson and with Edward Livingston, who prepared the final draft of the proclamation. Trist was the only person closely associated with Jackson who had already written numerous rebuttals of the nullification doctrine. He had been provided arguments against the doctrine by the ultimate authority on the U.S. Constitution, James Madison. At least seven paragraphs of the Nullification Proclamation contain language that is strikingly similar to language in Madison's letters to Trist or in Trist's letters to newspapers.

Trist's last published letter on nullification, which appeared at the end of 1833, dealt with the theoretical possibility that a single state would be so oppressed within the American Union that it would seek its salvation though independence. Trist had not yet considered the possibility that a number of states might secede together or that sectional conflict over slavery might be the cause of the separation. But Jackson had thought of these grim possibilities. "The nullifiers in the South," he wrote an old friend in the spring of 1833, "intend to blow up a storm on the slave question... These men would do any act to destroy this union and form a southern confederacy."[13]

In the spring of 1833, the U.S. consul in Havana died of cholera, and Jackson offered Trist the job. Havana was one of the largest and busiest ports in the Western Hemisphere. Cuba was still a Spanish colony, and the consul in Havana was the only representative of the U.S. government on the island. In that era, consuls derived their income from fees charged for services to shipmasters and others. Trist thought his income from the post would be two to three times his meager State Department salary, although this estimate proved excessive.

Trist served as American consul in Havana for eight years and lived in Cuba for three-and-a-half more years. During the first three years, his family remained in Virginia, and he returned there each year for the summer and early fall season, during which few American ships called at Havana and consular activities were limited. After her mother died in 1836, Virginia Trist went to Cuba with three children and two spinster sisters, but she was never happy there. She survived the torrid tropical climate and the stuffy Spanish society for three winters and two summers and then sailed to Europe in the spring of 1839 with their daughter and younger son; their older son was in a school for the deaf in Philadelphia. Virginia remained in Europe for more than two years, living mainly at St. Servan on the French coast. Nicholas Trist was left alone during a very difficult period in which he had to defend himself against charges that he had dealt unfairly with American mariners and aided those who wanted to use American ships or the American flag in the illegal trade in slaves.

More than 800 sugar plantations in Cuba were operated with slaves. Although Spain had outlawed the slave trade in 1820 under British pressure, the importation of slaves into Cuba continued with the secret support of the Spanish captains general, who held absolute power on the island. The U.S. laws prohibiting the slave trade were not energetically enforced, and the United States refused to condone British searches of ships flying the American flag, even if they were suspected of carrying slaves. As a result, slave-traders had more security under the American flag than any other. Moreover, American shipbuilders were building ships that were too fast to be caught by the slow British vessels patrolling the African coast. While it was illegal to build or fit a ship in the United States for the slave trade, there was no law against selling an American ship to slavetraders outside the United States.

British officials in Havana thought Trist had failed to prevent the use of the American flag by slavetraders. They assumed that because Trist had grown up in the slave states of Louisiana and Virginia, his professed hatred for the trade in slaves was insincere. But his grandmother and mother, Northern women from the free-soil state of Pennsylvania, had filled his mind with hatred of the slave trade and the institution of slavery.[14]

The readiness of British officials to make serious charges against an American consul was enhanced by the strong antislavery movement in Britain, which had resulted in the abolition of slavery in the British colonies in 1833, and by diplomatic tensions in the later 1830s. Relations between the United States and British governments, which were never very cordial in the nineteenth century, were especially strained in the late 1830s by American sympathy for an unsuccessful insurrection against the British in Canada and by boundary disputes on both ends of the U.S.-Canadian border.

In 1836, British commissioners stationed in Havana under a treaty with Spain charged that four American schooners, obviously fitted out for the slave trade, had been allowed to depart for Africa under the American flag. Trist refused to be drawn into correspondence on the matter, but the foreign secretary in London sent a protest to the American minister.[15]

In 1839 the British commissioners appealed to Trist to take action against the American ship *Venus*, which had reportedly landed 800 slaves on the Cuban coast and was expected momentarily in Havana. Trist replied that he could not act without legal evidence. Information on slave ships was easily obtained on the Havana docks, but it was only hearsay and no one would provide evidence that could be used in court against the slavetraders. In Cuba, Trist reported to the State Department, the slave trade was "a pursuit denounced in every way by law and upheld by an overwhelming public opinion."[16] The sugar planters needed slaves to work their plantations, and the Spanish officials ignored the violations of the law in return for a share of the profits.[17]

When the *Venus* arrived in Havana after discharging her cargo of slaves, she had a new name and was flying a Portuguese flag. She had made the trip to Africa too quickly to have obtained authentic Portuguese registry in a Portuguese port. The British commissioners insisted that Trist go on board to investigate, but he maintained he had no authority to check the papers of a ship flying the Portuguese flag.

In the fall of 1839, a British admiral on the African coast charged that the U.S. consul in Havana had aided the slave trade by signing blank forms which could be filled in later by shipmasters. This charge was forwarded by the Foreign Office to the State Department.[18] Trist challenged the British to produce any blank forms with his signature. The three forms provided by the British a year later turned out to be discharge certificates for seamen, with only the description of the seaman left blank.[19]

At first President Van Buren, for whom Trist had worked in the State Department, was inclined to ignore the British charges against Trist. In his annual message to Congress in 1839, Van Buren cited Trist as the source of recommended revisions of the laws to preserve "the integrity and honor of our flag." A British writer visiting Washington that winter wrote that the president and other officials "took occasion to speak to me of the merits of Mr. Trist and of the high opinion entertained of his character and services."[20]

Trist's principal problem with American mariners arose from his insistence on enforcing an unpopular provision of U.S. law that required a master discharging members of his crew in a foreign port to pay them three months extra wages.[21] American merchants and captains in Havana were outraged when Spanish authorities cooperating with Trist imprisoned an American captain for several months because he refused the extra pay due a discharged mate. In another case Trist supported the captain of the *William*

Engs, who was threatened by a mutiny, but the consul's role was criticized when the Spanish sentenced the mutinous crew to hard labor.[22]

Most of the American mariners were from the Northeast, where antislavery sentiment was strong, and they did not hesitate to protest actions of a consul from the South who had been charged by the British with aiding the slave trade. After meetings of shipmasters in New York and Boston sent resolutions critical of Trist to the House Committee on Commerce in Washington, President Van Buren sent a prominent Bostonian, Alexander Everett, to Cuba to investigate.

Trist requested a congressional hearing on the charges, but the House committee had little inclination to try to unravel the charges and Trist's responses. It had been overwhelmed with documents sent by the shipmasters and by the State Department, including copies of several of Trist's dispatches and letters and documents Trist had enclosed with them. On July 21, 1840, the day Congress adjourned, the committee submitted a brief report on the cases of Captain Wendell and the crew of the *William Engs*, accompanied by 475 printed pages of documents. The committee concluded that "the documents submitted to them do not at all affect the character of Mr. Trist for integrity and honor."[23]

This committee report ended the controversy over Trist's treatment of mariners, but the larger issue of his alleged aid to slavetraders was kept alive by a Senate resolution in July requesting the president to provide copies of all correspondence with British authorities concerning the slave trade, especially those related to the role of the U.S. consul in Havana. Van Buren did not respond to the Senate request until January 18, 1841, after he had been defeated by William Henry Harrison in the presidential election of 1840.

Everett's report on his investigation of the charges against Trist was based mainly on information from the British commissioners in Havana. It was highly critical of Trist, but most of the charges were undocumented.[24] Trist answered the principal charges effectively in a long rebuttal prepared while he was in Virginia during the summer of 1840. He insisted that there was no foundation for Everett's assertion that ships legally flying the America flag had brought slaves to Cuba. Although many American ships had been sold to foreign slavetraders in Africa, these sales were not illegal and were totally beyond the control of the consul in Havana. Trist flatly denied that any ship had left Havana under the American flag unless it had arrived there as a properly documented American vessel. Finally, he rejected Everett's claim that his certification of the accuracy of various routine papers for Portuguese ships in Havana during a gap between Portuguese consuls had any relation to the subsequent employment of some of these vessels in the slave trade.[25]

In January 1841, after the Senate received the documents on the slave trade it had requested the previous summer, the House requested all documents on the search and seizure of American vessels by British cruisers and all dispatches from Trist concerning the slave trade. This 766-page collection of documents, including Everett's report and Trist's rebuttal, was sent to Congress on March 3, 1841, the last day of Martin Van Buren's presidency.[26]

The nation had no career Foreign Service in the nineteenth century. Since the Democrats had lost the White House, a deserving Whig would undoubtedly have been appointed in 1841 to replace a consul identified with Jefferson and Jackson even if his service had been totally noncontroversial. The appointment of a new consul to replace Trist was delayed, however, by Harrison's death after only a month in office and by Tyler's subsequent conflicts with the Whig leadership in Congress. Secretary of State Daniel Webster wrote Trist on September 4, 1841, that a change was being made at Havana "on general grounds of propriety and expediency" without President Tyler having formed any judgment of the charges against Trist.[27]

Trist remained in Cuba as a private citizen for four years. He bought a small dairy farm in El Corro on the edge of Havana and lived a frugal life there until the summer of 1845. His wife and daughter returned from France and joined him at El Corro. His older son spent a year with the family there and then returned to school in Philadelphia. His younger son remained in school in Switzerland. Trist did part-time work for a commercial trading firm in Havana, wrote a treatise on dairy operations, raised a large garden, and sold milk and vegetables in the city. The Trists survived only by practicing "a most rigid economy."

What manner of man was it who walked the beach near El Corro and pondered his future and the nation's?

As Jackson had said, Nicholas Trist was a man of "integrity and honor." His early associations with Jefferson, Madison, and Jackson had contributed to his strong convictions that he must always tell the truth as he saw it and must always do what he thought was right without fear of the consequences. Jefferson appealed on his deathbed to Trist and other members of his family to honor him by living honest and truthful lives.[28] In Trist's mind, honesty and truthfulness required more than avoiding lies; they demanded the candid expression of the truth as he saw it, even when it was contrary to his own interests to do so. "If I am to have a fault," he wrote in 1848, "I would rather speak too harshly, and thrust forth truth unwisely, than to have played the hypocrite and held truth in."[29]

He also had to act on his convictions. "I claim the liberty of regulating my own conduct by what I deem right," he wrote to his friend Donelson in 1830.³⁰ This attitude was enhanced by his association with Andrew Jackson. Trist recorded several admiring anecdotes which describe Old Hickory as doing and saying precisely what he thought was right, without fear of "clamors."³¹ Later in Cuba, he wrote proudly of his inflexibility in enforcing unpopular laws, despite strong pressures to ignore them from the American community in Havana.

Trist had become accustomed to controversy and had emerged from several controversies with a large measure of success and vindication. In the early 1830s, the ideas in his antinullification letters had been strongly reflected in Jackson's Nullification Proclamation; in the end, the nullifiers had been defeated. Later in Havana, he learned patience and persistence in defending himself against unfair charges. The British government and the American mariners had failed to prove their charges against him, and his self-confidence remained unimpaired.

Like most American diplomats in all eras, Trist was sure that his understanding of the situation in the country to which he was assigned was infinitely greater than that of any official in Washington. Trist's close associations with three of the giants of the early nineteenth century — Jefferson, Madison, and Jackson — also contributed to his later willingness to defy the lesser mortal who was the eleventh president of the United States.

Trist's experience up to 1845 had prepared him to think independently, to make and rely on his own judgments, and to do whatever he thought was right without fear of the consequences. Two years later he would exercise his independent judgment and initiative to bring to an end America's first foreign war.

ONE

Our Flag Is Insulted

During the years of Nicholas Trist's childhood and youth in Louisiana (1804–17), its borders with the Spanish provinces of Florida and Texas were not clearly defined. In 1821, when he returned to Louisiana from West Point, the Spanish government had just ratified a treaty negotiated in 1819 by Secretary of State John Quincy Adams which ceded Florida to the United States. It established a border between U.S. and Spanish territory that ran from the Gulf of Mexico via the Sabine, Red, and Arkansas rivers to the 42nd parallel and then westward along that parallel to the Pacific. Spanish territory west and south of that border included all of the present U.S. states of Texas, New Mexico, Arizona, California, Nevada, and Utah as well as parts of the present states of Wyoming, Colorado, Kansas, and Oklahoma. Most of this vast region was arid; the Spanish settlements in the region were mainly on the upper Rio Grande in present-day New Mexico and on the California coast. But there were many tracts of fertile and adequately watered land across the Sabine River in the virtually uninhabited province of Texas.

Soon after the new border was accepted by the Spanish, it became the border between the United States and the newly independent republic of Mexico. The Mexican Constitution of 1824 established a federal system of government but made little allowance for the political inexperience of the Mexican people or the persistent authoritarian legacy from generations of Spanish rule in Mexico. The first decades of Mexican independence were a period of extreme political turbulence, with constant conflict between authoritarian centralists and more democratic federalists. Each group held the presidency for at least two periods, always under constant threat from the other.

During most of the quarter century between Mexican independence and the war between the United States and Mexico, the government of the United States was not well represented in Mexico. From 1822 to 1825, there was a Mexican minister in Washington, but the Monroe administration was not able to get a U.S. minister to Mexico. The Mexican post was turned down by a Louisiana senator and by General Andrew Jackson, and the appointment of an Illinois senator was withdrawn because of political controversy.[1]

In 1825, President John Quincy Adams appointed a South Carolina congressman, Joel Poinsett, as the first U.S. minister to Mexico. Although he was instructed to take every opportunity to explain U.S. political institutions to the Mexicans, Poinsett's enthusiasm for liberal and federalist principles carried him far beyond behavior acceptable in a diplomat. He encouraged the development of a liberal federalist party in Mexico to offset the centralist tendencies fostered by British influence, and he helped establish a number of York-rite Masonic lodges which became federalist strongholds. His vigorous advocacy of federal democracy in Mexico was resented by the centralists, and the outcry against his interference in Mexico's internal affairs ultimately led to his rejection by the Mexican government.[2]

The U.S. government's official relations with Mexico were not helped by the growing roles of individual Americans in the Mexican province of Texas. In January 1821, Moses Austin of Missouri had obtained permission from the Spanish government to bring a few American families into Texas. Although Moses died soon after receiving the grant, his son Stephen Austin obtained a confirmation of the grant from the new government of Mexico. This action by the government of the infant Mexican republic set the stage for a U.S.-Mexican conflict over Texas which persisted for a quarter century until it was resolved, at least from the legal standpoint, by the treaty Nicholas Trist negotiated in 1848.

In 1827, Henry Clay, Adams' secretary of state, instructed Poinsett to offer a million dollars for Texas and the eastern portions of New Mexico and Colorado or a half million for the northeastern half of Texas.[3] Poinsett was sure that these offers would be rejected and refused to present them. When Andrew Jackson became president in 1829, Poinsett was instructed to offer five million for a border which ran between the Rio Grande and Nueces Rivers to the Continental Divide and then along the highest mountains to the existing border at the 42nd parallel.[4] Poinsett was unable to carry out these instructions because he had been declared persona non grata by the Mexican government because of his interference in Mexico's internal affairs.[5]

Andrew Jackson's envoy to Mexico was also a failure, but for quite different reasons. Old Hickory appointed an army crony, Colonel Anthony Butler, as U.S. chargé d'affaires in Mexico. Butler was a land speculator with large holdings in Texas and a big personal stake in the U.S. acquisition of Texas. He was also an unprincipled schemer who was willing to use any means to get what he wanted. Butler was instructed to make the $5 million

ONE / *Our Flag Is Insulted* 19

offer for Texas, but word of the offer reached the press in the Mexican capital and was immediately spurned by the Mexican government.

Butler remained in Mexico for seven years, developing several new schemes to obtain Texas. In 1831 he pressed Jackson to increase the U.S. offer to $7 million.[6] Nicholas Trist, serving as Jackson's secretary that summer, prepared the coded reply containing Jackson's refusal to exceed the $5 million offer.[7] Early in 1833, Butler suggested that the United States make a substantial loan to the Mexican government with Texas as collateral, with the expectation that the United States would gain title to the province upon the inevitable Mexican default on the loan.[8]

Later that year Butler wrote Jackson that a treaty ceding Texas might be obtained by using half a million dollars secretly to put certain personages in Mexico in the "right humor." Jackson replied that Butler was not authorized to resort to corruption but added that "all the U.S. is interested in is the unencumbered cession, not how Mexico applies the consideration."[9] A few months later Butler again insisted that if negotiations for Texas were to be successful, "resort must be had to bribery [or] presents, if the term is more appropriate."[10] Jackson wrote on the letter, "A. Butler: What a Scamp. The Secretary of State ... will recall him." But the scamp's delaying tactics allowed him to remain in Mexico until the summer of 1835.

While Butler schemed and stalled, Mexico had been subjected to a dictatorship by General Antonio Lopez de Santa Anna. He had become a national hero in 1830 when he accepted the capitulation of fever-ridden Spanish troops who had attempted the reconquest of Mexico.[11] In 1833 he managed to get himself elected president of Mexico. In the spring of 1834, Santa Anna dismissed the Congress, abrogated the Constitution of 1824, and began to rule as a dictator.

In the summer of 1835, Anthony Butler returned to Washington with a letter from a Catholic priest, Ignacio Hernandez, who was a member of Santa Anna's inner circle. It stated that the United States purchase of Texas would be approved by Santa Anna's government if the priest was given $500,000 for secret distribution to a number of Mexican officials and legislators.[12] Jackson's response was similar to his reaction to Butler's first bribery proposal in 1833. He wrote on the Hernandez letter that "nothing will be countenanced by the executive to bring this government under the remotest imputation of being engaged in corruption or bribery," but he added that "we have no concern in the application of the consideration to be given; the public functionaries of Mexico may apply it as they deem proper to extinguish private claims."[13]

The similar caveats following Jackson's rejections in principle of the bribery proposals in 1833 and 1835 strongly suggest that Jackson would not have objected if money publicly paid to the Mexican government was subsequently used for payoffs to officials and legislators. In a recent study of Jackson's foreign policy, John M. Belohlavek wrote that "Jackson drew a pragmatic line between knowing what certain government officials might do with the $5 million after it was delivered and the prior act of paying bribes to Mexican officials to persuade them to cede the territory. If such activity were revealed in Washington, it would arouse the righteous indignation of an uninformed Congress — and destroy the possibility of annexation."[14]

Butler was allowed to return to Mexico for one more try to purchase Texas. New instructions to Butler from John Forsyth, Jackson's fourth secretary of state, stressed that "the President is resolved that no means of an even equivocal character shall be used" to obtain the desired alteration of the boundary.[15] But since Butler had insisted that payoffs provided the only chance for a successful negotiation, Jackson's decision to send him back to Mexico that fall lends credence to Butler's subsequent claim that Jackson was willing to permit the payoffs if they could be carried out without his official cognizance.[16] Nicholas Trist, on leave from his post in Havana, visited Jackson that summer and may have been told about Butler's scheme. If so, Trist's recollection of Jackson's attitude may have contributed to his positive response when similar payments to Mexican officials and legislators were proposed a dozen years later. Jackson's pragmatic attitude toward payments to Mexico probably also contributed to the persistent belief of his protégé, James K. Polk, a decade later that money was the key to an advantageous territorial settlement with Mexico.

Robert V. Remini, author of the most comprehensive biography of Andrew Jackson, concluded that "the Jackson administration botched the diplomacy necessary for any settlement [with Mexico], and the President himself deserves much of the blame. He should never have appointed Butler in the first place; then he should have replaced him early on, especially when he realized that his minister was a scoundrel. Jackson's fumbling only increased Mexican suspicion and hostility... It was a sorry diplomatic record."[17]

As it turned out, events in Texas in the fall of 1835 and early 1836 eliminated any chance that the United States could purchase Texas, with or without bribes. The American settlers in Texas had taken matters into their own hands.

By April 1830 the Mexicans had become concerned that the number of Americans in Texas was growing too rapidly. The Mexican congress passed a law which restricted American immigration into Texas, prohibited the importation of slaves into Texas, and imposed new duties on imports by Texans. The law was never adequately enforced.[18]

ONE / *Our Flag Is Insulted*

The northern Mexican provinces of Texas and Coahuila were jointly administered by a Mexican governor based at Saltillo, 500 miles from Austin's settlement on the Brazos. There was no way that Texas could be effectively governed from Saltillo, yet frequent petitions by the Texans for separate statehood were ignored. In 1832 and 1833, Texas conventions met at San Felipe to formulate new pleas for statehood, tariff reform, land reform, and schools. Stephen Austin took these appeals to the Mexican capital, where he was ignored for a while and then arrested and detained until the summer of 1835.

While Austin was being held, Santa Anna abrogated the Mexican Constitution. Texans were unwilling to live under a military dictatorship, and Austin returned to Texas in September 1835 to discover that a revolution was brewing. Santa Anna sent his brother-in-law, General Cos, to reestablish the authority of the central government in the rebellious province. Cos was besieged by a Texas force at the Alamo in San Antonio. Some of his troops deserted, the Texans attacked, and Cos surrendered.[19]

In November 1835 a new Texas convention proclaimed that as a result of Santa Anna's abrogation of the Constitution of 1824, the Texans did not accept the authority of his government to govern Texas. They stopped short of a declaration of independence and recognized the possibility that Texans might accept a future Mexican government operating under the federalist constitution of 1824.[20]

Santa Anna was determined to smash the Texas revolt and personally led a large Mexican army into Texas in the spring of 1836. This time it was the Texans who were besieged in the Alamo, and two hundred of them died there when the Mexicans attacked on March 6. Three weeks later the Mexicans massacred four hundred Texas volunteers who had surrendered at Goliad.

The government of the United States remained officially neutral in the conflict between Mexico and Texas, but the American people strongly supported the Texas revolution. American money, arms, and volunteers flowed to Texas. Even Andrew Jackson sent a personal contribution, while attempting to maintain an official posture of neutrality. American support for the Texas revolt was deeply resented by the Mexicans.

On April 21, 1836, Sam Houston's Texas army, crying "Remember the Alamo!" surprised the Mexicans during their siesta at San Jacinto and won a decisive victory. Santa Anna was captured and remained a prisoner in Texas for the remainder of the year. Jackson appealed to Houston to abandon a rumored plan to execute the former Mexican dictator. The captive signed a treaty recognizing the independence of Texas, but it was soon repudiated by the Mexican government.

Santa Anna was eventually sent to Washington, where in mid–January 1837 he was the special guest at a large dinner given by the president and at several receptions. The guests may have included the Speaker of the House of Representatives, James K. Polk of Tennessee. During informal talks at the White House, the two ex-generals discussed a possible treaty between the United States and Mexico that would give Texas and northern California to the United States. Santa Anna was sent back to Vera Cruz on a U.S. warship.[21]

In the last weeks of his presidency, Andrew Jackson pondered U.S. policy toward Texas. His talks with Santa Anna had increased his reluctance to approve U.S. diplomatic recognition of the independence of Texas because such recognition would declare that Mexico no longer had any jurisdiction in Texas and would eliminate any chance of a treaty between the United States and Mexico ceding Texas to the United States.[22] But Texas representatives in Washington expressed the strong desire of Texas to be annexed by the United States.

Although Andrew Jackson had long dreamed of Texas as a part of the Union, the aging and ailing president feared that any step toward annexation would lead to bitter sectional conflict in the United States, with dire consequences for the Union. Although there was strong support for annexation in the South and West, it was bitterly opposed in the North because admission of Texas would give the slavery bloc two additional votes in the Senate.

After both houses of Congress took actions supporting U.S. recognition of the independence of Texas, Jackson yielded. On his last day in the White House, March 3, 1837, Jackson nominated Alcee La Branche of Louisiana as chargé d'affaires to the Texas Republic.[23] The Senate immediately confirmed the nomination.

Meanwhile, U.S. diplomatic relations with Mexico had been suspended in 1836. The Mexican minister in Washington, Manuel de Gorostiza, had produced a stream of protests against the failure of the U.S. government to restrict support by Americans for the Texas revolution. Gorostiza was also very upset by the occupation in July of 1836 of Nacogdoches, a Texas community some 50 miles west of the Sabine River, by a small U.S. force under General Gaines. The Mexican minister demanded his passports. Before his departure he circulated a pamphlet containing insulting references to the people and government of the United States. Jackson was incensed by Gorostiza's conduct, and demanded that the Mexican government apologize for his insults.

Relations during 1836 between the U.S. envoy in Mexico and the Mexican government were less dramatic but not more fruitful than those in

Washington with the angry Mexican minister. In January 1836, Jackson finally replaced his "scamp" in Mexico, appointing Powhatan Ellis to succeed Butler as U.S. chargé d'affaires in Mexico. Ellis had been a member of the Mississippi Supreme Court, a U.S. senator, and a federal judge. He arrived in Mexico in May 1836, just before the Mexican capital learned of the Mexican defeat at San Jacinto. It was not an auspicious moment for the accomplishment of his primary mission, which was to obtain action by the Mexican government on the many claims by Americans against Mexico. Most of the claims involved the seizure of American ships, cargoes, or crews in Mexican ports or waters; the imprisonment of American citizens in Mexico, including several U.S. consuls; or unpaid bills for supplies delivered to Mexicans.

Secretary of State Forsyth wrote Ellis in midsummer that if he was unable to get a satisfactory Mexican response within a few weeks to twelve claims cases, he was to demand his passports and return to the United States.[24] Ellis soon concluded that there was little chance of settlement of the claims and withdrew as authorized.[25] "Our flag is insulted and fired upon," he reported to the president. "Our citizens in the pursuit of a lawful and peaceful trade [are] seized and imprisoned upon the most frivolous pretext. Their property [is] condemned and confiscated in violation of existing treaties and the acknowledged Laws of Nations."[26]

From the fall of 1836 to the spring of 1839, the United States had no diplomatic representative in Mexico, although there was some communication between the governments through the U.S. consul who remained in the Mexican capital. The State Department translator, Robert Greenhow, was sent to Mexico in the summer of 1837 with a letter demanding Mexican action on 35 categories of American claims, but there was no satisfactory response.[27] That fall the Mexican government promoted the Mexican consul in New Orleans to the position of minister to the United States, but he returned to New Orleans after President Van Buren told Congress in December that he had little hope of improved relations with Mexico.

In the spring of 1838, the Mexican government proposed that the American claims against Mexico be submitted to international arbitration. The two governments agreed to request the king of Prussia to serve as arbitrator, but the Prussian monarch declined. A new U.S.-Mexican treaty was signed in April 1839 which provided for the submission of the claims to a "mixed commission" of two Americans and two Mexicans.[28]

In May 1839, Van Buren sent Powhatan Ellis back to Mexico, this time as minister, with instructions to do everything he could to ensure Mexican ratification and implementation of the claims agreement.[29] It was ratified by the Mexican government in the spring of 1840. Over the next eighteen months, the mixed commission reviewed $8.5 million in claims by Americans against Mexico and found only about one in four of them to be valid.[30]

During the four years of the Van Buren administration (1837–41) and for about two years thereafter, the status of Texas received relatively little attention in the United States. Van Buren shared Jackson's desire to minimize sectional tensions in the United States. The government of Texas submitted a proposal for annexation in August 1837, but it was promptly declined by Van Buren because of U.S. treaty obligations to Mexico and constitutional questions concerning the power of the federal government to annex an independent state.[31] Rebuffed, the Texas republic withdrew its offer to join the Union and pursued an independent foreign policy which sought European recognition and support.

Early in 1842, President John Tyler appointed Waddy Thompson to replace Ellis as U.S. minister to Mexico. Thompson, a Whig congressman from South Carolina, had supported the U.S. annexation of Texas in a speech in Congress that contained disparaging references to Mexico. He later admitted in his memoirs that when he arrived in Mexico in April 1842 he was regarded with "distrust and dislike" and "as an enemy of the country."[32] But he studied Spanish, worked hard to gain the respect of the Mexicans, and gradually revised his estimate of the Mexicans and caused them to revise their opinion of him. In 1843, Thompson negotiated a new treaty which provided for the payment by Mexico of about $2 million in claims in quarterly installments over a period of five years, but only the first three installments were actually paid by the Mexican government. Although Thompson tried to promote more amicable relationships between the United States and Mexico, the time was not ripe for an easing of tensions between the two countries.

The main barrier to better relations was a renewal of the war between Mexico and Texas that had slumbered for more than five years. The conflict had been rekindled by an ill-fated Texas expedition to Sante Fe in the summer of 1841. Soon after Texas independence, the Texas Congress had declared that the Rio Grande was both the southern and western boundary of Texas, although the 650-mile stretch of high arid plains between San Antonio and Sante Fe on the upper Rio Grande was inhabited mainly by hostile Comanche Indians. In the summer of 1841, President Mirabeau Bonaparte Lamar of Texas sponsored an expedition to Sante Fe whose goal, in the words of the Texas representative to the United States, was "to open a trade with the people of that country and induce them, if possible, to become a ... part of Texas."[33]

The expedition consisted of a few traders and other civilians and 270 military men. They started too late in the season, soon ran out of pasturage and supplies on the scorched plains, and straggled into the upper Rio Grande Valley, where they were captured by Mexican troops based in Sante Fe. Some were executed, and the rest were starved and mistreated during a long and agonizing march to imprisonment in the Mexican capital. When news of the barbaric treatment of the "Sante Fe Pioneers" reached Texas, there was an outpouring of rage. The Texas Congress responded with a resolution extending the border of Texas to include the territory of all of the Mexican states just south of the Rio Grande plus California, but it was vetoed by Sam Houston, who had become president of Texas for the second time a few months earlier.

The Mexican government, headed again by Santa Anna since 1841, responded with forays across the Rio Grande. In March 1842, Mexican troops surrounded the small Texas garrisons at Refugio, Goliad, and San Antonio, forced their surrender, and then withdrew across the Rio Grande with a number of prisoners. In June a Texas volunteer force of about 200 men was attacked by 700 Mexican infantry and cavalry, who withdrew after a brief skirmish. The Texas Congress responded with a declaration of a war of invasion against Mexico, but President Sam Houston knew the Lone Star Republic lacked the resources for a major war against Mexico and again used his veto.

In September 1842, General Adrian Woll, a French general leading a Mexican army, attacked San Antonio with about 1200 Mexicans; about 60 men were killed on each side before the Mexicans retired. The furious Texans sent a volunteer force to Laredo in December, most of which withdrew after finding no Mexican soldiers. About 300 volunteers who remained on the Rio Grande were threatened by General Pedro Ampudia's army near Mier and surrendered. The Mier prisoners were treated in an even more barbaric fashion than the Sante Fe Pioneers. They were marched hundreds of miles across deserts and mountains toward the Mexican capital. When they escaped and were recaptured after nearly starving in the desert, every tenth man was shot on Santa Anna's orders on March 25, 1843.[34]

Americans were shocked by the Mexican treatment of the Sante Fe Pioneers and the Mier prisoners. Although the United States remained officially neutral in the renewed war between Texas and Mexico, the Texas question continued to cast a large shadow over U.S.-Mexican relations. Mexicans deeply resented the substantial though unofficial American support for the Texans in the resumed war, just as they had resented American support for the Texans in 1836. "The most painful, responsible, and expensive of my duties here," Waddy Thompson commented at the end of his first year in Mexico, "do not grow out of the relations of my own country with this, but from this Texas war."[35]

Another barrier to improved relations was the growing Mexican suspicion that the United States hoped to annex the Mexican province of California. U.S. trade with California had grown steadily. American ships traded New England manufactured goods for California hides, tallow, and furs. Some of these ships carried California products on to China, where they were traded for silk, tea, and other Chinese goods. Yankee whalers visited California ports to buy provisions for the long whaling voyages in the South Pacific.

By 1840 there was a small community of American traders in California. That summer most of them were suddenly arrested and transported in irons to prison.[36] Ellis, the U.S. representative in Mexico, was instructed to demand the immediate release of the American prisoners and the punishment of those responsible for the "gross outrage" and "palpable violation" of the code of civilized nations.[37] The Mexicans eventually released the prisoners, at first ordering them to leave California and then allowing them to return to their homes there.[38]

Mexican suspicions of American designs on California were greatly intensified in the fall of 1842 by an incredible act of the U.S. naval commander in the Pacific, Commodore Thomas Ap Catesby Jones. In September, Jones was in Peruvian waters with his fleet. He received copies of two May notes from the Mexican foreign minister to the U.S. secretary of state protesting actions by individual Americans and communities in support of the Texans in their war with Mexico.[39] Commodore Jones assumed from these strongly worded Mexican protests that war between the United States and Mexico was inevitable or had already begun. He sailed north, seized the California port of Monterey, and proclaimed that the United States was annexing California. Jones said later that he had wanted to forestall the occupation of California by a British fleet which had departed mysteriously from the Peruvian coast shortly before his departure. But the day after his occupation of Monterey, the commodore was greatly embarrassed to discover that U.S.-Mexican relations were no worse than usual. He lowered the American flag, apologized to the local Mexican officials, and sailed away.

When the Mexican government learned of Jones' action, it protested that Mexico "has suffered the greatest outrage which could be committed against an independent and sovereign nation."[40] The U.S. minister, now Waddy Thompson, replied that Jones had acted solely on his own responsibility and without orders from his government in Washington. The Mexican government demanded that Jones be punished, and Tyler ultimately yielded and removed the commodore from his command.[41] But the Mexicans persisted in the belief that Jones' seizure of Monterey indicated a plan by the U.S. government to gain control of California. There was no such plan in 1842, but Jones' action clearly reflected the growing American interest in California.

Shortly before the Monterey incident, Waddy Thompson had written the secretary of state that California was "the richest, most beautiful, and the healthiest country in the world" and that the harbor of San Francisco "is capacious enough to receive the navies of all the world."[42] Thompson wrote President Tyler that "the acquisition of Upper California ... will be by far the most important event that has occurred to our country."[43]

Tyler showed little interest in California but was beginning to formulate a plan to annex Texas. A Virginia slaveowner who had served as governor of Virginia and U.S. senator, Tyler was added to the Whig ticket in 1840 to increase its appeal to Southern Whigs and anti-Jackson Democrats in the South. When President William Henry Harrison died in 1841 after only a month in office, the Whigs discovered that the new President Tyler opposed the most important Whig principles. After Tyler vetoed bills for internal improvements and a new national bank, all of the original Harrison cabinet resigned except Secretary of State Daniel Webster. Tyler became a president without a party. With no hope of influence in domestic affairs, he turned to the area in which the president has the greatest power, foreign affairs.

Tyler shared the dream of many Southern expansionists that Texas, and perhaps other states carved from its western regions, would be admitted to the Union as slave states. The South saw that additional states without slavery would eventually have to be admitted from the territories in the northwest. The remaining areas south of the 36° 30' compromise line established in 1830 were territories reserved for the Indians, arid areas that were unsuitable for plantation agriculture and thus for slavery, and Texas. Texas had been settled primarily by Americans from the South and had a substantial cotton production and a sizable slave population. Southern leaders thought the admission of Texas offered the only chance to maintain a Southern veto in the Congress and to protect the South's "peculiar institution" against hostile measures advanced by the antislavery forces in the North.

As long as Daniel Webster of Massachusetts remained secretary of state, Tyler was unable to move toward annexation of Texas because Webster was totally opposed to the admission of Texas or any other slaveholding state. Tyler's continued interest in Texas was a major reason for Webster's resignation in May 1843. Tyler replaced him with a conservative slaveowner from tidewater Virginia, Abel P. Upshur. Later that year the president and secretary, both Virginia slaveowners, found an opportunity to use the antislavery policies of the British government to build support for the U.S. annexation of Texas.

Applying in North America the balance-of-power policy which was the

keystone of its foreign policy in Europe, the British government had welcomed the new Republic of Texas. The British thought an independent and perhaps enlarged Texas would bar U.S. expansion to the southwest and west and prevent the United States from becoming too powerful in the New World. There were also important economic reasons for British support for the continued independence of Texas. British imports of Texas cotton reduced British dependence on cotton from the American South. The conflict between Mexico and Texas threatened the very substantial British business interests in Mexico. The annexation of Texas by the United States might lead to war between the United States and Mexico, with devastating effects on the shaky Mexican economy. The continued independence of Texas offered the best chance for the era of peace and prosperity in Mexico desired by British merchants and by British holders of Mexican bonds.[44]

In the summer of 1843, Tyler sent Duff Green, editor of the *Telegraph* and a crony of John C. Calhoun, on a special mission to England. Green soon reported that the British foreign secretary (Lord Aberdeen) had told the Texas chargé d'affaires in London (Ashbel Smith) that the British government "desires to prevent the annexation of Texas by the United States and ... to accomplish that the minister would recommend a loan for the abolition of slavery" in Texas. The loan would be used to compensate slaveowners, following the British practice when slavery was abolished in the British possessions.

The story of the conversation between Aberdeen and Smith seems to have been fabricated by Duff Green, perhaps at the suggestion of his friends in Washington. While the British government hoped for the continued independence of Texas and for the abolition of slavery in all countries, it had made no proposal linking these goals.[45] But Tyler and Upshur thought that rumors of an alleged British plan to abolish slavery in Texas would promote support in the South for an annexation treaty that prevented Texas from becoming a refuge for escaped slaves and would increase support in both North and South for a treaty that prevented Texas from becoming a British satellite.

Although the Mexican government repeatedly stated that the U.S. annexation of Texas would result in war between the United States and Mexico, these threats were not taken seriously. When the Mexican foreign minister informed Waddy Thompson that an annexation act would be the equivalent of a declaration of war,[46] Thompson forwarded this assertion to Washington with the opinion that "it is only a characteristic piece of gasconade and ... they will recede from the threat made as they have heretofore."[47] By midfall Thompson was "entirely satisfied that the communication ... was solely intended for political effect" in Mexico.[48] In November the Mexican minister in Washington, General Almonte, wrote Upshur that "the Mexican government is resolved to declare war" if the United States proceeded with annexation.[49] Upshur replied that "the President sees no reason to suppose that Congress will suffer its policy to be affected by threats."[50]

In February 1844, Upshur was killed in the explosion of a naval gun during a firing demonstration aboard the warship *Princeton*. Tyler chose John C. Calhoun, the leading spokesman for Southern interests, to succeed Upshur as secretary of state. Calhoun was eager to continue negotiations with the Texans, and a treaty of annexation was signed on April 12, 1844. Texas was to be admitted to the Union as a territory, rather than as a state, leaving open the possibility that several states might ultimately be created from the vast but unspecified area of Texas. The treaty was sent to the Senate with documents selected to convince senators that annexation was the only way to prevent an unacceptable degree of British influence in Texas.[51] But one of the documents had an unexpected effect. It was a reply from Calhoun to Lord Aberdeen's denial that the British had a plan to abolish slavery in Texas. Calhoun's strong defense of the institution of slavery convinced antislavery men in the North that the annexation plan was a conspiracy of Southern slaveholders to increase their influence in the Senate by adding slave states to the Union.[52] While this Northern view of the annexation of Texas was essentially correct, it would be extended with much less justification to the next administration's goals to annex California, New Mexico, and perhaps other former Mexican provinces.

For the next six years — until the compromise of 1850 — the inseparably linked issues of the annexation of former Mexican territories and the extension of slavery dominated domestic politics in the United States.

TWO

A Common Destiny

The election of 1844 was the only U.S. presidential election in the nineteenth century that was fought mainly on an issue of external relations. The issue was the annexation of Texas.

Henry Clay of Kentucky, nominated by the Whig convention on May 1, declared against annexation of Texas without the consent of Mexico since otherwise "annexation and war with Mexico are identical." Former president Martin Van Buren of New York, ready to try for another Democratic nomination, also opposed annexation as long as the independence of Texas went unrecognized by Mexico. Former president Andrew Jackson, now a strong supporter of annexation despite earlier misgivings, was dismayed by Van Buren's stand on the Texas issue. Jackson withdrew his support for his former protégé and began to promote the nomination of a fellow Tennesseean, James K. Polk.

Polk was in Congress from 1825 to 1839, was Speaker of the House of Representatives for the last four of those years, and was governor of Tennessee from 1839 to 1841. Several members of Polk's family had been actively involved in the Texas war of independence, including two cousins who fought with Sam Houston. A great uncle in Texas wrote him a firsthand account of the aftermath of the fall of the Alamo and added, "James, you have an active tongue. Why not use it for Texas?"[1] But Polk, always mainly concerned with the political effect of any action, feared that an attempt to annex Texas would threaten the unity of the Northern and Southern wings of the Democratic party. Polk took no stand on the Texas issue until the spring of 1844 when, as a candidate for the vice-presidential nomination, he was forced to do so. By then a positive stand for annexation was the politically correct decision.

Jackson and his protégé stressed the danger that Texas would become a British dependency. Jackson, who defeated a British army in 1815, raised the specter of a new British army marching to the Mississippi from the Texas-Louisiana border and fomenting a slave insurrection in the lower South.

TWO / *A Common Destiny*

Jackson and Polk believed that Texas had been a part of the Louisiana Purchase and had been unwisely ceded to Spain by the treaty negotiated by Secretary of State John Quincy Adams in 1819. Polk wrote that British control of Texas was a prospect "which no American patriot, anxious for the safety and prosperity of this country, could permit to occur without the most strenuous resistance... Let Texas be re-annexed, and let the fixed policy of our Government be not to permit Great Britain or any other foreign power to plant a colony or hold dominion over any portion" of Texas.[2]

The Democratic convention, meeting in Baltimore in late May, adopted a new rule requiring a two-thirds majority for the presidential nomination. After failing to achieve the necessary majority on eight ballots, Van Buren withdrew. Polk's name was brought forward, and he became the first "dark horse" candidate to be nominated for the presidency of the U.S. The Democrats ended their convention with a candidate and platform supporting the annexation of Texas.

A week later, on June 8, the Senate voted on the annexation treaty. Senator James Buchanan of Pennsylvania, chairman of the Foreign Relations Committee, stressed the fear that Britain would control Texas if the United States did not annex it. But seven Northern and Western Democrats joined 28 Whigs to defeat the treaty, 35 to 16.

The Senate rejection of the treaty set the stage for a major debate on the annexation issue during the presidential election campaign. The critical difference between Whig and Democratic positions was on Texas. Polk, the Democratic candidate, strongly supported annexation. During the summer the debate on Texas was fueled by rumors of Mexican plans to invade Texas and of British and French pressures on Sam Houston to reject annexation.

Henry Clay, the Whig candidate, had opposed annexation in May. In the fall he declared that he would be glad to see Texas acquired "without dishonor, without war, with common consent of the Union, and upon just and fair terms." This declaration won him some votes in the South but cost him many others among antislavery voters in the North who were convinced that annexation was a plot hatched by Southern slaveowners. When the votes were counted, James K. Polk had won by a narrow margin. Although he won 170 of the 275 electoral votes, he received only 51% of the popular vote.[3]

While debating annexation and electing a new president, Americans paid little attention to reactions and developments in Mexico. For six crucial months in the spring and summer of 1844, the United States was represented in Mexico by only a chargé d'affaires ad interim, Benjamin E. Green. He was the son of Duff Green, who had started the rumor of British efforts to promote the abolition of slavery in Texas. On instructions from Secretary of State Calhoun, Green informed the Mexicans that the United States had signed an annexation treaty with Texas "in self-defense, in consequence of the policy adopted by Great Britain in reference to the abolition of slavery in Texas."[4]

Tyler appointed former Ohio governor Wilson Shannon to succeed Waddy Thompson as U.S. minister to Mexico. He was the first Northerner to fill the post, but he was a strong supporter of the annexation of Texas.[5] Shannon took his time about getting to Mexico but was finally on the job by mid-September. He was there in time to observe another change in the Mexican government.

Although Santa Anna had been reelected president under the centralist constitution proclaimed in 1843, the new Congress that assembled in January 1844 had a majority of *Moderados*.[6] The men of this faction were equally opposed to the extremes of monarchy and democracy, but especially abhorred the habitual despotism of Santa Anna.[7] General Paredes, an ally of Santa Anna's in 1841, turned against him, as did the mobs in the capital.[8] Santa Anna fled to Havana. On December 7, 1844, the Mexican Congress selected a Moderado, General Jose Joaquin de Herrera, as the new president of Mexico. Herrera was personally in favor of a peaceful settlement of the dispute with the United States, but his government was soon under heavy attack from the conservatives and it ultimately proved to be no more willing to negotiate a settlement with the U.S. than the preceding Mexican governments.

The news of a new moderate government in Mexico arrived in Washington in the first days of 1845 as the second session of the 29th Congress was debating a new annexation proposal. Although now a "lame duck" president, Tyler saw a final chance to go into the history books as the man who gained Texas for the United States. The Senate vote in June had shown that there was no chance of obtaining the two-thirds majority required by the Constitution for the approval of an annexation measure that was in the form of a treaty with Texas. But territories were normally admitted to statehood by a joint resolution, which required only a simple majority of each house of Congress. Tyler recommended that Congress admit Texas by a joint resolution of both houses. The chairman of the Foreign Relations Committee, Senator James Buchanan of Pennsylvania, told the Senate that the United States must admit Texas or find her a dangerous rival: "Texas will remain either to bless us by re-union and to promote harmony among the Anglo-Saxon race, or, like the Philistines to the Israelites of old, be a perpetual thorn in the side of this republic."[9]

Resolutions adopted in the House and Senate charted quite different

TWO / *A Common Destiny*

paths to the annexation of Texas. Under the House resolution, Texas would be annexed as soon as Texas accepted terms specified in the resolution. It was to join the United States as a state, skipping the status as a territory provided in the treaty in 1844. Congress consented to the admission of a new state consisting of "the territory ... belonging to the republic of Texas" without specifying its extent or boundaries. The resolution also stated that up to four additional states could be formed from this unspecified area, if the state of Texas gave its consent. The Senate approved a resolution offered by Senator Benton under which commissioners would be appointed to negotiate the terms of annexation with the Texans. A compromise plan emerged which allowed the president of the United States to choose between these two paths to annexation. President-elect Polk, although preferring the House plan, allowed Benton to think that he would support Benton's plan for negotiations with Texas.

The joint resolution containing the compromise plan was approved on February 27, 1845,[10] and was signed by President Tyler on March 1, three days before he relinquished the White House to James K. Polk of Tennessee. Although it had been assumed in Congress that Tyler would leave the choice of annexation plans to his successor, Tyler immediately instructed the new U.S. chargé in Texas, Andrew Jackson Donelson, to offer the Texans immediate annexation. Although Tyler essentially chose the House plan, he left open the possibility that some amendments might be suggested by the Texans.

In his inaugural address, the new president gave full support to the annexation process launched by his predecessor: "The Republic of Texas has made known her desire to ... merge her sovereignty as a separate and independent state in ours ... I regard the question of annexation as belonging exclusively to the United States and Texas." There was no reference to Mexico, and the only danger perceived by Polk was "the danger to our safety and future peace if Texas remains a independent state or becomes an ally or dependency of some foreign nation." There was also no direct reference to California, although the address included a veiled comment that U.S. laws and republican institutions should be extended to those who have settled in "valleys of which the rivers flow to the Pacific."[11]

After a brief hesitation, President Polk revised Tyler's instructions to Donelson to require him to insist on unconditional acceptance by the Texans of the terms of the Congressional resolution. General Juan Almonte, who had been Santa Anna's minister in Washington and had not yet been replaced by the Herrera government, denounced the bill annexing Texas as "an act of aggression."[12] But Polk thought the Herrera government would recognize that the loss of Texas was inevitable and that Mexico's broader interests required a settlement of the dispute with the United States. This was the first of James K. Polk's many misjudgments of Mexican attitudes and reactions during the next three years.

Polk decided to send a American dentist-merchant who had lived in Mexico for many years, Dr. William Parrott, back to Mexico as a confidential agent to explore the possibilities for rebuilding U.S.-Mexican relations. Polk probably did not know in advance that Parrott was not well regarded by some Mexican leaders. In the late 1820s, Parrott had helped Poinsett form York-rite Masonic lodges in Mexico that were hated by conservatives because they fostered decentralized democracy. As a merchant, Parrott had a very large claim against the Mexican government which Waddy Thompson thought was "exaggerated to a disgusting degree." Herrera's foreign minister subsequently stated that Parrott would not be acceptable as secretary to a U.S. minister.[13]

Parrott was the first of six men Polk would send south to communicate with Mexican leaders during his term as president. In addition to the dentist, he used a former Louisiana congressman, a U.S. naval officer, a former Spanish colonel, a New York newspaper editor, and finally the second-ranking officer in the U.S. Department of State.

The Herrera government was reconciled to the permanent loss of Texas, as Polk thought, but it was not willing to accept the annexation of Texas by the United States. Herrera's foreign minister, Luis Gonzaga Cuevas, feared "a long and costly war" with the United States and believed that Mexico should recognize the independence of Texas in return for a pledge that she would remain independent.[14] Anson Jones, who succeeded Sam Houston as president of Texas, had talked of just such an arrangement during his previous service as the Texas secretary of state. The Herrera government's willingness to recognize the permanent independence of Texas was communicated by the Mexican consul in New Orleans to Ashbel Smith, who was on his way home from England to succeed Jones as secretary of state of Texas. President Jones and Secretary Smith were eager to reach such an agreement with Mexico if they could count on British support.

On March 24, 1845, the British chargé in Texas, Captain Eliot, and the French representative, Count Saligny, received instructions from their governments to cooperate in efforts to resolve the Mexican-Texas conflict on the basis of the permanent independence of Texas. Eliot and Saligny rushed to the Texas capital, Washington on the Brazos, and worked out a secret agreement with Jones and Smith. The Texas officials would hold up action on the U.S. offer of annexation for 90 days. Eliot would go to Mexico with an offer from Texas to reject annexation by the U.S. in return for Mexican recognition of the permanent independence of Texas. On their way back to

TWO / A Common Destiny

Galveston, the British and French diplomats met Donelson, who was bringing the U.S. offer of annexation.[15]

While Eliot and Saligny were at the Texas capital, the Mexicans learned of the annexation bill passed by the U.S. Congress. The Herrera government was being strongly challenged by the conservatives, who were ready to pounce at any sign of weakness. The imperatives of Mexican politics required Herrera to continue Santa Anna's bitter opposition to the U.S. annexation of Texas.[16] Foreign minister Cuevas informed Shannon that Mexico would oppose annexation "with all the energy called for by its honor and sovereignty" and that the U.S. annexation action forced Mexico to break off diplomatic relations with the United States.[17] Shannon now became convinced that "it is utterly useless to think of arranging our difficulties with Mexico in an amicable way for the present or for some time to come." He added that "all parties here are clamorous for war."[18]

Eliot arrived in the Mexican capital in mid-April with Jones' plan for permanent Texas independence, and Cuevas presented it to the Mexican Congress on April 21, 1845. A few days later Polk's confidential agent, Dr. Parrott, also arrived in the capital. He soon reported that "war with the United States seems to be the desire of all parties, rather than see Texas annexed to the U.S."[19] On May 17 both houses of the Mexican Congress agreed to accept Jones' proposal. Eliot rushed back to Texas with this news, and on June 4 President Jones proclaimed that "peace with Mexico" had been achieved. But the conflict between Texas and Mexico was not to end so easily or quickly.

While Eliot was in Mexico, there had been a strong reaction in Texas against the proposed deal with the Mexicans. In the last weeks of his life, Andrew Jackson appealed to his old friend Sam Houston, and Houston declared his support for annexation. Donelson and other American agents in Texas had been cultivating support for annexation among former American citizens, who were the majority of the Texas population. (The following spring Polk introduced Donelson to Baron de Cyprey, the former French minister to Mexico, as the man who had "contributed largely to defeat the French and English policy in Texas.") By early May, Donelson was convinced that the Texas Congress and the subsequent popular convention would reject the proposed treaty with Mexico and accept the U.S. offer. "I consider the question settled, as far as Texas is concerned," he wrote to Polk's secretary of state, James Buchanan. "The opposition will be powerless compared with the mass of those who, proud of their kindred connections with us, are willing to share a common destiny under the Stars and Stripes."[20]

Nevertheless, the Texans were worried about the Mexican reaction. Donelson reported that Texas officials hoped that as soon as annexation was accepted by Texas, the United States would move troops to the border area. Donelson supported the Texas request.[21] Buchanan replied on May 23 that as soon as Texas acted, the U.S. Army would protect her from attack by any foreign power.[22] On May 28, the U.S. Army commander in the Southwest was told to prepare to defend Texas against a possible Mexican invasion. These orders set General Zachary Taylor on a road that would ultimately lead to the White House.

Zachary Taylor had spent his adult life in the frontier army fighting Indians—during the war of 1812, the Black Hawk War, and the war with the Seminoles in Florida. He had been commanding officer of the army's Department of the Southwest since 1840. In 1845 he was 61 years old and a plain, direct frontier general who was called "Old Rough and Ready" by his troops.

"Should the territories of Texas be invaded by a foreign power ... after her convention shall have acceded to the terms of annexation," the May 28 order to Taylor stated, "you will at once employ ... the forces under your command for the defense of these territories and to expel the invaders."[23] Further orders were set on June 15: "Your ultimate destination is the Western frontier of Texas, where you will select and occupy, on or near the Rio Grande del Norte, such a site as will consist with the health of the troops and will be best adapted to repel invasion and to protect what, in the event of annexation, will be our western border. You will limit yourself to the defense of the territory of Texas, unless Mexico should declare war against the United States."[24] In his war message the following year, Polk told Congress that he had ordered Taylor to the Rio Grande in January 1846 because of a threatened Mexican invasion, conveniently ignoring the fact that such orders were first issued in June 1845 before the Texas Congress acted on the annexation bill and more than a month before the president learned the Mexican response.

The orders to Taylor to occupy the area between the Nueces and the Rio Grande also preceded the arrival in Washington of rumors of Mexican troop concentrations on the Rio Grande. Donelson wrote Buchanan from New Orleans on May 24 that all the reports received there from Mexico indicated that a belligerent movement by the Mexicans was unlikely.[25] Although Donelson later forwarded several rumors of Mexican movements, they seem to have been spread by Polk's own agents in Texas.[26]

Polk had sent Charles A. Wickliffe, formerly Tyler's postmaster general, and Congressman Archibald Yell of Arkansas, to Texas as confidential agents to promote support for annexation.[27] Wickliffe joined the commander of the U.S. Navy squadron on the Gulf Coast, Captain Robert Stockton, and Texas militia general Sidney Sherman in promoting a new Texas expedition to

TWO / *A Common Destiny* 37

occupy the area between the Nueces and the Rio Grande before action was completed on annexation. Dr. Wright, a U.S. naval surgeon who claimed to be Stockton's secretary, visited President Jones with General Sherman on May 28. They urged Jones to authorize a volunteer force of 2,000 men which would take Matamoros with the protection and assistance of Stockton's ships in the Gulf.[28] Jones stated later that he had been assured that Polk supported the expedition "so that, when Texas was finally brought into the Union, she might bring a war with her."[29] A biographer of Polk, Charles Sellers, wrote that although Wickliffe and Stockton exceeded their instructions, they faithfully reflected the spirit of Polk's policy toward Mexico.

Rumors of Mexican movements near the Rio Grande were spread by Sherman and his American associates to build support for their plan to occupy the disputed territory between the Nueces and the Rio Grande before the Mexicans could do so.[30] Donelson wrote Buchanan on June 2 that it was widely believed in Texas that Mexico was concentrating troops on the Rio Grande; on June 4 he reported that General Sherman had told him that Mexico had about 7,000 men on the Rio Grande. Donelson's subsequent belief that the Mexicans had crossed the Rio Grande is indicated by his comment in a later dispatch to Buchanan that President Jones should have insisted on the withdrawal of Mexican troops to the southern bank of the Rio Grande before accepting the Mexican peace offer.[31]

Although Polk was probably unaware of the specific plan being hatched by his agents in Texas, there was no doubt about his determination to prevent the Mexicans from occupying the disputed area above the Rio Grande. "We will maintain all your rights of territory and will not suffer them to be sacrificed," Polk wrote to Sam Houston on June 6.[32] He wrote Donelson on June 15 that the Mexicans would not be permitted to "occupy a foot of the soil east of the Rio Grande."[33]

Historians have paid little attention to the reasons for Polk's insistence on the Rio Grande as the Texas border. The simplest explanation is that annexation could be completed only with the support of the Texans and they wanted the Rio Grande. Polk ignored the fact that the Texas claim to the Rio Grande as its southern and western boundary lacked a solid foundation.

The Spanish government had fixed the boundary between Texas and other provinces of New Spain at the Nueces in 1816, and this boundary was indicated on Spanish maps of colonial Mexico. Maps prepared in 1829 and 1836 by Stephen Austin, founder of the American settlement in Texas, showed the Texas boundary at the Nueces. In a map of Texas published in Cincinnati in 1836, the Nueces was the southern boundary of Texas and the area south of the river was marked "Droves of Wild Horses." Zachary Taylor would encounter the wild horses but no Texan or Mexican settlers when

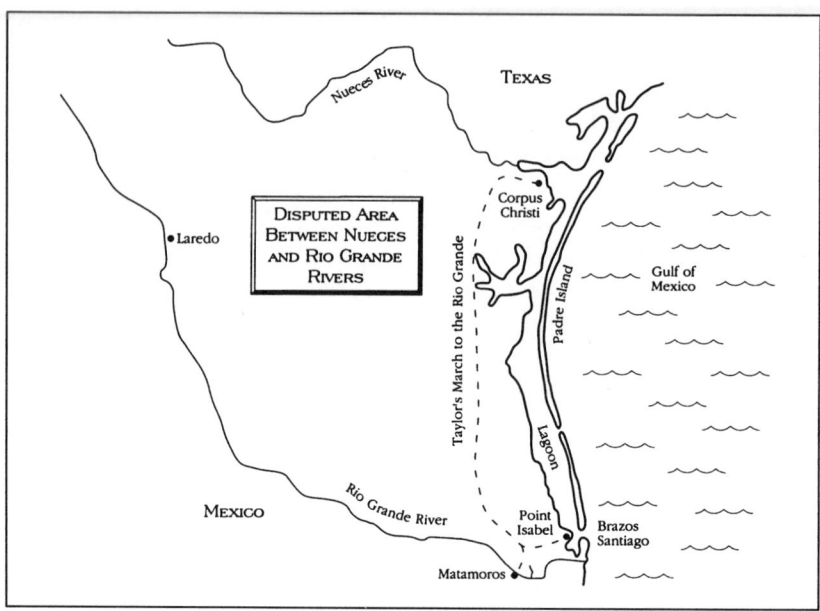

he marched across the area a decade later. The only settlement between the Nueces and the Rio Bravo (Rio Grande) shown on the 1836 map was the Mexican town of Laredo, just north of the Bravo but about 200 miles upstream from the Gulf of Mexico.[34] In 1845 there was still no settlement of Texans south of the Nueces.[35]

Some historians believe Polk insisted on the Rio Grande in order to provoke a war with Mexico. Charles Sellers commented that "this gratuitous insistence on an indefensible boundary claim was the clearest indication of the administration's anxiety to complete annexation not only at the earliest possible moment, but also as offensively to Mexico as possible."[36] Having accepted the Texas claim of the Rio Grande boundary, Polk then regarded any threat of a Mexican incursion north of the river as a potential attack on the United States.

The rumors of Mexican movements, although unfounded, contributed to the strongly skeptical reaction in Texas to President Jones' proclamation of "peace with Mexico." The majority of Texans were former American citizens with family and emotional ties to the United States. They were suspicious of the role being played in Texas by the British, who believed in monarchy and opposed slavery. When the Texas Congress met in mid-June, the Senate unanimously rejected the proposed treaty with Mexico and both Houses voted on June 21 to accept the U.S. offer of annexation. News of the unanimous acceptance of annexation by a popular convention in Austin on July 4 reached Zachary Taylor in New Orleans on July 22, just before he embarked for Texas.

Although General Taylor had been ordered to establish himself "on or near the Rio Grande," he decided to go only as far as Corpus Christi on the Nueces river about 150 miles north of the Rio Grande.[37] Donelson had written Taylor on June 28 that Corpus Christi, the most "western" point on the Gulf actually occupied by Texas, might be a proper objective for Taylor's force. He noted that "the occupation of the country between the Nueces and the Rio Grande ... is a disputed question."[38]

Taylor justified his decision to the War Department in purely military terms and didn't mention Donelson's advice.[39] The administration did not object to Taylor's decision, although the secretary of war wrote that at least a part of his force should be stationed south of the Nueces.[40]

For Polk and his cabinet, the summer of 1845 was a period of anxious waiting for news from the border area and from the Mexican capital, but there was very little news. Taylor, preoccupied with establishing his camp at Corpus Christi, neglected his communications with Washington but had hardly any information about the activities and intentions of the Mexicans 150 miles to the south of his camp.

The president grasped any straw of information or rumor that blew his way. In early August the Prussian minister in Washington, Baron Gerolt, told the secretary of the navy that he had authentic information that Mexico was preparing to invade Texas, that General Arista was marching to the Rio Grande with 3,000 men, and that General Paredes would soon follow with 10,000 men. The origin of Gerolt's report is unknown. The Prussian baron was well regarded by Polk, who later described him as "the only foreign minister at Washington ... whose feelings and opinions are with the Democratic Party of the U.S."[41] The baron's story was consistent with Donelson's reports and with a story in late July in a Washington newspaper, reprinted from a Mexican paper, that there were twelve to thirteen thousand Mexicans soldiers in the northern Mexican provinces, although they were badly equipped and poorly commanded.[42]

On August 7, Polk wrote to Buchanan, who was away in Pennsylvania, that "the strong possibility is that a Mexican army of eight to ten thousand men is now on the western frontier of Texas."[43] The secretary of war wrote to Taylor later in August "that there is reason to believe that Mexico is making efforts to assemble a large army on the frontier of Texas for the purpose of entering its territory and holding forcible possession of it." If Mexico crossed the river with considerable force, Taylor was to regard the movement as an invasion of the United States.[44]

There was no foundation in fact for Polk's belief that the Mexicans were assembling a large army on the Rio Grande that summer. Taylor heard in mid-August that General Arista had left Monterrey with about 1500 men,[45] but a "confidential agent" Taylor sent to Matamoros reported in early September that no extraordinary preparations or troop buildup had occurred there.[46] In this period Arista wrote Paredes that his troops were ill-clad, ill-fed, and in a state of "dreadful misery" and that an advance to Texas was impossible because of inadequate supplies.[47] One specialist on Mexican history has written that there were only 1300 Mexican soldiers on the borders of Texas in the summer of 1845.[48]

In late August of 1845, at a moment when the United States seemed poised on the brink of war with Mexico, Nicholas P. Trist became the second-ranking official in the U.S. Department of State. When Trist wrote Andrew Jackson in the fall of 1844 about a possible appointment, Jackson forwarded the letter to the president-elect with a strong endorsement: "Trist is ... a man of first rate talents, of unimpeachable moral character, of high honorable feelings and bearing.... He is worthy of your attention. ... Mr. Trist was of much use to me. Every confidence in him may be reposed."[49]

By the summer of 1845, no position had been offered to Trist, but upon his arrival in Washington from Havana in August, he learned that Polk's secretary of state, James Buchanan, was looking for a qualified person for the position of chief clerk in the State Department. Trist was ideally qualified for the job. He had worked in the department for two secretaries and had worked with the department as temporary secretary to President Jackson and as consul in Havana. During the decade he had spent in a Spanish colony, he had acquired a fluency in the Spanish language which would be very useful in a period in which relations with our Hispanic neighbor had reached a crucial stage. As a result of his early years in Louisiana, he was also fluent in French, which was still considered the most important language of diplomacy.

On August 28, 1845, Nicholas P. Trist was appointed chief clerk of the U.S. Department of State. In the 1840s the chief clerk was not a presidential appointee. The appointment was made by the secretary of state, and the incumbent served "at the pleasure of the Secretary." Thus Trist was Buchanan's man, not Polk's. This distinction would become important during Trist's mission to Mexico, when Polk would feel less need to support him than might have been the case if Trist had been one of his own appointees.

In 1845 the State Department had only about 20 employees. The five clerks in the Diplomatic Bureau had no authority to deal with any matter of substance. Three clerks in the Consular Bureau received reports from

American consuls around the world, but most of the consular reporting was useless because there was no one to organize and distribute the information. American diplomats and consuls complained that the State Department communicated with them seldom and tardily. About half of the State Department's clerks were in the Home Bureau, which handled domestic matters, including patents, copyrights, pardons, electoral procedures, and territorial administration.[50]

The title of "chief clerk" accurately reflected the duties of the incumbent, which were to supervise the work of the department's clerks and coordinate its paperwork. Trist commented that "everything that comes in passes through my hands in the first instance; everything that goes out passes through my hands in the last instance before receiving the Secretary's signature."[51] Trist developed a satisfactory relationship with the secretary, James Buchanan. He wrote later that "a close intimacy, personal as well as official, had grown up between us. Every proof of esteem and confidence ... was habitually extended to me."[52] Buchanan told Dolley Madison that the labors of the department would have killed him, but for Trist's assistance.

After Trist spent seven months as chief clerk, Buchanan recommended that the position be upgraded to an assistant secretary of state, appointed by the president and confirmed by the Senate, who would be authorized to transact under the general supervision of the secretary all the business of the department except that which was purely diplomatic in character.[53] No action was taken on this recommendation until 1853, however.

In that era the conduct of diplomacy was the exclusive responsibility of the president and the secretary of state, although the cabinet advised on diplomatic decisions. The State Department had no policy advisers, country experts, or other officials with substantive diplomatic responsibilities. The chief clerk did not participate in diplomatic decisions. Despite his decade of experience in a Hispanic country, there is no evidence that Trist had any opportunity to contribute to the policies of the Polk administration toward Mexico during the twenty months that he occupied the number two position in the U.S. Department of State.

In the same week that Trist returned to the State Department, James K. Polk began keeping a diary. During the rest of his presidency, he wrote in it nearly every day. The four volumes of the diary published in 1910 provide invaluable information on Polk's reactions to many political and diplomatic events, but they leave some important questions unanswered. Although he often recorded discussions with cabinet members and others in considerable detail, the diary contains no record of some of his most important decisions. Fortunately, it contains full accounts of Polk's decisions to send

Nicholas Trist to Mexico and to recall him, as well as Polk's reactions to Trist's most important dispatches from Mexico.

The diary clearly reflects the personal characteristics of the eleventh president. Justin Smith, who used the diary extensively in preparing a comprehensive history of the Mexican war published in 1919, found Polk "cold, narrow, methodical, dogged, plodding, obstinate, partisan, [and] very wanting in humor."[54] The diary reflects Polk's preoccupation with domestic politics and his limited previous experience in the diplomatic and military fields.

Although diplomatic and military issues dominated Polk's term as president, little in his previous background had prepared him to deal with such issues. As a student at the University of North Carolina from 1815 to 1818, he was passionately fond of mathematics and led his class in classics. After election to Congress in 1826, he was on the House Foreign Affairs Committee for five years (1827–32), but the House role in foreign affairs was quite limited in that era and these were not years of important challenges in U.S. foreign relations. For the next thirteen years, he occupied positions in which he focused exclusively or primarily on domestic issues. He was member and chairman of the House Ways and Means Committee (1832–35), Speaker of the House (1835–39), governor of Tennessee (1839–41), and a lawyer in private practice (1841–45). Biographies of Jackson and Polk provide no indications that Polk was significantly involved with the diplomacy of the Jackson administration. About the only recorded positions taken by Polk on foreign policy issues while he was a member of Congress were essentially isolationist positions. He strongly opposed the plans of John Quincy Adams and Henry Clay to participate in a conference in Panama of the newly independent republics of Latin America on the ground that it might "involve the nation in entangling alliances." In 1835, Speaker Polk contributed to the defeat of a fortifications bill which would have strengthened the hand of President Jackson during a diplomatic crisis with France.[55]

Polk was the first directly elected president of the United States who did not bring substantial diplomatic or military experience to the White House. Polk's limitations in the diplomatic area would have been less significant had his cabinet contained men with broad diplomatic experience. He rarely acted without consulting the six members of his cabinet — the secretaries of state, war, navy, and treasury, the attorney general, and the postmaster general. Important decisions were thoroughly discussed at one or more cabinet meetings, and the president and cabinet members sometimes came to the bedside of an ailing colleague to obtain his views on an important issue. Paul Bergeron, author of a recent study of Polk's presidency, wrote that "Polk's effective administering of the government was highly dependent upon the cabinet, whose advice, aid, and support he constantly sought.

There were differences, suspicions, and antagonisms from time to time, to be sure, but the prevailing theme was loyalty and duty."⁵⁶ There was more concern in the cabinet for loyalty and duty to the president than for the development of a foreign policy that would avoid war with Mexico. The cabinet members shared the president's expansionist outlook, and there was no advocate in the cabinet for a more restrained policy toward Mexico.

James Buchanan, Polk's secretary of state, was a Pennsylvania congressman for a decade and then minister to Russia for two years. This assignment, at a time when there were no important issues between the United States and czarist Russia, was the only prior diplomatic experience of any of the men attending Polk's cabinet meetings. Buchanan had been elected to the U.S. Senate in 1833. Although he chaired the Senate Foreign Relations Committee from 1837 to 1845, his interests were primarily political rather than diplomatic. During most of his term as secretary of state, Buchanan was either maneuvering for an appointment to the Supreme Court — which he subsequently turned down — or positioning himself to run for president. Polk, who stated before his election that he would not be a candidate for reelection, extracted from each cabinet member a promise that he would resign if he became a presidential candidate. Buchanan did not become an avowed candidate, but he calculated every major move in terms of its effect on his chances for the presidency.

Although usually more cautious than the president, Buchanan sometimes advocated more expansionist positions in order to win the political support of expansionists. Polk was often annoyed by Buchanan's self-serving maneuvers, but he did not want a stronger secretary of state and he kept Buchanan in the post throughout his presidential term. The secretary's most important instructions to U.S. diplomats were reviewed in draft — and often substantially modified — by the president, and they frequently contained phrases almost identical with those recorded by Polk in his diary.

The most outspoken expansionist in the cabinet was Robert J. Walker, the secretary of the treasury. He had been a Natchez lawyer and U.S. senator from Mississippi. His brother, a settler in Texas, died after his health was broken during imprisonment by the Mexicans. A biographer of Secretary Walker suggested that his strong advocacy of the U.S. annexation of all of Mexico in the later months of the war reflected in part a personal vendetta against the nation responsible for the death of his brother.⁵⁷

The secretary of the navy, George Bancroft, was also a consistent expansionist. He was a Boston historian who had studied in Germany and traveled widely in Europe. Although he had more overseas experience than any other cabinet member, it was as a student, not as a diplomat. Prior to joining the cabinet, Bancroft had published the first three volumes of a history of the United States. His research on the origins of the American nation had contributed to a highly nationalistic viewpoint similar to Polk's instinctive nationalism. Bancroft was a devoted adherent of the theory of Manifest Destiny and an early advocate of the U.S. acquisition of California.

William Marcy, the secretary of war, was governor of New York from 1833 to 1838. This very partisan Democrat coined the phrase "to the victor belongs the spoils" and shared Polk's distrust of the two most prominent generals, Winfield Scott and Zachary Taylor, because they were Whigs. His term as secretary of war was not a period of very effective civilian control of the military establishment. His previous service for two years on the joint U.S.-Mexican claims commission had exposed him to the wide range of American complaints and claims against Mexico. Although not an ardent expansionist, Marcy usually went along with the expansionist majority in the cabinet.

John Y. Mason, Polk's attorney general, had graduated from the University of North Carolina at the end of Polk's first year there. He was a Virginia congressman for six years, including a period as chairman of the House Committee on Foreign Affairs. As secretary of the navy in the last year of the Tyler administration, he had participated in Tyler's efforts to annex Texas. When Bancroft was appointed minister to Britain in September 1846, Mason moved back to his old job and administered the Navy Department for the rest of the war with Mexico. Mason was also an expansionist, although he later opposed the annexation of all of Mexico and supported the ratification of Trist's treaty.

Mason was replaced as attorney general in 1846 by Nathan Clifford, who had been attorney general of Maine and a Maine congressman. Clifford advocated the vigorous prosecution of the war with Mexico and a resolute policy on a peace settlement, so the substitution of Clifford for Bancroft did not change the nationalist and expansionist outlook of the cabinet.

The postmaster general was Cave Johnson, a former Tennessee congressman who was a long-time friend and political ally of Polk's. As was the case with most postmasters general, his responsibilities and influence were mainly related to domestic politics. The vice president, George Dallas of Pennsylvania, did not attend cabinet meetings or participate in policy making, although he sometimes advised Polk on relations with Congress.

During the Mexican crisis of 1845–46 and the subsequent war with Mexico, the men attending Polk's cabinet meetings were severely hampered by their limited understanding of Mexican conditions and developments, by inadequate and unreliable information on the reactions of the Mexican governments and people to American military moves, and by extremely poor intelligence on the dispositions and capabilities of the Mexican army.

The information problem arose in part from the lack of an effective communication system. The telegraph network, which would play a major role in the Civil War a few years later, extended no further south in 1848 than Petersburg, Virginia. The railroad network ran only as far south as central Georgia. From there travelers used horse-drawn post coaches for 104 miles and then 55 miles of railroad to reach Montgomery, Alabama, where they could get a steamboat to New Orleans. In the spring of 1847, Trist's hurried trip from Washington to New Orleans took nine days. Mail from the Gulf Coast to Mexico was even slower and more unpredictable. U.S. Navy ships carried mail to Mexican ports, but even during the war with Mexico there was no effort by the navy or army to develop a regularly scheduled courier service. As soon as the U.S. Army moved inland in Mexico, the forwarding of mail depended on the irregular movements of army units or other potential couriers that happened to be available. Because of the substantial distances and the inadequate means of communication, Washington's communications with its diplomats and generals in Mexico were extremely slow and unreliable.

The problem of transmitting information was compounded by major limitations on both the collection and the use of information. The United States had no professional diplomats, and the men representing the United States in Mexico had little experience with the collection and evaluation of political intelligence. Their dispatches to Washington were often inaccurate or misleading. When the war began, the U.S. Army had no organization and little procedure for acquiring military intelligence. The lack of information about the location, strength, and capabilities of Mexican army units contributed ironically to both a general underestimation of the Mexican ability to carry out a prolonged war and to the administration's inclination to give credence to unfounded rumors of large Mexican troop concentrations.

The government of the United States was also very poorly prepared to evaluate the inadequate and tardy reports it received from Mexico. Virtually all important decisions were made at the cabinet level, yet none of the men attending cabinet meetings had been in a Hispanic country or had any knowledge of the Spanish language or Hispanic mentality. There was no organization or staff within the government to evaluate information from abroad or provide advice to cabinet members on foreign affairs. The civilian government had only clerks, not policy advisers. About the only significant sources of policy advice were informal consultations during congressional sessions with a few friendly senators and congressmen.

The information problem was compounded by the impatient president's frequent unwillingness to wait for the best available information. On several occasions, after waiting for weeks for developments in Mexico, Polk made important decisions on the basis of inadequate information prior to receiving full reports from his diplomatic or military representatives in Mexico.

The inadequate information available to the president and his tendency to make snap decisions were major causes of the most remarkable feature of Polk's policy toward Mexico — repeated cyclical fluctuations between aggressive military moves and peace initiatives. In five distinct cycles during the three-year Mexican crisis, Polk would rotate between brandishing the sword and waving the olive branch.

The first shift from the sword to the olive branch began soon after Trist's return to the Department of State.

THREE

The Cup of Forbearance

Although Polk's show of force in Texas had brought the nation to the brink of war with Mexico in the summer of 1845, the threat of war receded that fall. General Herrera, who had served as interim president of Mexico since the end of 1844, was elected constitutional president of Mexico on August 5. He named a new cabinet that was opposed to war with the United States.[1] Two members of the new government would play crucial roles in Trist's mission to Mexico two years later. Manuel de la Peña y Peña, a prominent jurist, was foreign minister. Bernardo Couto, a respected lawyer, was minister of justice.

In late August, Polk's confidential agent in Mexico, Dr. Parrott, reported that "the present cabinet ... desires to settle the differences between the two governments by negotiations.... There is a desire, even publicly manifested, to receive a *commissioner* from the United States.... An Envoy possessing suitable qualifications ... might with comparative ease settle, *over a breakfast*, the most important questions."[2] Parrott's optimistic report accurately reflected the peaceful inclinations of Herrera and his cabinet but greatly underestimated the weakness of Herrera's political position and the extent of the opposition in Mexico to any concessions to the Americans.[3]

Despite Parrott's reference to a "commissioner," Polk recorded in his diary that Parrott had reported that the Mexican government "is desirous to re-establish diplomatic relations with the United States and that a Minister from the U.S. would be received." Polk also noted the concurrence of John Black, although the consul in Mexico City had written only that the new government was regarded as opposed to war with the United States. Polk and the cabinet decided on September 16 that it was "expedient to re-open diplomatic relations with Mexico" and that John Slidell, a Louisiana congressman, should be sent to Mexico as minister.[4]

Slidell was recommended for the diplomatic assignment by Buchanan. The secretary of state, like the president, carefully calculated the domestic political impact of every diplomatic move. Buchanan probably thought that

Slidell, a former New Yorker who was known as a political wire-puller in Louisiana, would be an asset in Buchanan's future presidential campaign. If he was able to obtain a treaty ceding California to the United States, the secretary of state who had sent him to Mexico would derive substantial political benefit from the mission. Although the extent of the relationship between Buchanan and Slidell in 1845 remains obscure, Buchanan's expectation that Slidell would become a valuable political ally proved accurate. As an influential U.S. senator, Slidell played an important role in Buchanan's election as president in 1856 and was one of Buchanan's most influential advisers during his presidency. Polk, who was in Tennessee until the last days of Slidell's term in Congress, probably had not met Slidell before his mission to Mexico. He accepted Buchanan's recommendation that Slidell, who spoke some Spanish, would be a suitable envoy.

From the beginning, there was confusion concerning Slidell's diplomatic role and status in Mexico. Although Polk was planning to send a minister "to re-open diplomatic relations,"[5] his secretary of state wrote Consul Black that he should ascertain whether the Mexican government would receive "an envoy from the United States entrusted with full powers to adjust all the questions in dispute between the two governments."[6] This language indicated that the U.S. government intended to appoint a special commissioner for a short-term negotiating assignment rather than a resident minister to resume normal diplomatic relations. Moreover, since the Mexicans thought the most important question in dispute between the two countries was the Texas question, it gave the Mexicans the erroneous impression that Slidell was authorized to negotiate concerning the status of Texas.

The reply from Peña, brought to Washington by the returning Parrott on November 9, indicated that the Mexican government was willing to receive a "commissioner" to negotiate a settlement of the disputes between the United States and Mexico.[7] But Polk again ignored the important distinction between a resident minister and a special commissioner, and he appointed Slidell as "Envoy Extraordinary and Minister Plenipotentiary" to Mexico. Such an envoy, not extraordinary at all, was the type of diplomatic representative sent to most nations. Mexican acceptance of Slidell as minister would have constituted a resumption of normal diplomatic relations before the resolution of any of the issues which had led to the break in relations and before the Mexicans heard the terms for a settlement that Slidell had brought to Mexico.

Two former U.S. diplomats in Mexico asserted later that they had told Polk and Buchanan prior to the Slidell mission that the Herrera government would not be willing to receive a regularly accredited minister prior to the resolution of the U.S.-Mexican dispute. Benjamin E. Green, U.S. chargé in

THREE / *The Cup of Forbearance*   49

Mexico before the Herrera government broke off diplomatic relations, claimed many years later that the Herrera government's unwillingness to receive a resident minister was fully explained to Polk and Buchanan prior to the Slidell mission. Joel Poinsett, former U.S. minister to Mexico, also claimed later that he warned the administration that Herrera could receive a commissioner but would not dare to receive a resident U.S. minister.[8]

Polk's biographers have not provided a satisfactory explanation of his insistence on appointing Slidell as minister to Mexico. Eugene McCormac suggested in 1922 that Polk did not realize the significance of appointing a minister rather than a special envoy: "It seems incredible that the President would deliberately jeopardize the success of a mission which promised to procure everything he could desire, even California, simply to gratify a whim of sending to Mexico the particular kind of a diplomatic agent which she did not want."[9] Charles Sellers wrote in 1966 that "it is impossible that Polk did not understand the significance of his insistence on the reopening of regular diplomatic relations."[10] Nonetheless, if the Slidell appointment is considered in the context of Polk's subsequent repeated misjudgments of Mexican reactions, it seems quite possible that he did not fully appreciate the important diplomatic difference between a special commissioner and a resident minister or that he did not understand why his appointment of Slidell as minister made it even more difficult for the shaky Mexican government to receive his envoy.

An appointment as minister required confirmation by the Senate. But since Congress was not in session, Polk could give Slidell a recess appointment without waiting for Senate confirmation. He tried to keep the mission secret to avoid meddling by the opposition Whigs at home and by the British in Mexico.[11] By the time Congress met in December, however, news of the Slidell mission had leaked and Polk sent the nomination to the Senate. Although there was some opposition, Slidell was confirmed by January 20.[12]

The primary objective of the Slidell mission was the purchase of California. Polk's strong interest in the acquisition of California was the most consistent thread of his early diplomacy and of his subsequent conduct of the war with Mexico.[13] It was derived in part from his mentor, Andrew Jackson, who had dreamed for years of an American empire extending from Atlantic to Pacific. Jackson had tried to buy northern California from the Mexicans in 1835. His last representative in Mexico, Powhatan Ellis, wrote in 1836 that "the bay of San Francisco is one of the largest and most secure in the world. Its acquisition would be of immense importance to the United States."[14] Before leaving the White House in 1837, Jackson secretly advised the Texans to claim California as a way to reduce opposition to the annexation

of Texas among Northeasterners, who wanted a Pacific harbor for their whaling ships.[15] In the early 1840s, expansion of trade with China intensified American interest in a Pacific harbor.

When Polk came to the White House, much less was known by Americans about California than about Oregon. The Oregon Trail, crossing the Rockies through South Pass, provided a road for covered wagons from the Missouri River to the Columbia River. There was no wagon route through the central Rockies to California, and the Mexicans prohibited exploration of possible desert routes south of the Rockies. But public interest had been stimulated by several accounts of visits to California by American seamen — notably Richard Henry Dana's *Two Years Before the Mast* — and by the widely read report by an army topographical engineer, John Charles Fremont, on his explorations of northern routes to California in 1843–44. Fremont had married the daughter of Senator Thomas Hart Benton of Missouri, who undoubtedly contributed to Polk's interest in California.

Forty years later George Bancroft wrote that Polk told him soon after his inauguration that the acquisition of California would be one of the "great measures" of his administration.[16] During the first year of his presidency, Polk's goal of acquiring California remained, however, a secret. On June 24, 1845, while Polk was still waiting for the Mexican reaction to the annexation of Texas, secret orders were sent to Commodore John D. Sloat, commander of the U.S. naval forces in the Pacific: "If you ascertain with certainty that Mexico has declared war against the United States, you will at once possess yourself of the port of San Francisco."[17] By the following spring, Polk's desire to annex California was known by General Zachary Taylor and some of his senior officers on the Rio Grande, but this vital aspect of the president's secret foreign policy remained concealed from his secretary of state until after the declaration of war with Mexico.

Thomas Ritchie, editor of the new administration paper, the *Union,* wrote an editorial on June 2, 1845, that undoubtedly reflected Polk's viewpoint:

> Who can arrest the torrent that will pour onward to the West? The road to California will open to us. Who will stay the march of our western people? Our northern brethren also are looking toward that inviting region with much more interest than those of the South. They, too, will raise the cry of "Westward ho!" However strongly many of them may now oppose annexation [of Texas], yet let California be thrown open to their ambition and the torrent even of their population will roll on westwardly to the Pacific.[18]

In mid–October, the arrival of a dispatch from the storekeeper in Monterey who served as American consul, Thomas O. Larkin, renewed old fears

THREE / *The Cup of Forbearance*

of British control of California. For a decade American representatives in Mexico had forwarded rumors of various schemes to expand British influence in California. Earlier in 1845 the Californians had revolted and forced Santa Anna's military governor to leave the province. Now Larkin passed on rumors that the Mexican government was organizing an expedition to restore its authority in the rebellious province and that the expedition was instigated and financed by the British in Mexico.[19] He also reported suspicious activities of newly appointed British and French consuls in California.

Suspicion of the British was a staple commodity in early nineteenth-century America. Andrew Jackson, victor in the last American battle with the British at New Orleans in 1815, undoubtedly contributed to Polk's strongly anti-British viewpoint. Even if California had been less attractive, Polk would have wanted to acquire it to prevent the British from doing so. His reaction to Larkin's report of increased British interest in California was to promote him to confidential agent and instruct him to warn the Californians of the dangers of British or French interference in their affairs. "Whilst … this government does not, under existing circumstances, intend to interfere between Mexico and California," Buchanan wrote to Larkin, "it would vigorously interpose to prevent the latter from becoming a British or French colony. If the people should desire to become one of the free and independent states of this Union … they would be received as brethren, when this can be done without affording Mexico just cause of complaint."[20]

In his first annual message to Congress in December, Polk revived and expanded the Monroe Doctrine with a new corollary that no European nation would be permitted to interfere with the decision of any republic or province in North America to join the United States. The "balance of power" concept must not be permitted any application on the North American continent. "We must ever maintain the principle that the people of this continent alone have the right to decide their own destiny."[21] Polk commented later that "in reasserting Mr. Monroe's doctrine, I had California and the fine bay of San Francisco as much in view as Oregon."[22]

The threat of British control of California was more apparent than real. The British minister in Mexico, Richard Pakenham, had proposed the establishment of a British colony in California in 1841, but the British government replied that it had little interest in new colonies which added financial burdens and complicated British relations with other major powers.[23] In 1844 the British vice consul in California, James Forbes, forwarded an inquiry from leading Californians concerning the possibility of a British protectorate. In May 1845, Forbes heard from London that the British government could not assist any insurrectionary movement in California, although it would "view with much dissatisfaction the establishment of a protectoral power over California by any other foreign state."²⁴ The British government, preoccupied with problems at home, was reluctant to take any action in California which might prevent a settlement of the long-standing dispute with the United States over Oregon.²⁵

Slidell had been instructed to make every effort to obtain California. The official instruction from Buchanan was backed up by a private letter from Polk to Slidell stating that he was "exceedingly desirous to acquire California."²⁶ Slidell was authorized to offer the Mexicans $25 million for a treaty that gave the United States the territories of New Mexico and northern California, including Monterey and San Francisco.²⁷ But Slidell had no opportunity to make this offer. The Herrera government was surprised by Slidell's prompt arrival in early December and was not prepared to receive him. The conservatives were ready to take maximum political advantage of any concession to the Americans, and the insecure moderate government was afraid that receiving Slidell as minister would lead to a revolution and a new conservative government.²⁸

A December 17 dispatch from Slidell indicating the government's reluctance to receive him as minister was received by Polk on January 12.²⁹ Although it did not indicate that the Herrera government had definitively refused to receive him, Slidell's dispatch convinced Polk that he was not going to gain his objectives in 1846 by diplomacy alone. He had waved the olive branch for several months; now it was again time to brandish the sword. The next day, January 13, orders were sent to General Zachary Taylor to occupy the territory between the Nueces and the Rio Grande.

Polk had realized from the beginning that Slidell's negotiations with the Mexicans might not be successful. A week after Slidell left for Mexico, Buchanan wrote him that the president hoped the negotiations could be completed before the end of the upcoming congressional session "so that, in the event of failure, prompt and energetic measures may be adopted on our part to redress the injuries which our citizens have sustained from Mexico."³⁰ But Polk was incensed by the unexpected reluctance of the Mexicans to begin negotiations, and he immediately decided that he should increase the pressure on the Mexicans by occupying the area between the Nueces and Rio Grande.

Ten days after the orders to Taylor, Polk heard from Slidell that the Herrera government had definitely declined to receive him as U.S. minister. Foreign minister Peña had informed Slidell on December 20 that he would be happy to receive him as a special commissioner to negotiate a settlement of the disputes between the two countries but could not receive him as resident minister. There is no indication that Slidell or Polk seriously considered the possibility of salvaging the mission by changing Slidell's status to that of special commissioner. Slidell now thought that his only remaining objective was "to throw all the responsibility and odium for the failure of negotiations on the Mexican government." He wrote Polk on December 29 that "this will place us upon the strongest possible ground and I have no doubt that if an appeal will be made by you to the country, it will be met with a hearty and unanimous response."³¹

There have been widely differing evaluations by historians of Polk's intentions concerning the Slidell mission. One view is that Polk was eager for peace and sincerely hopeful of successful negotiations with the Mexicans. Another view is that Polk did not want the Slidell mission to be successful, that the mission was designed only to establish a record of Mexican intransigence which would justify a declaration of war, and that Polk's real objective was to provide an excuse for the military conquest of California.

It is clear that Polk's first choice was to buy California from Mexico.³² He recorded in his diary on September 16 that he thought California and New Mexico might be obtained for $15 or $20 million but was willing to pay up to $40 million if they could not be had for less.³³ Polk's hope that he could buy California was an early example of his misjudgment of Mexican politics throughout the three-year Mexican crisis. "Already deeply aggrieved by the annexation of Texas," John H. Schroeder wrote in 1973, "no Mexican government could have then negotiated the cession of ... New Mexico and California."³⁴ But evidence that the president was naive and inept in his handling of the Slidell mission does not prove that he was insincere. Polk's unrealistic expectations of a successful negotiation in the fall of 1845, and again for a while in the spring of 1846, although ill-founded, are consistent with his unrealistic expectations from several other peace feelers during the next two years.

The instructions to Larkin and Slidell show that for a while in the fall of 1845, Polk's second choice was to wait for the Californians to follow the example of Texas and declare their independence from Mexico. Two months after the instructions to Larkin, Nicholas Trist sent Slidell a package of Spanish translations of the new state constitution of Texas. He suggested that Slidell forward them to Larkin, who could use them to show the Californians "what they would gain by a change."³⁵ Slidell forwarded the constitutions to Commodore Sloat at Mazatlan, who arranged their delivery in April in Monterey and San Francisco. In the words of Frederick Merk, the Californians were "offered the heady wine of the Texas compact as incentive to seek freedom."³⁶

David Pletcher has outlined a plausible scenario for the acquisition of California without war through a policy of gradualism:

> Polk might have sent Slidell to Mexico as a special envoy ... while Taylor's army, still at Corpus Christi, mounted guard over the disputed zone without offering an overt threat that would goad the Mexicans to cross the Rio Grande.... Tactful private warnings to Britain and the presence of Sloat's squadron cruising off the Mexican coast could have shielded an independence movement in California, which would establish a new state. At the least, an independent California could have maintained friendly relations for an indefinite period with the government in Washington. Eventually, the United States might have opened negotiations for annexation, choosing a time when Britain was fully involved in European affairs.... The revolutions of 1848 provided just such an opportunity, and there were others during the succeeding years.[37]

But Polk was unwilling to wait for the results of a policy of gradualism. He had already committed himself to serving only a single term as president, and he was unwilling to allow the credit for acquiring California to go to a future president who might be a Whig.

Polk's January 13 decision to send General Taylor to the Rio Grande was one of several important decisions regarding Mexico that Polk made too quickly with too little information and with inadequate consideration of the consequences. Although it was one of the most important decisions of his presidency, Polk did not mention it in his diary. Because of the lack of direct evidence, historians have rarely written about the reasons for the decision or Polk's expectations as to its consequences. Nevertheless, the indirect evidence supports two conclusions concerning the orders to Taylor.

First, the decision was not primarily motivated by a desire for the Rio Grande as the boundary with Mexico or by interest in the territory between the Rio Grande and the Nueces. On the map the Rio Grande, a long river running from New Mexico to the Gulf, appeared to be a natural boundary and barrier between Texas and Mexico, although it proved to be too shallow to impede those who wanted to cross it illegally. The Texans wanted a Rio Grande boundary because it would give them control of a buffer zone between Texan and Mexican settlements and would enhance their claim that Texas extended westward to Sante Fe on the upper Rio Grande. Polk, who usually gave domestic political considerations greater weight than diplomatic factors, supported the Texans in order to assure that the new state of Texas would vote Democratic in the next election. But the practical and political importance of the Rio Grande as a boundary was not great enough to risk a major military confrontation with the Mexicans for that reason alone. Interest in the land between the Rio Grande and the Nueces, an uninhabited desert of no known value, played no role in reaching the decision. The

THREE / *The Cup of Forbearance* 55

order to Taylor to occupy the disputed area was essentially a move in a diplomatic and military chess game with the Mexicans. The name of that game was the acquisition of California.

Second, Polk thought that a show of force on the Rio Grande would bring the Mexicans to the negotiating table without bloodshed. This conclusion is supported by his failure to make significant preparations for war, by his belief while Taylor was en route to the Rio Grande that the new Paredes government would receive Slidell, and by his similar misjudgments of Mexican reactions to several later U.S. military moves.

Two other factors probably contributed to Polk's unwillingness to wait for a more definitive Mexican response to the Slidell mission before ordering Taylor to occupy the disputed area. One was reluctance to leave Taylor's army in its unhealthy location at Corpus Christi until the onset of the next "sickly season." The troops had been decimated by sickness after their arrival there during the previous summer. Taylor had written in November that much more sickness was to be expected when warm weather returned and that "winter is the best time for operations in Texas."[38] Polk may have thought that if he waited too long, Taylor's troops might not be ready when they were needed for a show of force on the Rio Grande.

Another factor adding urgency was Polk's desire to bring the Mexican affair to a stage permitting a definitive message to Congress before it adjourned in early summer, returning only in December after the midterm congressional elections. There were several references to such a message in his diary and in dispatches to and from Slidell, but these contain no indication of the expected purpose or content of the message. In the event of the bloodless victory he anticipated, such a message would have allowed him to proclaim his resolute and successful handling of the Mexican situation to the country in time to benefit Democratic candidates in the fall congressional elections. Or, if the Mexicans were still dragging their feet, the message would have provided a new opportunity for tough talk to the Mexicans and for the building of congressional and public support for a strong policy toward Mexico.

Polk may have realized that by the time such a message could be delivered in the spring or early summer, the Mexican situation might require urgent congressional action that could not be deferred until the next congressional session in December 1846. He may also have foreseen that the Whigs would capture control of the House of Representatives in the congressional elections in the fall of 1846 and concluded that he should seek congressional support for his Mexican policy while the Democrats still controlled both houses.

In his message in May recommending a declaration of war, Polk defended the January 13 orders to Taylor on the grounds that the area north of the Rio Grande had become a part of the United States through the admission of Texas to the Union and that "invasion was threatened" from across the river. Neither claim was valid. The assumption that the area between the Nueces and Rio Grande was a part of the United States was based only on unsubstantiated claims by the Texans. But once he had ordered Taylor to occupy the area, Polk had to insist that it was American territory or admit that he had ordered an invasion of Mexico.

Rumors of a Mexican crossing of the Rio Grande during the previous summer had proved to be without foundation. Parrott, arriving back in Washington in November, reported that many of Arista's officers had returned to the capital from the Rio Grande "in a state of utter poverty."[39] There was no hint of a threatened Mexican invasion in the reports Polk received prior to January 13 from Slidell and Black in Mexico or from General Taylor in Texas. Taylor's reports from Corpus Christi repeatedly stated that he had no intelligence from below the Rio Grande.

Even though he expected a bloodless victory, Polk recognized that the orders to Taylor could lead to war. He did not prepare for it, but he did not flinch from it. "It is not designed, in our present relations with Mexico, that you should treat her as an enemy," Taylor was told by the secretary of war on January 13. "But, should she assume that character by a declaration of war, or by an open act of hostility toward us, you will not act merely on the defensive, if your relative means enable you to do otherwise."[40] Slidell was informed by the secretary of state on the twentieth that the president had ordered the "army of Texas" to the Rio Grande and sent a strong fleet to the Gulf and "will thus be prepared to act with vigor and promptitude the moment the Congress will give him the authority."[41] But the January 13 order to Taylor gave the rustic frontier general, who totally lacked political or diplomatic experience, authority to judge whether the Mexicans had engaged in "an open act of hostility" that required him to begin offensive operations.

A week after the orders to Taylor, Polk learned that General Mariano Paredes had issued a "pronunciamento" against the Herrera government on December 14 in San Luis Potosí and had marched toward the capital.[42] Although Polk knew little of Paredes or his supporters, he immediately guessed that the Herrera government had already been overthrown. In a January 28 dispatch revised by the president, Buchanan told Slidell that he should not leave Mexico until the expected new government had decided whether it would receive him as minister. "Should the Mexican government ... finally refuse to receive you," Buchanan wrote, "the cup of forbearance will have been exhausted.... Nothing can remain but to take the redress of the injuries of our citizens and the insults to our government into our own

THREE / *The Cup of Forbearance*   57

hands.... Should war become inevitable, the President will be prepared to conduct it with vigor."⁴³ But the secretary and the president didn't think war was inevitable, and the dispatch provided additional instructions for the negotiations that they hoped Slidell could conduct with the new government.

Similar language about "taking redress into our own hands" was used in five entries in Polk's diary in the coming weeks.⁴⁴ None of them indicated the type of redress Polk had in mind, and the repeated use of this vague phrase probably reflected Polk's uncertainty about the actions which might be necessary and appropriate as the Mexican crisis unfolded. In his second annual message to Congress in December 1846, Polk noted that this phrase was from Andrew Jackson's special message to Congress on relations with Mexico in February 1837.⁴⁵ Jackson had written that although the United States had sufficient cause for war with Mexico, another opportunity should be given to Mexico "to atone for the past, before we take redress into our own hands."⁴⁶ Old Hickory, who had been about to leave the White House, had chosen an ambiguous phrase to cover the failure of his administration to deal effectively with Mexico. Polk used the same phrase to maintain an appearance of resolution while avoiding a commitment as to his future course of action.

News soon arrived that Polk had guessed right. On New Year's Eve, the troops in the Mexican capital had pronounced against the government, Herrera had resigned and fled, and a new government had been formed with General Paredes as president. Paredes headed a conservative coalition supported by the army, the Catholic clergy, and the sizable monarchist faction that believed Mexico should be ruled by a European prince.⁴⁷ This alcoholic and ineffective president presided over the Mexican government for seven crucial months that included the beginning of the war between the United States and Mexico.

Before leaving the Mexican capital to wait for further instructions nearer the coast in Jalapa, Slidell conveyed to Paredes through an intermediary the idea that his government's acute financial embarrassment "might be relieved if satisfactory arrangements for boundary could be made."⁴⁸ It was not the first time, nor the last, that a U.S. representative in Mexico concluded that money was the key to peace with Mexico.

Meanwhile, Polk received a visit from Colonel Alexander A. Atocha, a former Spanish officer who lived in New Orleans. Atocha, who had recently talked with Santa Anna in his exile in Havana, told Polk that if Santa Anna returned to power in Mexico, he would be willing to sign a treaty giving the United States all the territory north and east of the Rio Grande and north of San Francisco in return for a payment of $30 million. Although Polk was not sure Atocha could be trusted, he nonetheless accepted the idea that an advantageous peace settlement could be obtained if Santa Anna returned to power.⁴⁹

After hearing of the overthrow of the Herrera government, the Polk administration waited for six weeks before communicating again with Slidell. This uncharacteristic hesitation was due to the acute tension in this period between the United States and Britain over Oregon.⁵⁰ For nearly a year, Polk had juggled two simultaneous crises of his own making—a diplomatic confrontation with Britain over the border in the Northwest and a diplomatic and military confrontation with Mexico over the border in the Southwest. Although the Mexican crisis ultimately led to war, the Oregon crisis attracted far more public and congressional attention until very shortly before the beginning of the war with Mexico.

The status of the "Oregon country" in the Pacific Northwest had remained unresolved for nearly half a century. Americans had established settlements south of the Columbia River, while a British company—the Hudson Bay Company—carried on fur trading operations in the unsettled territory north of the river. A U.S.-British treaty in 1827 confirmed the joint occupation of the territory. Several efforts to draw a boundary between United States and British territory in the Northwest had been unsuccessful. In the early 1840s, as the westward movement of settlers on the Oregon Trail increased rapidly each year, settlement of the Oregon boundary became increasingly urgent. When Polk was inaugurated in March 1845, three thousand additional settlers were poised along the Missouri River for the trek to Oregon.⁵¹

In the summer of 1845, Polk renewed the U.S. proposal that the Oregon country be divided along the 49th parallel, although many American expansionists wanted a border much further north at 54°40'. Polk's proposal was rejected by the British minister—the same Richard Pakenham who had proposed a British colony in California—because it did not include British rights to navigate the Columbia River. Polk angrily withdrew the offer and recommended to Congress in December 1845 that the United States give notice of the termination of the joint occupation of Oregon, as allowed by the U.S.-British treaty of 1827. The belligerent tone of the message was intended to convince the British that they should compromise,⁵² but it also convinced many Americans, including General Zachary Taylor, that war with England was imminent.⁵³

During the nearly five months that the Oregon issue dominated public attention, the Congress, press, and public paid very little attention to relations with Mexico. Polk's diary contained almost daily references to discussions with cabinet members and congressional leaders about the Oregon crisis, but

THREE / *The Cup of Forbearance* 59

there were few references to Mexico. The Congress did not learn about the orders to Taylor until March, and his movement to the Rio Grande was not mentioned in the president's diary until April 29, a month after Taylor's arrival on the river.

When Polk secretly ordered Taylor to the Rio Grande in mid–January, he expected that congress would act promptly on Oregon and that the British reaction to the congressional action would be known before Taylor reached the river. But the Oregon debate dragged on. Although Taylor took his time getting to the Rio Grande, the Oregon and Texas crises threatened to reach the boiling point at about the same time. When Buchanan finally wrote to Slidell again on March 12, it was to instruct him to make a formal request to be received as minister by the Paredes government. The president and the secretary wanted to make sure that if the Slidell mission failed, there was a clear record of Mexican rejection of the American olive branch. "On your return to the United States," Buchanan wrote, "energetic measures would at once be recommended by the President and these might fail to obtain the support of Congress if it could be asserted that the existing government had not refused to receive our Minister."[54] Slidell was urged to return to the Mexican capital from Jalapa to make the request to Paredes in person.

For a while in late March and early April, Polk and his cabinet thought the Paredes government would receive Slidell. Polk recorded in his diary on March 28 that dispatches from Slidell "rendered it probable that he would very soon be received by the existing government of Mexico in his character of Minister of the U.S."[55] This was a great exaggeration of the mildly hopeful outlook Slidell had conveyed in two dispatches in February. Slidell had written on February 6 that if U.S.-British negotiations on Oregon were resumed with a good chance of success, "pretexts will not be wanting for a reconsideration of the decision of the Herrera cabinet" to refuse to receive him. On February 17, Slidell wrote that Taylor's march to the Rio Grande "may exercise a salutary influence upon the course of this Government" but also expressed the opinion that Paredes would not be able to hold power for very long.[56]

Polk's belief that he could strike a deal with Paredes may have been derived in part from a conversation on March 27 with Waddy Thompson, the former U.S. minister to Mexico. Polk made no comment in his diary about the talk with Thompson, but he told the cabinet the next day that Paredes' main problem was money:

> If our minister could be authorized upon the *signing* of a treaty to pay down a half million or a million of dollars it would enable General Paredes to pay, feed, and clothe the army and maintain itself in power until the

> Treaty could be ratified by the U.S. and subsequent installments which might be stipulated in the Treaty paid.... Such a sum might induce him to make a treaty which he would not otherwise venture to make. In these views there seemed to be a concurrence. The question followed how an appropriation could be obtained from Congress without exposing to the public and foreign governments its object.[57]

Polk discussed the idea of such a secret appropriation with Senators Benton, Allen, and Calhoun. He noted on April 3 that Calhoun had advised him against requesting money for a payment to Mexico "at present."[58] Polk put the idea aside in the spring but would attempt to implement it in the summer.

"Our affairs with Mexico appear to be going very well," Secretary of the Navy Bancroft wrote on March 29 to the U.S. minister in London. "Our little army of occupation is advancing to the Del Norte. No resistance is apprehended, and in Mexico itself a better spirit toward us is prevailing.... The prospect of an adjustment is better than ever."[59]

Responding on March 24 to a Senate inquiry whether relations with Britain or Mexico required an increase in U.S. naval or military force, Polk said "a wise precaution demands such an increase" but pledged to pursue policies calculated to preserve an honorable peace with both nations.[60] The following week Polk told Marcy that he should reduce the estimates prepared by the bureau chiefs in the War Department.[61] The only logical explanation for this action, just as Taylor was arriving at the Rio Grande, is that Polk believed Taylor's march would convince the Mexicans to accept the "adjustment" desired by the United States. "The President was of the opinion," Bancroft wrote some years later, "that the appearance of our land and naval forces upon the borders of Mexico and in the Gulf would deter Mexico alike from declaring war or invading the U.S."[62]

Polk's optimism in late March and early April about the prospects of a deal with Paredes is another example of his tendency to jump to unwarranted conclusions on the basis of slim and incomplete evidence of developments in Mexico. Until only a month before war was declared, he still thought he could obtain the treaty he desired by waving the sword without using it.

But the fate of the Slidell mission had been sealed before this burst of optimism in Washington. Slidell had written the Paredes government on March 1 that "the President wishes by exhausting every honorable means of conciliation, to demonstrate to the civilized world that if its peace shall be disturbed, the responsibility must lie with Mexico alone."[63] On March 12 the Mexican foreign minister wrote Slidell that Paredes was unwilling to receive him as minister. To do so while the Texas question was still pending would involve "prejudging it without even touching it."[64]

THREE / *The Cup of Forbearance* 61

This news reached Washington on April 7. "Be assured that nothing is to be done with these people," Slidell wrote, "until they have been chastised."[65] But the Oregon crisis had reached a critical point, and Polk was not quite ready to chastise the Mexicans. Slidell had been told in March that in the event of the failure of his mission, his premature return to Washington might "produce considerable alarm in the public mind and might possibly exercise an injurious influence on our relations with Great Britain" on the Oregon issue.[66] The rejected envoy returned to his home near New Orleans and awaited further instructions.

By mid–April there were indications that Congress would soon adopt a conciliatory resolution on Oregon. Congress was expected to adjourn by June; Polk was running out of time to obtain congressional action on the Mexican issue before Congress reconvened in December. On April 17, Polk summoned Slidell to Washington. He promised to delay action until Slidell arrived, thus allowing several more weeks for congressional action on Oregon and for news from the Rio Grande before he had to decide on his next move in Mexico.[67]

FOUR

Hostilities May Be Considered as Commenced

The January 13 order to occupy the area between the Nueces and the Rio Grande reached General Zachary Taylor at Corpus Christi on February 3. Although he was ordered to make the move "as soon as it can be conveniently done with reference to the season and the routes by which your movements must be made," the order did not convey a great sense of urgency. Taylor took another month to make his preparations, including a reconnaissance of a possible route via Padre Island, which extends parallel to the coast between Corpus Christi and the Rio Grande. He eventually chose an inland route and began the march from Corpus Christi on March 3, 1846.

The land along the 196-mile route was populated only by herds of wild horses, some small game, and a great many centipedes, tarantulas, and rattlesnakes. Taylor thought the Mexicans might resist his crossing of the Arroyo Colorado, a shallow river near the present town of Harlingen, which he reached on March 19. The Mexican commander at Matamoros, General Francisco Mejia, issued a proclamation calling for resistance to "the degenerate sons of Washington." Taylor was met by Mexican officers who told him that his crossing of the arroyo would be considered to be a declaration of war by the United States.[1] He ignored the warning, crossed without incident, and marched on toward the Rio Grande. He established a supply base at Point Isabel near the Brazos de Santiago, the inlet between Padre and Brazos islands which admitted ships to a sheltered lagoon.

Taylor reached the Rio Grande opposite Matamoros, a small Mexican town about 30 miles southwest of Point Isabel, on March 28. Taylor sent his second-in-command, General William J. Worth, and five lieutenants across the river under a white flag. General Mejia refused to meet Worth but sent his second-in-command, General Vega. None of the American officers spoke Spanish, and none of the Mexicans admitted to understanding English.

FOUR / *Hostilities May Be Considered as Commenced*

Worth's "interpreter," Lt. Knowlton, translated Worth's remarks into French, and this version was then translated into Spanish by one of the Mexican officers.

Minutes prepared by the five lieutenants indicated what they thought had been said by and to the Mexicans:

> General Vega remarked that "we" felt indignation at seeing the American flag placed on the Rio Grande, a portion of the Mexican territory. General Worth replied that ... the army had been ordered to occupy its present position by its government; it has come in a peaceable rather than belligerent attitude, with a determination to respect the rights and customs of those on the right bank of the Rio Grande.... General Taylor was well aware of the importance of Brazos Santiago to the commerce and business community of Matamoros ... and would freely grant entrance and exit to all Mexican and other vessels trading with Matamoros on the same terms as before its occupation by the United States, leaving all questions arising therefrom to be settled hereafter by the two governments.[2]

Despite this and earlier statements that the army had come in a peaceable attitude, Taylor built a strong fort in a bend of the river opposite Matamoros. Its battery of four 18-pounders covered the ferry crossing and was within range of the town's public square. Taylor thought the threat of demolishing the town would restrain the Mexicans "from any enterprises upon our side of the river."[3] During their first two weeks on the Rio Grande, Taylor and most of his officers thought there was a good chance for a peaceful resolution of the dispute. "If they remain quiet, we shall not come to blows," Taylor wrote his daughter on April 7.[4] Lt. George C. Meade, a future Union general, also thought it would be a "bloodless war."[5]

On April 11, General Pedro Ampudia arrived at Matamoros with 2,400 men. After the remainder of his force arrived on April 14, the total Mexican force at Matamoros was about 4,400 men and was about equal in size to Taylor's army.[6] Ampudia was greatly disliked by Mexicans along the river and was especially hated by Texans for his barbaric treatment of the Texas prisoners captured at Mier in 1842. He immediately demanded that Taylor withdraw to the Nueces; if he did not, "arms and arms alone must decide the question."[7] Taylor replied that his orders would not permit him to "retrograde from the position I now occupy."[8] Ampudia prepared for an attack but canceled his plans when he received orders from General Mariano Arista, who was en route to Matamoros to take over the chief command on the river, to take no action until he arrived.[9]

Arista had a much better reputation among northern Mexicans and Texans than Ampudia.[10] He had lived for a time in Cincinnati, spoke English, and had married an American woman. Several reports had reached Washington that Arista hoped the conflict with the United States could be settled by negotiation.[11] Colonel Atocha told Polk in February that Arista was friendly to the United States and favored the annexation by the United States of Mexico's northern states.[12] Rumors that Arista was coming to the Rio Grande as a "pacificator" reached Taylor's camp as early as April 2.[13]

On April 15 a Mexican from Matamoros told Taylor that an express had just arrived from the Mexican capital; Arista would supersede Ampudia and Mexican operations against the Americans would be suspended until June 1. The same morning Taylor received New Orleans newspapers reporting the optimistic outlook in Washington in late March and suggesting that Slidell had been received by the Mexican government. These reports were consistent with a letter from Commodore Connor, commander of the squadron off Vera Cruz, who had written Taylor on March 2 that "I have it on very good authority that it is probable that [Slidell] will be received by the Mexican government." The reports received on April 15 conflicted, however, with a rumor received the previous week that Slidell had left Mexico in late March.[14]

The news received on the morning of April 15 from the Mexican and American capitals convinced Taylor and his officers that negotiations were about to begin or were already under way. "It looks very much as if the Mexicans have received him and fixed this period (June 1) for the termination of negotiations," Lt. George C. Meade wrote his wife on that evening.[15] Major Philip Barbour was convinced that "there will not be a hostile gun fired."[16] "It is now the opinion of many," Lt. Ulysses S. Grant wrote home a few days later, "that our difficulty with Mexico will be settled by negotiation."[17] In fact, Slidell had left Vera Cruz on April 2 and had been back in New Orleans since April 9. He had no instructions to keep the U.S. commander on the Rio Grande informed on the status of his mission. News of Paredes' refusal to receive Slidell had reached Washington on April 7, but it did not reach Taylor until April 19.[18]

Although Polk later told Congress that Taylor had been given "positive orders to abstain from all aggressive acts toward Mexico and Mexican citizens,"[19] Taylor's response to the prospect of U.S.-Mexican negotiations was to order a naval blockade of the mouth of the Rio Grande. Since most of the provisions for Matamoros and its garrison were brought in by ship, the blockade made it impossible for the Mexicans to maintain a large force for very long at Matamoros.

Taylor had been instructed by the secretary of war in January to "enforce and maintain our common right to navigate" the Rio Grande,[20] although the common right of Mexicans and Americans to navigate the river would not be established until the treaty negotiated by Nicholas Trist in 1848. The Mexicans believed they had the exclusive right to navigate an interior river in their national territory. At first Taylor thought Marcy's instruction meant he should not interfere with Mexican commerce on the river. Assurances that the Rio Grande would remain open were given by Taylor in February to traders from Matamoros,[21] by the American officer who reconnoitered Padre Island in February to a Mexican customs officer, and by General Worth on March 28 to General Vega.[22] Despite these promises, Taylor eliminated freedom of navigation on the river on April 15.

In a message to the House of Representatives in 1848, Polk stated that "in prosecuting a foreign war ... duly declared by Congress, we have the right by 'conquest and military occupation' to acquire possession of the territories of the enemy.... It is from the same source of authority that we derive the unquestioned right, after the war has been declared by Congress, to blockade the ports and coasts of the enemy."[23] But General Zachary Taylor ordered the blockade of the Rio Grande nearly a month *before* the U.S. Congress declared that the United States was at war with Mexico.

There is no evidence that the blockade was suggested or ordered by the president or secretary of war. Since it took about three weeks for a dispatch or letter to reach Taylor from Washington, any such communication would have had to be written in Washington before about March 25. At that time Taylor had not yet arrived at the Rio Grande; a blockade order would have been inconsistent with Polk's belief at that time that he could strike a deal with Paredes and with his urgent need to prevent the Mexican situation from boiling over until the Oregon crisis was resolved. By the time Polk heard in early May about Taylor's blockade, however, Paredes had refused to receive Slidell and the Oregon crisis was receding, so Polk was not unhappy that his general had taken the Mexican bull by the horns.

The blockade has been ignored or barely mentioned by most historians and Taylor biographers, but a few historians have considered it the first act of war in the U.S.-Mexican conflict.[24] In 1994, Secretary of State Warren Christopher rejected proposals for a naval blockade of Castro's Cuba on the ground that such a blockade would be "an act of war."

One possible explanation for Taylor's blockade decision is that he intended to provoke a war with Mexico and provide an excuse for the U.S. seizure of New Mexico and California. But there is no substantial evidence that this rustic Whig general was acting to advance the geopolitical goals of the Democratic president. Indeed, Taylor's letters to his son-in-law that summer contain several disapproving comments on Polk's territorial ambitions, including his "outrageous" plan to take permanent possession of California.[25] A more credible explanation for Taylor's blockade is that he hoped by forcing the Mexicans to withdraw from Matamoros to avoid a long stalemate on the Rio Grande that would seriously undermine the health, morale, and effectiveness of his troops.

While still in Corpus Christi in November, Taylor had warned the War Department that widespread sickness among his troops should be expected with the coming of warm weather: "A summer movement would be attended with great expense of health and life."[26] Now in mid–April he was 150 miles further south on a coast known for the ravages of diarrhea and the *vómito*, yellow fever.

A prolonged stalemate would also accelerate other personnel and manpower problems. During the three weeks he had been on the river, Taylor had lost four senior officers. His egotistic second-in-command, General Worth, had departed with the intention to resign because of his resentment of a presidential ruling that permanent rank took precedence over brevet rank. Lt. Col. Ethan Allen Hitchcock departed on sick leave. Col. William Whistler was sent home because of drunkenness. The quartermaster, Col. Trueman Cross, was murdered by bandits or guerrillas while he rode outside the camp.

During the same period, Taylor had lost a considerable number of enlisted men through desertion. Many men in the ranks were recent immigrants with only a slight attachment to their adopted country. They were dazzled by the pretty señoritas, who could be seen bathing nude across the river, and by enticements offered by the Mexican generals, including a promise of 320 acres of land to each man crossing the river. Taylor reported on April 6 that these enticements "have met with considerable success"; the following week a Mexican newspaper in Matamoros claimed that 43 soldiers and 6 slaves had deserted from the American army. Taylor wrote later that "the evil of desertion" had "increased to an alarming extent" and that his ranks were being "daily thinned" before he ordered pickets to shoot deserters attempting to swim the river.[27]

By ordering the blockade, General Zachary Taylor acted to bring the confrontation on the river to a speedy end without waiting for diplomatic progress in the Mexican capital. He did what he thought was best for his troops. In a dispatch to the War Department, Taylor expressed confidence that the blockade would "compel ... the Mexicans either to withdraw their army from Matamoros, where it cannot be subsisted, or to assume the offensive on this side of the river."[28]

Taylor believed the Mexicans would choose the first option—withdrawal. He had spent his life fighting Indians, who usually avoided a pitched battle. He knew little and understood less about the Mexican army. In that era the U.S. Army had virtually no foreign intelligence capability. Before leaving Corpus Christi, Taylor wrote the War Department that "exaggerated

FOUR / *Hostilities May Be Considered as Commenced* 67

accounts of Mexican preparations to resist our advance" were being spread by persons who wanted the American army to remain in Texas; "I do not believe that our advance to the banks of the Rio Grande will be resisted."[29] After he reached the Rio Grande without encountering resistance, he could not believe that the Mexicans would cross it to attack his army.

Two subsequent statements document Taylor's belief that the Mexicans would not fight. When he sent Captain Thornton with two companies of dragoons on April 24 to investigate rumors that the Mexicans had crossed the river, Thornton's second-in-command reported that Thornton had been "prepossessed with the idea that the Mexicans had not crossed, and if they had, that they would not fight."[30] This conviction could only have come from his commander. Taylor reported later that when he learned that Arista had in fact sent a large force across the river, "I could not believe that even with 4,000 men he would make an attempt upon my camp opposite Matamoros." He assumed that Arista's objective was to capture the American supply depot at Point Isabel because "provisions had become exceedingly scarce in Matamoros since the blockade of the river," rather than an attack on the main American army.[31] The diaries and letters of several of Taylor's officers indicate that they also thought that the Mexicans would not fight.

Taylor's blockade decision was made very quickly with no recorded discussion with his senior officers. There is no indication that he realized that the blockade would eliminate any possibility that the U.S.-Mexican dispute could be resolved without war. "That Taylor, one of the least sensitive senior officers in the army, should be charged with the delicate responsibility for command along the Rio Grande in 1846," K. Jack Bauer wrote in the most recent biography of Taylor, "is one of the ironies of American history."[32]

Two days after the blockade order, the U.S. Navy stopped two schooners that were about to enter the river with supplies for Matamoros. When Ampudia protested, Taylor replied that the blockade was "the natural result of the state of war so much insisted upon by the Mexican authorities as actually existing at this time."[33] By then the Mexican government had decided to send its troops across the river. Although General Arista strongly advised against it, orders to attack the Americans were issued in the Mexican capital on April 4.

The decision to attack Taylor's army was influenced by the hostile attitudes of influential Mexicans towards Americans and their government, by excessive confidence in the capabilities of the Mexican army coupled with a substantial underestimation of the capability of the American army, by the belief that Northern leaders in the United States would not support a war with Mexico, by expectations of European support, and by Paredes' belief that a war with the United States was the only way to maintain himself in power in Mexico.

Justin R. Smith summarized in 1919 the reasons for the hostile attitudes of Mexican leaders toward the United States:

> The principal cause [was] the supposed misconduct of our government in the settlement, revolution, and successful resistance of Texas, and in the recognition and annexation of that republic ... but other strong reasons cooperated.... It was believed that we intended to pursue the Texas method progressively, until all of Mexico should little by little become ours.... It was alleged that we ... did all we could to hinder its agricultural, industrial, and commercial development ... and it was even believed that we incited the Indians to ravage the northern frontiers.... The privileged classes dreaded the influence of our democratic ideas. The clergy were afraid that Protestantism, or at least free thought, might cross the border.... The numerous misunderstandings and clashes with the United States ... had produced an enduring resentment, and in particular our claims and our efforts to have them settled were commonly deemed artificial and unjust.[34]

The overconfidence of the Mexican leaders in the capacity of the Mexican army was compounded of national pride, the self-serving statements of individual commanders, the lack of a civilian authority to oversee and evaluate the Mexican army, and the favorable comments about the Mexican army by European diplomats and important European newspapers. Mexican cavalry units were much more numerous than the American dragoons, and their horses and horsemanship were deemed much superior. Mexican artillery was thought to be excellent. The Mexican soldier was used to rapid movements on foot through bad country with limited rations. The Mexicans would also have the advantages of interior lines of communication, shorter supply lines, and support from the local population.[35]

The American army, on the other hand, was regarded as small, poorly disciplined, preoccupied with Indian-fighting and other frontier duties, incapable of long marches on foot, and weak in both artillery and cavalry. These previous perceptions of the American army were enhanced by reports from Matamoros after Taylor's army reached the Rio Grande, but most of these were received after the decision to attack had been made in the Mexican capital only seven days after Taylor's arrival at the Rio Grande.

The negative Mexican evaluation of the U.S. Army was bolstered by the belief that the American invasion of Mexico would not be supported by Northern leaders in the United States who thought the invasion was part of a plot by slaveowners to extend slavery. General Juan Almonte, Mexican minister in Washington from 1842 to 1845, reported in 1844 that conversations with northeastern congressmen and senators indicated that New England and perhaps other northeastern states would not support a war with

FOUR / *Hostilities May Be Considered as Commenced* 69

Mexico. Almonte returned to Mexico in 1845 and became Paredes' most trusted adviser.[36]

On the other hand, Mexican leaders thought Mexico could expect important support from England and perhaps other European powers during a war with the United States. In a recent study of the monarchists in 1845–46, Miguel E. Soto concluded that "the monarchist conspirators thought that with the support of the European powers, Mexico would emerge quite successfully from the conflict with the United States."[37] John Black, U.S. consul in the Mexican capital, reported a few days after the war began that it was confidently believed in the capital that Paredes had a good understanding with the English and that in return for ceded territory and an advantageous commercial treaty, England would give Mexico a large loan to finance the expenses of the war with the United States and would offer to guarantee a new U.S.-Mexican border, perhaps at the Nueces.[38] Mexican expectations of a major British role in an eventual peace settlement persisted throughout 1846 and 1847, until these hopes were shattered by a newly arrived British envoy.

In addition to all these reasons to attack the American invaders, the decision to attack was also influenced by the personal attitudes and ambitions of General Paredes. He used support for war with the United States to gain power late in 1845 and to retain it in the spring of 1846. In launching his revolution against Herrera in December 1845, he had accused the Herrera government of willingness to accept the loss of Texas in order to avoid "a glorious and necessary war" with the United States. Miguel E. Soto's study of the monarchists concluded that "the Paredes government ... had come to rely upon the first results of the war for its very survival."[39]

The order to attack was issued on April 4 by General Jose Maria Tornel, who had succeeded General Almonte as minister of war.[40] If Taylor had not cut off supplies to Matamoros, Arista might have found excuses to delay implementation of the order. But by the time Arista arrived in Matamoros, the town was becoming untenable. On April 23 a proclamation issued by Paredes informed the nation that he had ordered Arista to "attack the army which is attacking us, to answer with war the enemy who makes war on us."[41] The next day, April 24, although he had not yet heard of Paredes' proclamation, Arista warned Taylor that "hostilities have commenced, and ... you must not be surprised that the troops under my command should wait for no further signal."[42] Taylor replied that "if hostilities are to ensue, the responsibility must rest with them who actually commence them."[43]

On the day Taylor responded to Arista, the U.S. Congress removed the principal reason for presidential restraint in dealing with Mexico. Northern

Whigs and Southern Democrats agreed on April 25 to a joint resolution containing a conciliatory form of notice to the British of the termination of the joint occupation of Oregon. Unlike Polk's belligerent message in December, the congressional resolution was designed to promote a compromise with the British on the Oregon border issue and it eliminated any danger of war between the United States and Britain. The British government was preoccupied with a food crisis resulting from cold, wet weather that ruined much of the grain harvest in England and from a blight that destroyed half of the potato crop in Ireland. The food shortages had led to a major political crisis over the repeal of the Corn Laws, and the government was in no mood for a major struggle with the United States.[44] Within two months after the congressional action on Oregon, U.S. and British representatives would sign a new treaty providing that the northern border of the United States would run along the 49th parallel from the Lake of the Woods to Vancouver Island.

After the congressional resolution on Oregon, Polk felt free to make the next move toward his goal of obtaining California. His intention to send a message to Congress regarding Mexico was noted in his diary on April 7 — the day he heard that Paredes had refused to receive Slidell — and on April 9, 10, 11, 21, 25, and 28. But his thinking remained masked in the diary by vague comments about the need "to take the remedy for the injuries and wrongs we have suffered into our own hands."[45]

The available evidence indicates that Polk concluded during April that a short war between the United States and Mexico would speed the downfall of Paredes, eliminate any threat that Mexico would be governed by a European monarch, and lead to the early return of Santa Anna, who would be willing to sign a treaty ceding California to the United States.

Consul Black had reported on December 30 that it was widely believed in Mexico that Paredes had overthrown the Herrera government in order to pave the way for the establishment of a monarchy and that this plan was supported by England, France, and Spain.[46] The idea of a European prince on a Mexican throne was anathema to Polk. It conflicted with the Monroe Doctrine, which he had recently reaffirmed and expanded, and with his hope for the development of democratic political institutions in Mexico.

Buchanan wrote Slidell on March 12 that reports of the monarchists' plans had been received in Washington from several quarters and that Prince Henry of Spain was regarded as the most likely candidate for a Mexican throne. Although Buchanan thought "these may be, and probably are, idle speculations," he stated that an attempt by European powers to put a European prince on a Mexican throne would be "resisted by all the power of the United States."[47] But Polk had not allowed the reports of Paredes' monarchist

FOUR / *Hostilities May Be Considered as Commenced*   71

leanings to inhibit his enthusiasm for a deal with Paredes during the period in late March and early April when he thought such a deal was possible.

The news that Paredes had refused to receive Slidell was accompanied by indications that Slidell did not give great credence to the monarchist threat. On February 6 he had written that the establishment of monarchy was unpopular in the army, as every general including Paredes hoped to place himself at the head of a despotic government.[48] He noted on February 17 that the idea that the new monarchist journal, *El Tiempo*, reflected Paredes' views was contradicted by the existence of two other ministerial journals that opposed monarchy.[49] After the Paredes government refused to receive him, Slidell commented on March 18 that a "prompt and decisive action with Mexico" by the United States would prevent Britain and France from supporting the installation of a monarch while Mexico was engaged in hostilities with the United States.[50]

In the same dispatch, Slidell reported the prospect that the "Federal party" in Mexico, supported by leading military men, would invite the ex-dictator, Santa Anna, to head a new liberal movement. This idea was supported by a March 19 dispatch from Black indicating that the monarchist movement might be thwarted by "federalists" who objected strongly to European influences in Mexican affairs.[51] The idea that if Santa Anna returned to power, he would be willing to sign an acceptable treaty had been planted in Polk's mind in February by Colonel Atocha, and Polk held to this belief until it was shattered by events later in 1846.

Polk brought up the Mexican question again in the cabinet on April 28. "It was the unanimous opinion of the cabinet," Polk recorded, "that a message should be sent to Congress ... recommending that measures be adopted to take redress into our own hands for the aggravated wrongs done to our citizens ... by Mexico."[52] There was still no indication in the diary of the kind of the measures he was considering. No action was taken, pending Slidell's arrival in Washington and further news from the Rio Grande.

During the first week of May, the country was edging toward war, but there was no atmosphere of crisis in Washington. On Saturday, May 2, Polk noted that he had "nothing much of importance to submit to the cabinet."[53] The next day he told Senator Benton that the United States had "ample cause of war," that he was eager to avoid it "if it could be done honorably and consistently with the interests of our injured citizens," but that he "could not permit Congress to adjourn without bringing the subject before that body."[54] On Wednesday, mid–April dispatches arrived from Taylor describing Ampudia's threat of war if Taylor did not withdraw to the Nueces and Taylor's blockade of the Rio Grande. Polk recorded no comment on the blockade, noting only that "no collision has taken place, though the probabilities are that hostilities might take place soon.["55](#) On Thursday, Polk heard from the American minister in London that the British foreign minister thought that congressional moderation on the Oregon question paved the way for resumed negotiations.[56] This news strengthened Polk's conviction that he could now deal with the Mexican situation without worrying about war with Britain.

The next day, Friday, John Slidell arrived in response to Polk's summons on April 17. His last dispatches from Mexico had contained several statements of his conviction that the Mexicans would never agree to U.S. demands until "they have been chastised," "they have been taught to respect us," "we have given them a good drubbing," and "they have been made to feel our strength." The only record of his meeting with Polk is the note in Polk's diary that Slidell had urged him to take matters "in our own hands."[57]

Saturday, May 9, 1846, was the day the question of war or peace was decided in Washington. In the regular cabinet meeting that morning, Polk posed the question "of what was the duty of the Administration in the present state of our relations" with Mexico:

> I stated that ... we had ample cause of war ... I then propounded the distinct question ... whether I should make a message to Congress on Tuesday and recommend a declaration of war against Mexico. All except the Secretary of the Navy gave their advice in the affirmative. Mr. Bancroft dissented but said if any act of hostility should be committed by the Mexicans, he was then in favor of immediate war. Mr. Buchanan said he would feel better satisfied ... if the Mexican forces ... should commit any act of hostility, but as matters stood we had ample cause of war against Mexico and he gave his assent to the measure. It was agreed that the message should be prepared and submitted to the cabinet in their meeting on Tuesday.[58]

Polk directed Buchanan and Marcy to have their clerks begin copying the correspondence with Slidell and Taylor for submission to Congress with the message. The cabinet adjourned at about two o'clock.

Like most of Polk's important decisions regarding Mexico, the decision to recommend a declaration of war was made with grossly inadequate information. He had heard of the events on the Rio Grande during Taylor's first two weeks there, but he had no idea what had happened during the ensuing three weeks and had received no indication of the Mexican government's reaction to Taylor's arrival on the Rio Grande. But the impatient president wanted to send a message to Congress before the last days of the session and was unwilling to wait for additional information from Texas and Mexico.

The president and cabinet had decided to recommend that Congress

FOUR / *Hostilities May Be Considered as Commenced* 73

declare war on a neighboring country on the stated grounds of two decades of rather unsatisfactory diplomatic relations, sporadic harassment of American citizens and shipping, and about $3 million in unpaid claims by Americans against Mexico. An idea of the message Polk would have sent to Congress, if fate had not intervened to provide a stronger basis for a declaration of war, can be derived from his annual message to Congress that December. He reviewed "the wrongs we had suffered and patiently endured from Mexico," which included "unlawful seizures of American property," "insults to our flag," imprisonment of American citizens for insufficient causes, and "lawless seizure and confiscation of our merchant vessels and their cargoes."[59]

Polk was spared the harsher judgments by historians that would have been inevitable if he had recommended a declaration of war based only on the complaints against Mexico as of that morning. At 6 P.M. that evening, the adjutant general of the army arrived at the White House with an April 26 dispatch from General Taylor:

> I regret to report that a party of dragoons ... became engaged with a very large force of the enemy, and after a short affair in which some sixteen were killed and wounded, appear to have been surrounded and compelled to surrender. Not one of the party has returned, except a wounded man sent in this morning by the Mexican commander, so I cannot report the particulars of the engagement.... Hostilities may now be considered as commenced.[60]

Taylor also reported receiving a letter from Arista, not yet fully translated, stating that he considered hostilities commenced. Yet Taylor's conclusion that hostilities had in fact commenced was based entirely on the "very confused idea of the affair," as it was described by one officer, from a wounded dragoon who thought Captain Thornton and a lieutenant had been killed although they were only prisoners. But the missing "particulars of the engagement" were of no interest to the impatient president. Mexico had shed American blood on soil that he claimed as American, and he needed no more details or justification for the strong message to Congress that he had been contemplating for more than a month.

Polk immediately summoned the cabinet to meet again at 7:30 P.M. "The cabinet was unanimously of the opinion," he recorded, "that a message should be sent to Congress on Monday ... recommending vigorous and prompt measures to enable the Executive to prosecute the war."[61] Polk, Buchanan, and Bancroft labored all day Sunday on the war message. It was delivered to Congress at noon on Monday, May 11, 1846:

> The cup of forbearance had been exhausted even before the recent information from the frontier of the Del Norte. But now ... Mexico has passed

the boundary of the United States, has invaded our territory, and shed American blood on American soil. She has proclaimed that hostilities have commenced and that the two nations are now at war. As war exists, and nothwithstanding all our efforts to avoid it, exists by the act of Mexico herself, we are called upon by every consideration of duty and patriotism to vindicate with decision the honor, rights, and interests of our country.[62]

The message contained no reference to Polk's primary objective, the acquisition of California.

Democrats in the House immediately introduced a bill authorizing the president to call for 50,000 volunteers. The preamble of the bill stated that "by the act of the Republic of Mexico, a state of war exists between that Government and the United States." This language created a dilemma for many Whigs who believed that the Nueces was the southern boundary of Texas and that Polk had brought on the war by ordering Taylor to the Rio Grande. But they were given little opportunity to speak and no time to examine the 144 pages of documents accompanying the president's message. When a vote was forced by the Democratic majority after only two hours of debate, 174 members supported the bill but 14 courageous members voted against it and 35 members abstained.

The Senate, accustomed to a slower pace, took until the next day to approve the war bill. Senator Benton, chairman of the Senate Military Affairs Committee, initially opposed "aggressive war on Mexico" but later succumbed to administration pressure and assurances that the war would be over in 90 to 120 days.[63] Several Whigs urged the removal of the offensive preamble, but without success. Calhoun declared in an emotional speech that he could no more vote for the preamble than plunge a dagger into his own heart. When the bill came to a vote, it was approved by forty senators, including some who actually opposed the war. Two senators from Delaware and Massachusetts voted against it; three senators including Calhoun, abstained; and eleven senators were conveniently absent.[64] The bill was signed by the president that afternoon, scarcely more than twenty-four hours after Congress received his war message, and the United States was officially at war with Mexico.

Meanwhile, the first battles of the war had already been fought on the Rio Grande. On April 24, General Arista sent 1600 men across the river with orders to cut the road between Matamoros and Taylor's supply base at Point Isabel; some of these Mexican troops ambushed Captain Thornton's dragoons the next morning. Taylor, assuming that Arista hoped to capture his supply base, moved his main force to Point Isabel and left only a small

FOUR / *Hostilities May Be Considered as Commenced* 75

garrison at the fort he had built opposite Matamoros. But on April 30, Arista crossed the river with the rest of his army and lay siege to the fort. Taylor marched back with his main force and supply train to relieve the besieged fort. On Friday, May 8, Taylor's army won a major battle with Arista's larger army at Palo Alto. On Saturday, May 9, while Polk and his cabinet were pondering the question of war or peace in Washington, Taylor won another victory at Resaca de la Palma that gave him control over the lower Rio Grande valley. But the president and Congress would not hear of these battles for several more weeks. The decision to declare that the United States was at war with Mexico was based entirely on earlier complaints against Mexico and on Taylor's preliminary report of the Mexican ambush of Captain Thornton's dragoons.

The two crucial decisions that led to the war between the United States and Mexico — President Polk's order to General Taylor to march to the Rio Grande and President Paredes' order to General Arista to attack Taylor's army — were made by ambitious men who were primarily concerned with their own domestic agendas. Each gave little thought to the effect of these orders on his soldiers or his people. Each made totally unrealistic assumptions concerning the effectiveness of his own army, the logistical and operational problems that would be encountered, and the duration of the war.

These crucial decisions and others were made too quickly on the basis of inadequate, outdated, and often misleading or inaccurate information. Although there were some surprises, the impatient men on both sides were often fully aware that they lacked information and yet acted anyway without waiting for better information. Polk ordered Taylor to the Rio Grande before he knew the final result of the Slidell mission. Paredes ordered an attack on Taylor's army before receiving any substantial information on Taylor's actions after he arrived at the Rio Grande. Taylor blockaded the river before he knew the results of the Slidell mission and before he had any reliable indication of Mexican intentions. Polk and his cabinet decided to ask the Congress to declare war on Mexico prior to receiving news of any Mexican attack on Taylor's army. The U.S. Congress declared war on the basis of Taylor's incomplete report of the attack on Captain Thornton's dragoons, without knowing that by then the first two major battles of the war had already been fought.

Each of these brash actions can be justified only by subsequent events or under the assumption that war between the two nations had become inevitable. But the war of 1846–48 was not inevitable. Since gold had not yet been discovered there, Polk's sense of urgency about acquiring California in 1845 and 1846 was entirely a result of his personal ambition and his commitment to serve only a single term as president. He had not exhausted the diplomatic or political possibilities for acquiring California. He did not attempt to negotiate the purchase of California through a special commissioner, the only type of envoy the Mexicans were willing to receive. He was not willing to wait for the rebellious Californians to declare and maintain their independence from Mexico.

Nor was the war as it would be fought inevitable or necessary from a purely military standpoint. American invasions of the Rio Grande valley and central Mexico were not essential prerequisites for the achievement of Polk's primary goal, the U.S. acquisition of California. As later events demonstrated, New Mexico and California could be captured by small American army and navy units. In both Taylor's campaign below the Rio Grande and Scott's campaign in central Mexico, the primary objectives were political and diplomatic rather than military. The war in the Rio Grande valley provided an excuse for the seizure of New Mexico and California. The subsequent campaign in central Mexico was intended to force the Mexicans to accept a treaty recognizing the U.S. acquisition of these provinces.

If California had still been a Mexican province in 1848, both the American desire to acquire it and Mexican determination to hold on to it would have been dramatically enhanced by the discovery of gold in the province. The resulting conflict would have been very stark and intractable, and a "gold war" for California might have become inevitable. Such a war would probably have been more focused in California, would have involved smaller units and fewer casualties and costs than the war fought in 1846–47, would have had a more limited impact on internal conditions in each country, and would perhaps have left a less bitter legacy in Mexico than that remaining from American invasions of heavily populated areas in northern and central Mexico.

FIVE

A Peace Must Be Conquered

The active phase of the war with Mexico lasted for sixteen months until September 1847, but the war's end was not proclaimed until more than two years after it began. Although a short war by modern standards, it lasted much longer than James K. Polk had expected.

The day after war was declared, Secretary of State James Buchanan proposed in a cabinet meeting that foreign governments be advised that the United States had not gone to war with Mexico to acquire territory. The secretive president had kept even his secretary of state in the dark regarding his intentions. Polk, who had gone to war to acquire California, was appalled by Buchanan's proposal. "I told Mr. Buchanan," he recorded in his diary, "that though we had not gone to war for conquest ... in making peace we would if practicable obtain California and such other portions of the Mexican territory as would be sufficient to indemnify our claimants on Mexico and to defray the expenses of the war."[1]

Polk wrote a new paragraph on U.S. war aims for the circular to foreign governments that ignored the question of territorial acquisitions: "We go to war with Mexico solely for the purpose of conquering an honorable and permanent peace.... We shall bear the olive branch in one hand, the sword in the other."[2] But cabinet members were left in no further doubt about Polk's intentions. He told them that his war aims were "to acquire for the U.S. California, New Mexico, and perhaps some others of the northern provinces whenever peace was made.... To secure that object, military possession should with as little delay as possible be taken of all these provinces."[3]

Later the same day, a very general strategic plan was agreed upon at a meeting of the president, the secretary of war, and the general-in-chief of the army, Winfield Scott. Its essential elements were (l) to occupy the territories the United States wanted to acquire — New Mexico and California — as quickly as possible before the thin Mexican forces in these areas could be reinforced and (2) to occupy temporarily some additional territory below the Rio Grande, primarily as a means of convincing Mexicans to agree to the "indemnity in territory" the president wanted.[4]

Although the occupation of New Mexico and California required only a small percentage of the U.S. forces deployed during the war, this clear-cut objective received priority attention from the president and cabinet. New Mexico was important mainly because it provided an access route to California — including a route for an eventual railroad — that avoided the highest ranges of the Rockies and Sierras. The real goal was California, especially the great bays of San Francisco and San Diego.

In June 1845, nearly a year before the war began, the U.S. naval commander in the Pacific, Commodore John D. Sloat, had been ordered to seize San Francisco if Mexico declared war on the United States as a result of the U.S. annexation of Texas.[5] A few days after war was declared by the United States, Sloat was instructed that "the most important public object [is] to take and hold possession of San Francisco, and this you will do without fail."[6] By June 23, when this order was still en route to Sloat, Bancroft hoped he had already taken San Francisco and Monterey pursuant to the contingency order in 1845. "Our people consider California and New Mexico as ours," he wrote to the U.S. minister in England. "They will not easily give them up."[7]

Aside from the contingency order to Sloat, virtually the only military planning prior to the declaration of war was for a military expedition across the southwestern deserts to California. In April 1845, a few weeks after Polk's inauguration, Colonel Stephen Kearny at Fort Leavenworth was ordered to take five companies of dragoons to the Rockies, and to return by a southern route near the U.S.-Mexican border. Kearny proved that cavalry units could operate effectively at great distances from their bases, and he gained firsthand knowledge of more than half of the route from Fort Leavenworth to Sante Fe.[8] Before Kearny returned that fall, the commissary officer in St. Louis was ordered to prepare a logistical plan for the conquest of New Mexico. As soon as war was declared, Kearny was ordered to take infantry and cavalry units along the Sante Fe Trail, occupy New Mexico, and then make the "thousand mile leap" over the deserts to California.[9]

Before Kearny could arrive in California, the province was seized by the U.S. Navy and by American settlers recruited by the American explorer John Charles Fremont. The explorer arrived in northern California in the spring of 1846 after finding a new route from the Rockies to the basin of the Columbia River. There he met Marine Lt. Archibald Gillespie, who had been sent to California via Mexico with Polk's October instructions to Consul Larkin to encourage California separatism. Some historians had suggested that Gillespie also brought secret instructions to Fremont, but this mystery has remained unresolved. Fremont proceeded to the large American settlement

FIVE / *A Peace Must Be Conquered* 79

on the Sacramento River and gave these Americans the impression that a revolt would be supported by the U.S. government. Although they did not know that the United States was already at war with Mexico, the Americans proclaimed the Bear Flag Republic and, led by Fremont, attacked and captured a Mexican post at Sonoma on June 15. With 90 American riflemen, Fremont drove Mexican dragoons from the area north of San Francisco Bay. Fremont's actions eliminated any chance of success for Polk's October strategy of encouraging a revolution by native Californians. These Mexicans saw the Bear Flag Republic and the military moves of Fremont and his volunteers as the beginning of the American conquest of California, and they resisted the conquest as long as they were able.

Meanwhile, Commodore Sloat arrived at Monterey. He had heard rumors of fighting on the Rio Grande in early May but had not received official confirmation that the United States was at war with Mexico. After learning that Fremont's volunteers had attacked Mexican units, the cautious commodore decided to occupy Monterey. Sloat, who was ill, soon turned over his command to newly arrived Commodore Robert Stockton. On August 12 a small group of Stockton's marines and Fremont's volunteer riflemen occupied Los Angeles, which had also been abandoned by the Mexican authorities. Stockton proclaimed possession of California on behalf of the United States and appointed Fremont as governor.

Kearny, promoted to brigadier general, left Ft. Leavenworth on June 30 and captured Sante Fe on August 19. He began the thousand-mile march across the unmapped deserts with about 200 dragoons on September 25. Two weeks later he met Kit Carson, who had been sent east with the news that California was already under the control of Stockton's marines and Fremont's riflemen. Concerned about feeding his men on the way across the deserts, Kearny sent half of them back to Sante Fe and proceeded toward San Diego with about 100 men and Kit Carson as guide. After entering California, Kearny was attacked at San Pasqual on December 6 by 150 Mexican lancers; 18 Americans were killed and 14 were wounded.

By then news of the American capture of Monterey, San Francisco, and Los Angeles had reached Washington. Marcy wrote Polk on December 5 that "the whole province was yielded up to the United States, and is now in our military occupancy." By mid–January, after several more small engagements with the Californians, Marcy's premature statement proved correct. Polk's paramount objective had been achieved in the first nine months of war by very small U.S. navy, army, and volunteer units.[10]

The second part of the strategic plan Polk approved in May involved much larger forces but much less well-defined objectives. While Kearny was on his way to California, General Taylor would advance up the Rio Grande valley, and smaller forces under General John Wool and Colonel Alexander Doniphan would invade Chihuahua from San Antonio and El Paso.[11] The goal of these movements was diplomatic rather than military. Polk had no plans, then or later, to annex territory below the Rio Grande, although he toyed with the idea of additional annexations later in the war. These aggressive movements in northern Mexico were expected to convince Mexico that it could gain nothing by continuing the war and that it should agree to the cession to the United States of New Mexico and California.

Polk had not yet seriously considered the possibility of sustained warfare between the United States and Mexico over a period of more than a few months. On July 14 he wrote his brother William, then in Italy, that he should not resign his diplomatic post there to join the army because the war would be over before he could arrive in New York.[12] The president's initial conception of a short and relatively painless war was based on a substantial underestimation of the patriotism and military capabilities of the Mexican people and of the manpower, supply, and health problems that would be encountered by American forces operating in Mexican territory. The president's naive assumptions concerning the war brought him into conflict with the general-in-chief of the U.S. Army, Major General Winfield Scott.

Except for Andrew Jackson, Scott was the most distinguished American soldier between the Revolution and the Civil War. He entered the army in 1807 and won a congressional medal and a commission as major general at age 30 during the war of 1812-14 with England. He commanded U.S. forces in the Black Hawk War in 1832 and in the Seminole War in 1835. Scott had also played key roles in South Carolina in the nullification crisis of 1832–33 and in the U.S.-Canadian conflict on the Maine border in 1839. In the phrase of Gilbert and Sullivan, Winfield Scott was the very model of a modern major general. But these accomplishments were much less important to the Democratic president than the fact that Scott was a Whig who had received 68 votes for the presidential nomination in the Whig convention in 1840.

Polk assumed that the forces necessary to carry out his strategic plan could be created almost immediately through the enlistment of large numbers of volunteers and that the war would be over before the expiration of their rather short enlistments. General Scott knew that effective military forces could not be created, trained, equipped, and transported to the Rio Grande in only a few weeks. He proposed that most or all of the summer be used to recruit and train an effective volunteer force to supplement Taylor's regulars, before beginning active operations in the Rio Grande Valley in the fall. Secretary of War Marcy tried to convince Scott that the public demanded immediate military moves that summer and that many of the

FIVE / *A Peace Must Be Conquered*

volunteers would be unwilling to enlist for more than three months. When a private letter from Scott containing critical remarks about Polk found its way to the president, Polk informed Scott that he was expected to remain in Washington and leave the field command to General Zachary Taylor.

The Polk Administration could never make up its mind what it wanted Taylor to do in northern Mexico. "You are advised to prosecute the war with vigor, in the manner you deem most effective," Marcy wrote Taylor on May 28. "I am anxious to hear your views as to the measures you propose to execute."[13] On June 8, Marcy wrote Taylor that "a peace must be conquered in the shortest space of time practicable" and that the campaign was to be prosecuted with vigor in order to "dispose the enemy to desire the end of the war."[14] Although the capture of Monterrey, Mexico's second largest city, was stated as the immediate objective of Taylor's campaign, there was no decision about further military objectives. Marcy asked Taylor whether he thought he should attempt a movement to the Mexican capital. Taylor replied that it would not be possible to maintain a 1000-mile line of communications from the Rio Grande to the capital.[15]

While Kearny and Taylor were brandishing the sword, Polk and Buchanan were waving the olive branch. Polk's first move was to send a Spanish-speaking naval officer, Commander Alexander Slidell Mackenzie, to see Santa Anna in Havana.[16] Mackenzie, a younger brother of John Slidell who had taken the name of their mother's family, was instructed to say that Polk sought an early peace but would prefer to negotiate with a new Mexican government headed by Santa Anna. The U.S. naval squadron in the Gulf of Mexico had been ordered to allow Santa Anna to pass through the U.S. blockade of Mexican ports. If he returned to power in Mexico, the United States would be willing to suspend hostilities and send a minister to negotiate a settlement of the difficulties between the two nations. Mexico would be asked to cede part of her territories in return for an "ample consideration" in ready money.[17] Mackenzie gave these messages to Santa Anna in Havana on July 6, 1846.

Before Mackenzie returned, Polk received a dispatch from Consul Black in Mexico indicating his belief that the Paredes government wanted to settle the dispute with the United States.[18] Polk immediately decided on another peace initiative. Buchanan wrote to "the Minister of Foreign Affairs of Mexico" so that the letter could be answered by either Paredes' foreign minister or his successor if there was a new government by the time the message was received. "It is deemed useless, and it might prove injurious, to discuss the causes of the existing war," Buchanan wrote. "This might tend to delay or defeat the restoration of peace."[19] The letter again proposed negotiations by a U.S. "Envoy Extraordinary and Minister Plenipotentiary," ignoring the unwillingness of both the Herrera and Paredes governments to receive such a normally accredited resident envoy until the difficulties between the two countries had been resolved. As had been the case with the Slidell mission, the Polk administration was asking the Mexican government to resume full diplomatic relations with the United States before any substantive issues had been discussed or resolved. The message was sent to the commander of the U.S. naval squadron at Vera Cruz with orders to transmit it under a flag of truce to the governor of the province.

Polk thought the key to a peace settlement was a sizable cash payment to be paid upon the signature of the treaty. On March 28, a few weeks before the war began, he had told the cabinet that he believed he could obtain a treaty if the U.S. minister was authorized to pay a half million or million dollars to enable Paredes to pay, feed, and clothe the army and maintain himself in power until the treaty could be ratified by the United States.[20] Polk apparently discussed an appropriation for this purpose in late March with Senators Benton, Cass, and Allen but did not press for action at that time.[21]

On August 1, just before learning the results of the Mackenzie mission, Polk told the cabinet that he had decided to ask Congress for $2 million for unspecified expenses in connection with the termination of the war. He hoped the House leadership could ram the bill through the House with minimal discussion in the last days of the session and that he might get Senate action after a secret debate in executive session.[22]

Mackenzie's report on his talks with Santa Anna and a memorandum from Santa Anna arrived on August 2. The ex-dictator pledged that if he returned to power he would support republican principles and a liberal constitution and enter negotiations for a peace treaty defining new boundaries. There was no reference to money, but Polk assumed that Santa Anna had not missed the promise of an "ample consideration" in return for territory.[23]

Two days later, Polk sent a confidential message to the Senate asking for an appropriation of $2 million to cover a payment to be made to Mexico immediately after the signature of a peace treaty. The Whigs in the Senate refused to consider a confidential request for the appropriation, and on August 8 Polk publicly asked both Houses for $2 million for an initial payment to Mexico. The House passed a bill appropriating the $2 million but containing a proviso proposed by Representative David Wilmot of Pennsylvania banning slavery from any territory gained from Mexico. This was the opening bell for the controversy over slavery in territories gained from Mexico that would dominate American politics for the next four years. The Senate was embroiled in debate on the Wilmot Proviso when the legislative session expired at noon on August 10 per prior agreement.

FIVE / *A Peace Must Be Conquered*

"Had the appropriation been passed," Polk wrote in his diary that night, "I am confident I should have made an honorable peace by which we should have acquired California, and such other territory as we desired, before the end of October."[24] The idea that a peace treaty could have been achieved with a faltering Paredes government or with a new government headed by Santa Anna in only 2½ months—scarcely more than the time required for one trip to and from the Mexican capital—was ridiculous, and the comment clearly reflects the Polk's naive misjudgment of the Mexican situation.

Polk did not need the $2 million in 1846 or even in 1847. Santa Anna was returning to Mexico, with Polk's assistance, but he was not yet ready for peace on American terms.

Two days after the U.S. Congress declared war, the secretary of the navy had sent an order to Commodore Conner at Vera Cruz: "If Santa Anna endeavors to enter the Mexican ports, you will allow him to pass freely."[25] These orders preceded Mackenzie's visit to Santa Anna and were apparently based on Atocha's statement in January that Santa Anna desired a settlement of the dispute with the United States. The commodore complied with these orders on August 16 when Santa Anna arrived at Vera Cruz on a British steamer. There he learned that Paredes had surrendered executive authority in late July to the vice president, General Nicholas Bravo, who had been replaced as interim president by General Jose Salas. The latter general proclaimed support for Santa Anna, who was escorted back to the capital.[26]

Santa Anna proclaimed that he had returned to save Mexico from monarchy. He proposed the readoption of the federal constitution of 1824 and promised to act as the "slave of public opinion."[27] He quickly perceived that public opinion in Mexico was not ready for peace negotiations with the American invaders. Accepting the supreme executive power and the command of the army, he proclaimed that he would hold these powers until he could bring "laurels plucked on the banks of the Sabine" to a newly elected Congress.[28]

The August week in which Santa Anna threatened a Mexican thrust to the Texas-Louisiana border was hardly a propitious one for the arrival of Buchanan's note offering negotiations. Santa Anna's new foreign minister, General Manuel Rejon, replied that the Mexicans could not accept Buchanan's statement that the cause of the war was merely "a thing that is past and belongs to history." Since negotiations involved the national honor and the territorial integrity of Mexico, the question must be referred to the new Congress to be convened on December 6.[29]

Meanwhile, Buchanan went to Saratoga Springs in search of a cure for a bile problem, and Nicholas P. Trist was acting secretary of state for a month. On September 10 the British minister brought Trist an offer of British mediation in the U.S.-Mexican conflict. Trist attended a cabinet discussion of

Polk's reply to the British offer. Although he declined the mediation, Polk said he would welcome any British efforts to convince the Mexicans that they should negotiate.[30] Months later in Mexico, when Trist needed help in delivering a new U.S. proposal of negotiations, he would remember the British offer and Polk's response.

Polk's hopes of negotiations in 1846 were shattered on September 19, when Trist brought him Rejon's note of August 31. Polk did not record his reaction, but the next day he began to plan the invasion of central Mexico.[31] Trist commented later that "Santa Anna's return to Mexico, that master stroke of policy on the part of the Administration, turned out to be one of the greatest blunders ever perpetrated by political tricksters.... Santa Anna's presence there proved to be ... a most serious hindrance to the restoration of peace."[32] Bancroft's biographer agreed that the order to allow Santa Anna to return to Mexico was "one of the worst mistakes of judgment made by the Polk Administration."[33]

The idea of an invasion of central Mexico had been considered for several weeks before Polk learned of the Mexican rejection of his peace initiative. An attack on Vera Cruz, Mexico's most important seaport, followed by a thrust inland toward the Mexican capital, was discussed in several cabinet meetings beginning in late August. Polk told the cabinet on August 29 that he had learned that an army landing below Vera Cruz could lay siege to the city without coming under fire of the guns of San Juan d'Ulloa, an island fortress designed to protect the harbor from naval attack. This important intelligence was received in Washington prior to July 9, when it was communicated to Taylor. It was apparently brought from Santa Anna by Colonel Atocha in January and confirmed during Mackenzie's July visit to Santa Anna.[34] The feasibility of an end run around the fortress was also confirmed by the former U.S. consul in Vera Cruz, F. M. Dimond, who was summoned to the White House on October 17.[35]

In mid–October Polk learned that Taylor had attacked Monterrey, captured most of the town, and then agreed to an eight-week armistice because he lacked rations and forage for further operations. Polk thought the armistice was inconsistent, however, with the aggressive war policy he had adopted after Santa Anna's rejection of the offer of negotiations.[36] Marcy wrote Taylor that the war should "be prosecuted with the utmost vigor, to the end that they might be made sensible of the evils of its continuance."[37]

Taylor's armistice at Monterrey, plus evidence of dissatisfaction in his army, convinced Polk that Taylor was not the right man to lead an invasion of central Mexico. Neither of the major generals who were Democrats, Patterson and Butler, had the necessary military experience. This left only

FIVE / *A Peace Must Be Conquered*

General Winfield Scott. Polk feared, however, that if an invasion commanded by Scott was successful, the Whig general would be catapulted into the presidency in the upcoming election in 1848.

Nonetheless, Polk needed a competent commander to handle a difficult amphibious landing on an enemy shore and subsequent operations in the heart of the enemy's country, and Scott was by far the best qualified man available. Although Polk had made very negative comments about Scott in his diary in September and October, he reluctantly chose Scott in November to lead an invasion of central Mexico. It was about the only time that Polk put the national interest ahead of his perceived political interests, and he soon regretted the decision.

Scott outlined his views on the conduct of the war in central Mexico in a memorandum to the secretary of war on November 12. After the capture of Vera Cruz, the principal objective "would be to open a new and better line of operations upon the enemy's capital. To reach that point, or to place it in imminent danger of capture, an army of more than 20,000 men may be needed."[38] His memorandum was considered by the cabinet on November 17. Buchanan opposed the march on the capital on the grounds that the administration couldn't finance a large enough army. Polk recorded his support for an effort to capture the Mexican capital, if the United States had a sufficient force in the field and no peace had been made.[39]

Scott was sent to Mexico with only the vaguest of instructions. "It is not proposed to control your operations by definite and positive instructions," Scott was told in a very brief letter of instructions from the secretary of war, "but you are left to prosecute them as your judgment ... shall dictate....The objects which it is desirable to obtain have been indicated, and it is hoped that you will have the requisite force to accomplish them. Of this you must be the judge when ... the time for action has arrived."[40] The letter contained no reference to a march to the Mexican capital or to any other specific military objective. By giving Scott unlimited discretion in the conduct of the campaign, the Democratic president and secretary were making sure that the Whig general could be blamed for anything that went wrong.

The general objectives of the war were summarized on December 8 in Polk's second annual message to Congress: "The war will continue to be prosecuted with vigor, as the best means of securing peace.... It has been carried into the enemy's country ... with a view to obtain a honorable peace and thereby secure ample indemnity for the expenses of the war, as well as to our much injured citizens who hold large pecuniary demands against Mexico."[41]

Having prepared an invasion of the Mexican heartland, Polk thought he should also prepare for the peace agreement which he assumed would follow the brandishing of the American sword in central Mexico. His first move was to renew his request to Congress for money to be paid to the Mexican government in a peace settlement, increasing the request to $3 million. Polk eventually got his "three million dollar bill," but the bill had very negative ramifications in both the United States and Mexico. The bitter debate on the Wilmot Proviso to the bill showed the depth of the sectional division on the issue of slavery in the territories to be gained from Mexico, and it intensified opposition to the acquisition of such territories in both House and Senate. In Mexico, Santa Anna's many political enemies feared he would use a cash payment in various ways to consolidate his political power. The prospect of such a U.S. payment to Santa Anna upon the signature of a treaty enhanced their determination to oppose any peace agreement with the Yankee invaders.

While Scott was preparing to invade central Mexico, Polk was sending two men to Mexico to wave the olive branch again. The first of these was Moses Y. Beach, publisher of the expansionist *Sun* in New York. Beach traveled with his daughter and a Spanish-speaking companion, Mrs. Jane Storm, ostensibly on private business connected with his banking interests. His contacts in Mexico were mainly with aristocrats and clergy who opposed Santa Anna. Without authority from the president, Beach discussed with these Mexicans the outlines of a peace treaty, including a boundary at 26° which would give the United States substantial territory below the Rio Grande, the cession of a transit route across the Isthmus of Tehuantepec, and a $15 million U.S. contribution to the cost of a railroad or canal across the isthmus. A member of his family claimed in 1879 that Beach had been told to expect the arrival of an official U.S. envoy who would take advantage of the groundwork he had laid. In fact, Beach's unauthorized discussion of a boundary at the 26th parallel contributed to the Mexican government's unwillingness to enter into peace negotiations. When Santa Anna returned to the capital, Beach left in a hurry to avoid arrest as a spy.[42]

Polk's second agent in Mexico that winter was Colonel Atocha. He visited the president again in Washington in mid–January 1847. This time he brought a November letter from Santa Anna indicating his desire of peace and his interest in learning U.S. peace terms.[43] Polk enlisted Atocha as a confidential courier to deliver another note from the secretary of state to the foreign minister of Mexico. The rejection by three Mexican presidents of his proposals to appoint a minister had finally convinced Polk that a peace treaty would have to be negotiated *before* the resumption of normal diplomatic relations. Buchanan conveyed an offer to appoint a distinguished citizen or citizens as commissioners with full powers to conclude a treaty of peace, as soon as the Mexican government indicated its desire to appoint commissioners.[44]

FIVE / *A Peace Must Be Conquered*

The offer to appoint "distinguished citizens" as peace commissioners reflected Polk's hope to use his friend Senator Thomas Hart Benton of Missouri, chairman of the Senate Military Affairs Committee, in a combined military and diplomatic role in Mexico. Before Scott was given the command in central Mexico, Benton suggested that Polk ask Congress to create the position of lieutenant general which would outrank both the prominent Whig generals, Taylor and Scott. Polk couldn't wait for congressional action and sent Scott to Mexico, but he recommended creation of the new rank in a message to Congress in late December.

Scott was furious when he learned that Polk planned to give Benton both the top military rank and responsibility for peace negotiations. David Pletcher wrote that the effort to elevate Benton was "one of the most discreditable acts of Polk's whole career, for it amounted to direct betrayal of Scott."[45] The Whigs refused to cooperate, and the bill to create a lieutenant general died when the 29th Congress expired on March 4. But Scott's feeling of betrayal contributed to his hostile reaction two months later when he learned that responsibility for peace negotiations had been given to the chief clerk of the State Department.

Like the two preceding peace initiatives, Buchanan's January 18 letter suggesting negotiations arrived in Mexico at an inauspicious moment. Santa Anna had been reelected president by the Mexican Congress on December 23 but was in the north assembling a new army to meet Taylor. Vice President Gomez Farias was acting president. Although Buchanan's letter contained no indication of peace terms, Gomez Farias informed the Mexican Congress that the United States demanded the cession of all of northern Mexico down to the 26° line.[46] Although such a boundary had been advocated in the cabinet by Secretary of the Treasury Walker, there had been no decision to demand territory below the Rio Grande. Gomez Farias' assertion of this American claim was apparently based on Beach's unauthorized discussions of a boundary at 26°.

The acting Mexican foreign minister replied to the Buchanan letter on February 22, 1847. He wrote that the acting president would not consider appointing peace commissioners unless the United States lifted the blockade of Mexican ports and evacuated all Mexican territory.[47] Atocha returned to Washington on March 20 with this reply. Trist translated the note and read it to the cabinet. "I at once declared to the cabinet," Polk recorded, "that the preliminary conditions required were wholly inadmissible and that no alternative was left but the most energetic crushing movement of our arms upon Mexico."[48]

Ten days later, on April 1, dispatches arrived from Taylor with details of a new American victory in a battle with Santa Anna at Buena Vista on

February 22 and 23. Meanwhile, Scott had made his landing below Vera Cruz on March 7 with 200 ships and 14,000 men. He began a siege which lasted twenty days until the garrison surrendered on March 27. This news reached Washington on April 10. In the three weeks since he had vowed "the most energetic crushing movement of our arms upon Mexico," the president had learned of major victories by Taylor at Buena Vista and by Scott at Vera Cruz. Polk immediately concluded that there was now a good chance for a treaty.

In December, Polk had discussed with Senator Benton a peace commission of three or four persons that might include Benton, Senator John Crittenden of Kentucky, Governor Silas Wright of New York, and perhaps the previous minister-designate to Mexico, John Slidell.[49] This discussion reflected the fact that the only previous American peace treaties — those ending the first and second wars with Britain — had been negotiated by large and distinguished delegations.

In January, however, when Buchanan expressed interest in heading an eventual peace commission, Polk said he would prefer that Buchanan go alone so that "the administration ... would be entitled to the whole credit for the arrangement."[50] As usual, Polk was giving priority to domestic political considerations. But sending the secretary of state would be feasible only if the Mexicans were ready to negotiate without delay.

Now in April uncertainty about Mexican intentions obviously precluded sending the secretary, but other factors pointed to the designation of a single commissioner. Because of the adjournment several weeks earlier of the final session of the 29th Congress, it was not feasible to obtain congressional agreement on a multimember peace commission that would have to include representatives of various political factions. The appointment of a confidential executive agent could be made without Senate confirmation. Polk hoped that he could keep the appointment of a single commissioner a secret to avoid or minimize criticism if the mission proved abortive and, if the Mexicans were willing to talk this time, to permit secret negotiations without the knowledge of those in Mexico and the United States who opposed a peace settlement.

Polk wrote a full account in his diary of the decision on a commissioner in the cabinet meeting on April 10, 1847:

> I had several times mentioned to Mr. Buchanan the importance of having a commissioner [at] the headquarters of the army ready to take advantage of circumstances as they might arise to negotiate for peace. I stated to the cabinet today that ... it [was] more important since the news of the recent victories.... All members of the Cabinet present concurred. I preferred that

FIVE / *A Peace Must Be Conquered* 89

the Secretary of State should be the sole commissioner ... but ... he could not attend the headquarters of the army for an indefinite period.[51]

Buchanan, who could not go himself, thought he would derive the maximum political advantage from the peace mission if his deputy at the State Department were appointed commissioner.

> Mr. Buchanan then suggested that Mr. N. P. Trist, the chief clerk of the Department of State, might be deputed secretly with plenipotentiary powers to the headquarters of the army and that it might be made known that such a person was with the army ready to negotiate. Mr. Trist, he said, was an able man, perfectly familiar with the Spanish character and language.... It was unanimously agreed by the Cabinet that it would be proper to send Mr. Trist and that he would take with him a treaty drawn up by the Secretary of State and approved by the cabinet, which he should be authorized to ... conclude with them if they would accept it.[52]

Trist was working at his desk in the State Department when Buchanan entered and requested that Trist accompany him to the White House. Trist commented later that until the president told him he had been selected for an important mission in Mexico, "I had as little thought of going to Mexico as of going to the moon."[53] But he accepted the mission instantly.

Buchanan was given only Sunday and Monday to prepare the draft treaty and a letter of instructions to Trist; they were approved by the cabinet on Tuesday, April 13. The treaty draft provided that the United States would receive Texas (including of course the territory between the Nueces and the Rio Grande), New Mexico, and both Upper and Lower California. If the Mexicans would also give the United States transit rights across the Isthmus of Tehuantepec, the narrow strip of Mexican territory separating the Atlantic and Pacific, the United States would pay up to $30 million. The payment was to be reduced to a maximum of $25 million if Trist could not obtain either lower California or the transit rights across the Isthmus, but not both. If neither of these could be obtained, the payment was not to exceed $20 million.[54] Aside from these provisions, the instructions left Trist little room for negotiation or compromise with the Mexicans.

As with several other of Polk's important decisions related to Mexico, the decision to send Trist to Mexico was made very quickly without adequate consideration. Polk acted after receiving news of two American military successes in Mexico but before receiving any indication that the Mexicans were ready to negotiate. Because of the recent American victories at Buena Vista and Vera Cruz, James K. Polk thought he was now in a position to dictate the peace terms.[55] Polk had known Trist mainly in subordinate roles as translator, interpreter, copier of secret dispatches, and bearer of dispatches and messages to and from the president. The assignment in Mexico involved similar functions — delivering and translating for the Mexicans the president's peace terms. Polk did not send Nicholas Trist to negotiate with the Mexicans. He recorded later in his diary that Trist's "simple duty ... was to submit and enforce the ultimatum of his government."[56]

Nicholas Trist was soon to discover that his duty in Mexico was not nearly as simple as the president thought.

SIX

Bread Upon the Waters

Nicholas Trist arrived in Vera Cruz on the cutter *Ewing* on the morning of May 6, 1847. On arrival he learned that on April 17, the day he left Washington, Scott's army had met the Mexicans at a mountain pass called Cerro Gordo. In a short but deadly battle, the Americans had stormed the Mexican defenses, thrown the Mexicans into a disorganized flight, and captured more than 3,000 prisoners. Santa Anna had fled across the mountains to Orizaba, where he was reorganizing his scattered forces. Scott had moved up to Jalapa, which was 4600 feet higher and much healthier than Vera Cruz.

Trist thought the American victory at Cerro Gordo might provide a new opportunity for peace negotiations, and he was eager to provide for the rapid delivery to the Mexicans of the offer of negotiations he had brought from Washington. A large wagon train and about 1,000 men were about to leave Vera Cruz but would take a week to make the 75-mile trip to Jalapa. The delivery of the American offer of peace negotiations seemed too urgent to await his own arrival at Scott's headquarters with the slow wagon train. He thus accepted the offer of Colonel Childs, commander at Vera Cruz, to rush Buchanan's letter and a letter from Secretary of War Marcy to Scott by a platoon of Tennessee dragoons. Trist did not feel strong enough to make a fast trip on horseback so soon after the rough voyage from New Orleans. The hard-riding Tennessee dragoons made the trip to Jalapa in just over twenty-four hours. But this speedy delivery contributed to a misunderstanding of Trist's mission by General Scott and to a bitter feud between the two men that lasted for more than a month.

Buchanan's letter to the Mexicans was sealed; the secretary of war had assumed Scott would read the copy of Buchanan's letter in Trist's possession at the same time that he read Marcy's accompanying letter. Marcy wrote Scott that "Mr. Trist is clothed with diplomatic powers as will authorize him to enter into arrangements with the government of Mexico for the suspension of hostilities," but he failed to make clear that the suspension of hostilities

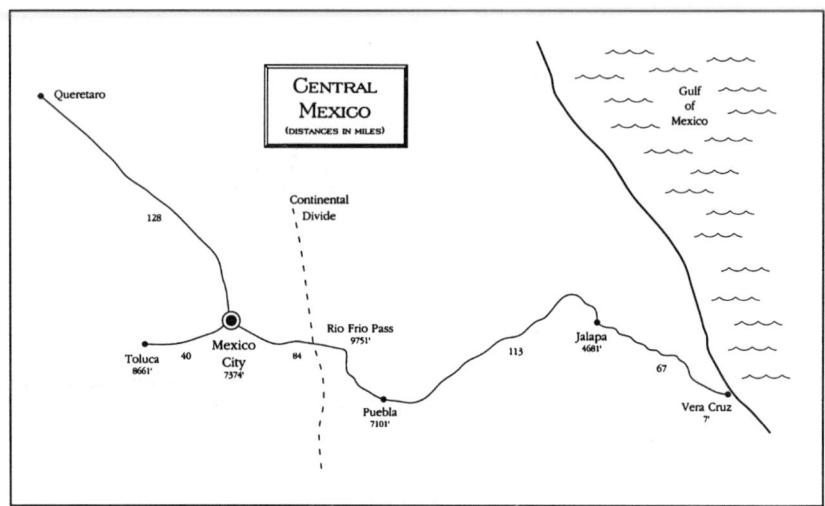

was to take place only after the Mexicans had ratified a treaty of peace. Scott was instructed that he should regard notification from Trist that "the contingency had occurred" as an order from the president to suspend hostilities, but Marcy did not define the contingency.[1] Trist commented later that in Marcy's letter "the intentions of the Government were so lamely expressed as to convey to the General's mind a totally erroneous conception" of the intended relationship between the general and himself."[2]

Scott was infuriated by the secretary's letter and sent a stiff note to Trist the next day by the returning dragoons:

> The Secretary of War proposes to degrade me by requiring that I, the commander of this army, shall defer to you, the chief clerk of the Department of State, the question of discontinuing hostilities.... Here in the heart of a hostile country ... this army must take military security for its own safety. Hence the question of an armistice or no armistice is, most peculiarly, a *military* question appertaining of necessity ... to the commander of the invading forces.... The safety of this army demands no less.[3]

Scott's hostile initial reaction to the Trist mission did not result from a lack of sympathy with the goal of a negotiated peace. He fully shared the administration view that the only purpose of military operations in Mexico was to "conquer a peace." His correspondence contains many references to his hope that a peace settlement might be achieved before the army reached the Mexican capital. The secretary of war's instructions to Scott in November had contained no reference to the capture of the capital or to any other specific military objective; Scott had been left free to conduct operations "as

SIX / *Bread Upon the Waters*

your judgment ... shall dictate."⁴ His judgment was that the United States should make peace with Mexico as soon as possible.

The Whig general did not expect that the Democratic president would give him full responsibility for peace negotiations. But he recalled that before he left Washington, Polk had hinted that Scott might serve as a peace commissioner along with a distinguished Democratic senator from New York, Silas Wright.⁵ Scott was furious when he learned a few weeks later that Polk hoped to give both the military and diplomatic responsibility to another Democratic senator, Thomas Hart Benton of Missouri. Now in May he was informed by the secretary of war that the exclusive responsibility for peace negotiations had been given to a minor official, the chief clerk of the State Department. When Polk learned of Scott's hostility to Trist's mission, he noted in his diary that Scott "desired to be invested with this power himself."⁶

Scott also recalled in his memoirs that in the mail brought by the dragoons, "I received the most reliable information from Washington that [Trist's] well-known prejudice against me had much weight in his appointment."⁷ Trist was prejudiced against Scott, although his attitude toward Scott was probably not a factor in his selection for the peace mission. Although he had only met Scott socially two or three times and had never exchanged a word with him, Trist had absorbed the hostility of his Democratic superiors—Polk and Buchanan—toward the Whig general the president had so reluctantly sent to Mexico. Trist wrote later that "his character had been so entirely misconceived by me, as to make it the reverse of what I now know it to be."⁸

Trist left Vera Cruz on May 8 with the wagon train and received Scott's letter when the returning dragoons met the train the next day at San Juan del Rio. Stunned by the general's angry response, Trist began a letter to Scott by candlelight that night in his tent. At first he explained that the "contingency" in which hostilities were to be suspended was the ratification by the Mexican government of a peace treaty. But then he allowed his anger to get the best of him, stating that Scott's letter raised the question whether the U.S. government was to be permitted by General Scott to conduct its international relations in its own way and by its own agents.⁹

Trist's letter did not reach Scott for nearly two weeks. On the way up to Jalapa, Trist suffered a moderately severe attack of the diarrhea which was sweeping through the army.¹⁰ His illness probably accounted for his failure to call on Scott after his arrival in Jalapa on May 14 and contributed, as Scott indicated in his memoirs, to the "offensive tone" of Trist's May letters. On May 20, Trist wrote Scott that he was acting in the same relation to the president "as one of your aides-de-camp to yourself, when entrusted with a verbal order to a subordinate officer." He then proceeded to inform Scott that it was the command of the president that the secretary's of state's letter be transmitted immediately to the Mexicans under a flag of truce.[11]

Scott received Trist's May 9 and May 20 letters as he was departing for Puebla, Mexico's second largest city, which had been captured by General Worth's division on May 15. It had been built by the Spaniards in a beautiful high valley at 7,000 feet; it was far above the hot country of the coast, yet separated by the Rio Frio range of mountains from the "Valley of Mexico" that contained the Mexican capital. The pleasant atmosphere of the carefully planned mountain city did not improve Scott's humor. He sent a scorching reply to Trist on May 29. Trist was warned that "if you dare use the style of orders or instructions again ... I shall throw back the communication with the contempt and scorn which you merit at my hands."[12]

Scott was also sickly on his arrival in Puebla. But the larger reason for his bad temper was the precarious status of his campaign in Mexico. Although he had landed at Vera Cruz with approximately 10,000 men, his effective force had dwindled rapidly through sickness, battle casualties at Cerro Gordo, and the return to the United States from Jalapa of a large number of twelve-month volunteers who refused to reenlist. By May 28 about 3,200 men were sick at Vera Cruz, Jalapa, Perote, and Puebla, and Scott's effective force was down to about 5,300.[13] He had no choice but to wait in Puebla for additional reinforcements before beginning a march across the Continental Divide into the Valley of Mexico.

One Mexican historian has suggested that Scott's failure to forward Buchanan's offer of peace negotiations may have resulted from the general's desire to use American military might to force Mexican acceptance of the American proposals.[14] In fact, Scott had no idea in May what proposals Trist had brought to Mexico, and all the evidence indicates that Scott would have greatly preferred a negotiated settlement to risking his small and sickly army in a continued campaign in the heart of the enemy's country.

By the end of the month, Trist had recovered sufficiently to make the 116-mile journey up to Puebla from Jalapa. He received Scott's blast of May 29 on his arrival in Puebla in the first days of June. It was now obvious that he could not rely on Scott to forward Buchanan's letter and that he must find some other way to deliver it to the Mexicans. In newspapers from the Mexican capital, left in a stable by travelers, Trist learned that the Mexican Congress had been reconsidering the previous British offer of mediation in the U.S.-Mexican conflict.[15] Earlier in the 1840s, the British government had tried to prevent the American annexation of Texas and American control of California. But once the war between Mexico and the United States began, the British accepted U.S. acquisition of these provinces as irreversible. The British began to work for an early peace settlement which would prevent other Mexican territorial losses and protect the substantial British economic interests in Mexico.[16]

Trist was acquainted with Charles Bankhead, the British minister in Mexico, who had been secretary of the British Legation in Washington when Trist was in the State Department in the early 1830s.[17] He assumed that Bankhead would be motivated to help by both the official policy of the British government and by the strong desire of the British businessmen in Mexico to avoid an American attack on the capital that might end in the sack of the city.[18] Trist recalled that in September, when Polk rejected the British mediation offer, he had nevertheless stated that he would welcome British help in convincing the Mexicans that they should negotiate for peace. Trist thus assumed that the president would approve of a request for British help in the delivery of the U.S. offer of peace negotiations. Although British officials had made harsh accusations against Trist when he was consul in Havana, that experience did not deter him from asking for British help in the very different situation in Mexico. So on June 6, Trist wrote Bankhead to ask for his assistance in forwarding Buchanan's note to the Mexican government.[19]

Bankhead responded immediately by sending a young officer of the British Legation, Edward Thornton, to Puebla to meet Trist and pick up Buchanan's note. Thornton, the son of a British diplomat, was well launched on his own diplomatic career which would culminate in the 1870s with service as British minister in Washington. Although Thornton was ordinarily the third-ranking member of the British Legation, the first secretary, Percy Doyle, was on leave in England. Moreover, the minister, Bankhead, was suffering from an illness that limited his activities and would eventually require him to return to England.

Thornton briefed Trist on recent developments in the Mexican capital. On April 21 the Congress had passed a law stating that "every individual is declared a traitor which ... shall treat with the government of the United States."[20] The law had been strongly supported by members opposed to Santa Anna, who thought any treaty would include a large payment for ceded territory and that Santa Anna would use the money to maintain himself in power in Mexico. But there had been a secret debate in late April on a motion to reconsider the previously rejected British offer of mediation. Santa Anna's foreign minister, Manuel Baranda, had supported mediation as the only way to save the capital from attack by the Americans and had resigned after the mediation motion was defeated in the Congress on April 30.[21]

Although formal British mediation had been rejected, Bankhead was still eager to use British influence to prevent an American attack. "The

English Minister ... offered ... to act as Scott's emissary for any [peace proposals] that he might make," another former foreign minister wrote on May 7. "He further promised that the American army would not advance, and thus some agreement could be arrived at. It was hoped that the Congress would be pacified by such a step, when it saw England's sword flung in the balance."[22] Bankhead had no authority to threaten British military intervention, but he may have hinted at that possibility in his eagerness to convince the Mexicans that they should negotiate. The idea that the British government might play an important role in an eventual peace settlement persisted in Mexico until December, when the British government's unwillingness to intervene was clearly stated by Bankhead's successor.

After the American capture of Puebla, the Mexican Congress, fearing that Santa Anna would use the crisis to reestablish a dictatorship, readopted the Constitution of 1824, which included severe limitations on the power of the executive. Santa Anna acquiesced, and the revived constitution was proclaimed on May 21.

Thornton told Trist that Santa Anna would not be able to convince Congress to lift the ban on negotiations unless ample funds were available to purchase the support of recalcitrant members. He said it was widely believed in the capital that "the grant of the U.S. Congress of three millions of dollars for the conclusion of a treaty ... was destined to bribe certain members of the Government."[23]

During his years as consul in the Spanish colony of Cuba, Trist had learned that bribing politicians and officials to obtain desired actions was "a universal rule and practice" in present and former Spanish colonies. But he explained to Thornton that he had no money that could be used for this purpose. The State Department's fund for secret expenses was very small, and he had no authority to draw on it. All other expenditures of public funds had to be recorded in the public accounts. Trist thought the necessary funds could be provided by the British and other foreign merchants in Mexico, who had a large stake in avoiding an American attack on the capital. But Thornton was thinking of a larger fund than could be collected from the merchants, and he feared the peace effort would fail because of the lack of money for bribes.[24] Thornton also visited General Scott on June 11, but apparently did not raise the question of purchasing support in the Mexican Congress for a peace treaty. He left Puebla that evening bearing Buchanan's letter to the Mexican foreign minister.

Trist's discussions with Thornton convinced him that the best chance for peace lay in negotiations conducted while the American army remained in Puebla. He wrote Buchanan on June 13 that if the Mexican capital were captured, the Mexican government would flee to some remote location and

SIX / *Bread Upon the Waters* 97

the opponents of peace would have many opportunities to delay or prevent negotiations.[25] His apprehensions in June were remarkably close to the actual situation that developed in October and November.

Trist resolved to express these views in a new letter to Scott, taking "particular care that my communication offers no basis whatsoever for the pretense that he had been dictated to, or interfered with, in the discharge of his duties."[26] But before he could write to the general, Trist was struck down by a more severe attack of diarrhea and was forced to remain inactive for ten days until another visit by Thornton to Puebla on June 24.[27]

Thornton was accompanied by Ewen Macintosh, a British merchant-banker in the capital who was also British consul general, and a Mr. Turnbull, a British merchant in Puebla. The British visitors told Trist that Buchanan's note had been delivered on June 12 to Santa Anna, who had expressed a strong desire to open peace negotiations. But since the Mexican Congress had branded as a traitor anyone who negotiated with the enemy, Santa Anna had no choice but to refer Buchanan's offer to the Congress.[28]

The British visitors doubted that the Mexican Congress would approve of peace negotiations when it reassembled unless money was spent to purchase the support of some members. Trist again insisted that he had no money for secret expenditures. Before returning, Thornton met again with General Scott and, at Trist's request, imparted to Scott everything he had communicated to Trist, including the need for money to bribe Mexican legislators.[29]

The next day, June 25, Trist summoned what strength he had to write a conciliatory letter to Scott. There was no reference to purchasing support for peace, but Trist raised the possibility of an armistice to facilitate peace negotiations while the army remained in Puebla. Trist also sent Scott a copy of Buchanan's April 15 letter to the Mexicans and the original "full powers" document authorizing Trist to negotiate a treaty.[30]

Scott was pacified by the polite tone of Trist's letter, by the appeals of General Persifor Smith who had been trying to end the feud between Trist and Scott, and by the belated opportunity to examine the Buchanan note proposing negotiations.[31] But Scott's reaction to the opportunity for negotiations was primarily based on his further assessment of the military situation. He had only about 5,000 men fit for duty in Puebla. He had ordered his commander in Jalapa, Colonel Childs, to wait for the last reinforcements of which he had news and then abandon Jalapa and bring its garrison up to join the main force at Puebla. Scott was waiting for reinforcements under General Gideon Pillow due in Puebla in early July and for a force under General Franklin Pierce expected later that month. With these arrivals he would have an operational force of about 10,000 men. But he had received reports that Santa Anna's force around the capital might be around 30,000 men.[32] Scott was in the heart of the enemy's country with only a small army and serious supply, communications, and health problems. He could not ignore a chance to end the war without further bloodshed.

Scott's reply to Trist's letter has not survived, but his response was summarized by Captain Robert Anderson (later commander at Fort Sumter in 1861) after a talk with Scott on the twenty-seventh: "Mr. Trist having forwarded in a *proper* letter the documents presenting him in his official capacity, General Scott ... states that he is willing to confer with Mr. Trist, either by writing or orally, on all questions entrusted to him."[33] Trist recorded that Scott also "offered to remove the obstacle presented by my inability to make secret expenditures which, he said, was a matter of no difficulty for him."[34]

When Scott's letter was delivered on the twenty-sixth, Trist was again very sick. Trist commented later that "my death was, for several weeks, expected from day to day."[35] But he summoned his strength again to write Thornton on July 3. He told him that Scott had offered to provide the secret fund Thornton had suggested. "If there is any person, who, in your opinion, could be safely entrusted with the whole affair, I should be very glad to put it into his hands."[36]

On July 6, Scott sent Trist a box of guava marmalade, apparently intended as a substitute for the crackers and dried figs which Trist had used for diarrhea many years earlier at Monticello.[37] Some writers have claimed that the gift of the marmalade ended the feud between Scott and Trist, but improved relations began two weeks earlier with Trist's June 25 letter to Scott and the general's reply the next day. Scott probably sent the marmalade after his first meeting with Trist, earlier on the sixth.[38] The marmalade must have helped, as Trist wrote the next day that he was "decidedly convalescent," and two weeks later he was well enough to join General Worth on a eight-mile trip to the pyramid of Cholula.[39]

Both Trist and Scott regretted their feud, and both wrote to their superiors in Washington during July to urge that the evidence of their quarrel be suppressed.[40] Now the time had come for the general and the diplomat to work together for the peace they both sought.

The day after Scott sent Trist the marmalade a wagon train arrived from the coast with mail, reinforcements, and the president's close friend, Major General Gideon J. Pillow. The former Tennessee lawyer-politician had played a crucial role in the maneuvers leading to Polk's nomination by the Democratic convention in 1844. Pillow had received a slight wound at Cerro Gordo and had returned to the United States, but Polk had urged his friend to return to the army as soon as possible.

SIX / *Bread Upon the Waters* 99

Newspapers that arrived with Pillow indicated that public opinion in the United States was taking a harder line on any peace settlement with the Mexicans. "Already in the U.S.," Trist wrote to Thornton, "a strong public opinion has been formed ... which demands that the futile attempts to bring the Mexican government to reason be desisted from.... It demands that the U.S. should select a line of boundary as may suit themselves."[41] Trist began to realize that if there was to be a negotiated peace settlement with the Mexicans, it must be done quickly before the hardliners in the United States and in Mexico made negotiations impossible.

Two days after Pillow arrived, Trist received a coded report from Thornton: "The government is certainly trying all means to make Congress meet. If it meets, the peace party has the better [chance]." But Thornton thought, "the delay of the march makes a bad impression here. Four thousand men at the Rio Frio or San Martin would quicken proceedings much. Santa Anna fears but wishes to make peace." He again raised the question of money to purchase support for a peace treaty: "200,000 to 300,000 dollars might do good, not less."[42]

Trist began to give serious consideration to Thornton's suggestion. He had several reasons for believing that the president might not object to secret payments, if they produced the kind of peace settlement the president wanted. One may have been his recollection of Andrew Jackson's attitude toward such payments. Trist had visited President Jackson in the summer of 1835, not long after Jackson's envoy in Mexico had been in Washington to press his plan for obtaining Texas by bribing Mexican officials. Jackson had sent Butler back to Mexico to make one more try for Texas, even though Butler had insisted that the bribery plan offered the only chance for success.[43] The circumstances support Butler's later claim that Jackson had been willing to go along with the payoff plan, if it could be kept secret. Jackson may have given his former secretary some indication of this attitude during Trist's visit to the White House in the summer of 1835.

Trist also had reason to believe that the current president was not adverse to the use of secret payments to achieve diplomatic objectives. Trist was back in the State Department in 1846 when charges were made in Congress that President Tyler had used the appropriation to the State Department for secret "contingent expenses of foreign intercourse" to muzzle opposition in the Maine press to the northeastern boundary settlement with Britain in the Webster-Ashburton treaty. Trist and Buchanan brought the confidential records on Tyler's use of the appropriation to Polk, who subsequently refused to comply with a House resolution demanding copies of the presidential certificates for payments from the appropriation. Polk explained to the Congress that "the experience of every nation on earth has demonstrated that emergencies may arise in which it becomes absolutely necessary ... to make expenditures the very object of which would be defeated by publicity."[44] Trist probably knew that Tyler had used the secret fund for payoffs and that Polk had approved of this use of the fund.

Trist knew that Polk thought money was the key to peace in Mexico. He knew that Slidell had been authorized in 1845 to inform President Paredes in some discreet manner "that the U.S. were both able and willing to relieve his administration of pecuniary embarrassment, if he would ... settle the question of boundary between the two Republics."[45] Trist was undoubtedly aware of Polk's belief in the summer of 1846 that a peace could be obtained by promising a substantial payment to a new government headed by Santa Anna. Trist thought that considering Polk's earlier comments on secret expenditures, he might go along with a secret effort to purchase support for a peace treaty. There was no time to consult Polk, but the president's close friend, General Pillow, had just arrived in Puebla.

Before Trist left Washington, Polk asked him to brief Pillow concerning his mission. Pillow's arrival in Puebla gave Trist the first opportunity to comply with the president's request. Neither Trist nor General Scott knew in July that over the next few months Gideon J. Pillow would seriously complicate and threaten the missions of both men in Mexico. Pillow's letters to Polk from northern Mexico had already contributed significantly to the president's negative assessment of the performance of General Zachary Taylor and to Polk's reluctant decision to appoint Scott rather than Taylor as the commander of the invasion of central Mexico.[46] After joining Scott's army, the newly promoted major general took every opportunity to minimize Scott's reputation and to promote his own. His actions in Mexico and his letters to Polk reflected an intense mixture of extreme partisanship, egotism, ambition, and self-promotion.

But in July these characteristics were not yet evident to Trist and Scott. They welcomed the president's friend and took him into their confidence. Trist briefed Pillow on his mission, the obstacles that blocked the road to peace, and the plan to "purchase a peace." At first, as Pillow recalled later, he opposed the plan: "I expressed myself as ... decidedly opposed to the whole scheme as being wrong in principle and as a measure of policy, impolitic."[47] A few days later Trist arranged for Pillow and Scott to meet in Trist's quarters. Pillow recalled in 1848 that Scott had said "the thing was not in itself immoral, that it was not corrupting these men for the very fact that they were in the market and offered to take the money was evidence that they were already corrupt."[48] This use of plural forms supports other evidence that the discussion at Puebla was on the purchase of support for peace among members of the Mexican Congress. (Ten years later Pillow

SIX / *Bread Upon the Waters*   101

claimed that the money was to be paid directly to Santa Anna and that Scott had said "we are not corrupting Santa Anna, for the fact that he was found in the market, asking a bribe, was proof that he was already corrupted."[49]) Pillow was swayed by Scott's presentation. "Entertaining great respect for General Scott's opinions and regarding the precedents ... that such was a usage sanctioned by the practice of our government, I changed my position...and gave it my sanction."[50]

On the evening of July 17, General Scott invited Generals Pillow, Shields, Quitman, Twiggs, and Cadwalader to his quarters. The best account of the meeting was written by Major General John A. Quitman:

> The prospects of peace were now slight, but ... he was informed by some foreign residents in Mexico that this desirable result would certainly be attained by the application of a considerable sum of money; that the Mexican leaders expected the negotiations to be attended by a *douceur* [bribe]; ... that the use of money for such purposes was justified by the practice of other nations; that, considering the great good it would bring to our country, he regarded the means as moral and proper; ... that ... he, General Scott, had credit ... to raise a million or a million and a half of dollars to apply to this purpose, a sum sufficient to insure the success of the negotiations; that he had already expended ten or twenty thousand dollars, which he regarded as "bread thrown upon the waters."[51]

Scott then read a note from Trist covering similar ground and ending with the statement that "the only alternative ... is an early movement upon the capital [which would] augment the hindrances to negotiations.... The adoption of this plan will, it is hoped, ultimately supersede the necessity for the occupation of the capital."[52]

Colonel Ethan Allen Hitchcock, who also attended the meeting, recorded further details on the payment plan:

> The General also mentioned that $10,000 had actually been dispatched to a particular individual in the government (not Santa Anna); and that ... the sum of one million dollars had been placed in position in the capital to be offered from a secret service fund (not to be alluded to in the treaty); but this sum is not to pass under the orders of Santa Anna til the treaty shall be formally ratified.[53]

The reactions of the generals varied. Hitchcock said Pillow "came out very fully and eloquently in support of the measure," but Pillow claimed in 1848 and 1858 that he had stated that the course advocated by Scott was the lesser of two evils. General Quitman vigorously opposed the plan. He thought such a transaction "neither could nor should be concealed from the people of the United States [who would] condemn a treaty obtained by corrupting the rulers of a sister republic."⁵⁴ Brigadier General James Shields also opposed the plan "as wrong in principle and humiliating for the U.S. to be compelled to purchase a peace from a vanquished country."⁵⁵ (After his return to the United States in December, Shields told Polk that bribery had not been suggested or considered at the July 17 meeting.⁵⁶) Hitchcock recorded that Brigadier General David Twiggs had "approved of the whole scheme,"⁵⁷ but other accounts agree that Twiggs declined comment on the ground that it involved a political question which was beyond his competence as a career officer in the regular army. Pillow and Hitchcock recorded that Brigadier General George Cadwalader also declined to comment, but Quitman stated that Cadwalader had joined Shields in opposing the plan.

Scott was not deterred by this lack of support for the plan by the generals other than Pillow. He thanked the generals for their advice and said he would take full responsibility for continuing the effort to purchase support for a peace treaty. Later that evening he summarized his position in a letter to Trist which repeated most of the points made in the meeting and added one more justification: "We cannot certainly know that the money we may silently pay ... would not go into the same channels and to like uses with that which our government is willing to pay by a public treaty."⁵⁸

Neither Trist nor Scott ever submitted a report on the plan to "purchase a peace." Trist began a letter to Buchanan of the subject on July 21, but the surviving incomplete draft is limited to explanations of the origin of the plan.⁵⁹ On February 6, 1848, Scott wrote the secretary of war that "I have not reported on the subject of secret disbursements ... because of the uncertainly of our communications with Vera Cruz and the necessity of certain explanations which, on account of others, ought not to be reduced to writing." He maintained that "I have never tempted the honor, conscience, or patriotism of any man, but have held it as lawful in morals and in war to purchase valuable information or services voluntarily tendered me."⁶⁰

Both Scott and Trist refused to testify regarding the plan to purchase a peace before the court of inquiry established in the spring of 1848. Scott wrote to the court that "not a dollar was paid by me or by my order consequent on or connected with the subject [of the July 17 meeting] to any member of Santa Anna's government, civil or military" except small sums to bearers of messages and some paroled officers. Scott admitted that "there was a confidential arrangement or understanding to pay public money on a contingency that never happened," but refused to give details.⁶¹ The court of inquiry was unable to obtain proof of the payment of money, but it agreed with Scott's assertion that the arrangements with the Mexicans had not in any way affected the operations of his army.⁶²

SIX / *Bread Upon the Waters*

Polk recorded in his diary in the fall of 1848 that the secretary of war had told him that Scott spent between "two and three hundred thousand dollars" for secret service expenses in Mexico and that Scott offered to make only verbal explanations of these expenditures.[63] There is no record of Scott ever making such explanations. When charges of an attempt to bribe Santa Anna were raised a decade later in 1857, Scott again denied that he had paid money directly to Santa Anna; the denial as written did not apply to payments to an agent outside the Mexican government that were to be used for bribes to members of the Mexican Congress.

Evidence assembled here for the first time indicates that the agent was Ewen Macintosh, the British consul general in Mexico. In the nineteenth century, British consuls combined consular functions with private business activities. Macintosh was a principal in a merchant banking firm, Manning & Macintosh, which had close ties to the Mexican government. His firm had played a major role in the consolidation of Mexico's foreign debt in 1845. It was charged later that he had made "a million and a half" on the debt refunding as a result of a bribe to General Herrera's foreign minister, Julius de la Rosa, and the payment of $400,000 to Santa Anna when he returned to power in 1846. Macintosh's profit was in Mexican bonds, so he had a large stake in maintaining the value of these securities.[64] Macintosh's firm was in a group of investors that had acquired rights to construct a transit route across the 125-mile Isthmus of Tehuantepec between the Atlantic and Pacific.[65] Because of his varied business interests in Mexico, Macintosh had, as Trist reported, "immense interests ... at stake upon the restoration of peace."[66]

Trist's incomplete draft report on the plan to purchase a peace describes a crucial role played by an unnamed individual "whose interest in the restoration of peace is direct and personal.... The opportunities afforded by his position and long established relations could not be surpassed [including] very extensive business relations, a long residence in the country, and ... the most familiar footing with Santa Anna."[67] The description fits Macintosh perfectly.

Coded references to Macintosh were removed in the published versions of two of Trist's dispatches. On July 23 he quoted Thornton's first message to him after the $10,000 was received at the capital: "Macintosh can do nothing with him [Santa Anna], even with the aid he possesses from you."[68] A month later Trist wrote of his conviction that "aided by money advanced by Macintosh," Santa Anna would omit no effort in his power to procure ratification of a peace treaty.[69]

General Pillow told the court of inquiry in 1848 that the agents by whom the negotiations with the Mexicans had been conducted while the army was still in Puebla were Macintosh and Thornton.[70] Two of George W.

Kendall's dispatches to the New Orleans *Picayune* refer directly to Macintosh as the fiscal agent behind the peace movement. The first of these stated Kendall's belief that the major forces for peace were Santa Anna's desire for peace and the efforts of "Macintosh, Thornton, and company" representing British interests. He added that "Thornton, during the illness of Mr. Bankhead, does the talking on the English side; Macintosh acts as banker and general agent." A few days later Kendall referred to Macintosh as "the broker and disbursing agent of all the moneys appropriated toward purchasing a peace."[71] When Scott presented an accounting of the appropriated funds he had used for "secret service" expenditures, he listed the July 16 payment of $10,000 as to "___ & ___".[72] Macintosh's firm, Manning & Macintosh, was the only firm using the ampersand in its name which had any connection with events in Mexico in that period.

As it turned out, the opportunity for purchasing support for a peace treaty in the Mexican Congress had passed by the time Scott presented the plans to the American generals on July 17. Four days earlier, a quorum having at last been obtained, the Congress adopted a report by its Committee on Foreign Relations reaffirming that under the reinstated Constitution of 1824 the executive had full power to conduct foreign relations and the Congress's role was limited to the approval or disapproval of treaties submitted to it by the executive.

On July 16, the day before Scott met with his generals, Santa Anna appealed to the Congress for the repeal of the resolution of April 21 branding anyone a traitor who negotiated with the enemy. "The Executive expressly requests of Congress that it declare if it be the will of the nation not to listen to propositions of any sort which may come from the United States."[73] But the Congress took no further action, the shaky quorum soon dissolved, and the Congress as a body played no further role in the events of that important summer in Mexico. Nonetheless, the attitudes of members of Congress remained of the utmost importance because the Congress would have to ratify any peace treaty that might be negotiated.

Even as he was hoping for a negotiated peace without further bloodshed, Santa Anna was not neglecting the preparations for the defense of the capital. Macintosh was also hedging his bets. Colonel Hitchcock recorded later that "we know that [Macintosh] had advanced Santa Anna money for the support of his army at the very time when he was holding out hopes of peace to detain us at Puebla. His object was to gain time for Santa Anna to raise, equip, and discipline his troops and to equip himself with cannon."[74]

Macintosh did not help Santa Anna without extracting a quid pro quo. On July 17, the day Scott met with his generals, Santa Anna approved the

SIX / *Bread Upon the Waters* 105

contract transferring to Macintosh and associates the rights of colonization on the strategic Isthmus of Tehuantepec.[75] An American paper in Mexico, the *North American*, reported the following spring that "on the 18th of July, when Santa Anna found himself unable to raise the necessary funds to carry on the fortification of the capital, the English house of Manning and Macintosh stepped forward and offered the handsome little sum of $600,000 [which was] spent upon works and fortifications which were intended to keep the Yankees out of the capital."[76]

But Santa Anna still hoped to avoid a battle. Ironically, the best chance for peace now seemed to lie in an American march toward the capital. Since the Mexican Congress had refused to take responsibility for negotiations, Santa Anna thought he could negotiate only if the capital were closely threatened by the American army. Thornton sent Trist a coded message on July 21: "Santa Anna is afraid to make peace now.... [He] now says, secretly, that he shall allow your army to approach this city, even as far as the Peñon, and then endeavor to make peace."[77] El Peñon was a large fortress about ten miles southwest of the capital.

Thornton's message arrived in Puebla along with newspapers containing Santa Anna's proclamation for the defense of the city. Together they dashed the American hopes for peace. Thornton's message convinced Scott that he had no choice but to continue his advance into the Valley of Mexico. "This intelligence decides that the movement upon Mexico [City] must now take place," Trist wrote Buchanan on the twenty-fifth. "Nevertheless ... I consider the probabilities of an early peace very strong."[78] The same day Hitchcock recorded his understanding that "we must advance on the capital and ... we will be met by a flag before we reach the Peñon."[79]

On the twenty-seventh Santa Anna assembled his generals to seek their sanction for negotiations. But his old enemy, General Valencia, arrived in the capital the day before with his Army of the North and vigorously opposed negotiations. The meeting of the Mexican generals ended with the conclusion that there should be no negotiation until after another opportunity to retrieve Mexico's fortunes on the field of battle.[80] A hint of this meeting reached Scott on the twenty-ninth. "Everything now shows," Hitchcock recorded, "that the Mexicans intend to carry out the war to the utmost of their ability, and the probability now is that our attempt to enter the capital will be met with most determined opposition." He added, however, that "the English minister, Mr. Bankhead, thinks our advance to Chalco [a lake near the capital] would bring about a peace."[81]

Thornton wrote Trist on July 29 that Santa Anna "has been saying ... that he must let General Scott advance even close up to Mexico [City] and, since he is now abandoned by Congress, must then as a military chief endeavor to make peace. There is no doubt that he is very anxious for peace, for he knows well what will be the fate of his army if he risks another battle." Thornton still believed that "proceedings would be much accelerated here by the advance of your army" but was "entirely opposed in this position by Mr. M[acintosh]." He added that Bankhead "thinks it is his duty to tell you that ... he is no party directly or indirectly to any advice or communication sent from hence which does not emanate immediately from this Legation."[82] At that time a British consul was not a member of a British legation, and this message from Bankhead to Trist is another indication that Macintosh was playing a role with which the British minister could not be officially associated.

Trist reported to Buchanan that he had seen a letter from the capital containing a crucial message from Santa Anna that the U.S. army must not only approach the capital but must also capture some of the outer defenses of the city before Santa Anna could begin peace negotiations. The message was apparently in a letter from Macintosh to Turnbull, the English merchant in Puebla who had been with Macintosh and Thornton when they visited Trist on June 24. Trist wrote Buchanan of his conviction that "we are ... not destined to enter the city. After trying his fortune, not without hope it seems that she may smile upon his at the Peñon or whatever point we may decide upon first carrying, ... [Santa Anna will] contrive to have himself entreated to armistice for the appointment of commissioners."[83]

Pillow wrote in 1848 that Trist told him the message from Santa Anna was "that we should attack their outer works and if we carried them that our army should halt and allow time for making proposals and negotiate [and] that Scott had agreed to this additional proposal but required that before halting this army a 'flag of truce' should meet him, but Santa Anna was not willing to take the initiative by sending a 'flag of truce.'"[84]

Pillow subsequently claimed that he had strongly opposed this arrangement with Santa Anna. He thought if the Americans carried Santa Anna's outer defenses, an armistice for negotiations would give him time to reorganize his army and strengthen his inner works. If the Americans were repulsed, the Mexicans would put the Americans to the sword. He talked to Scott, and the next day Scott read him a letter which he proposed to send to the capital.[85] Both Pillow and Hitchcock described the letter in terms which are highly consistent with those of an unidentified draft in Trist's papers:

> If this army should ... carry any of the outer defenses or beat the enemy in a battle, it may be impossible for me to restrain the ardor and impetuosity of the conquerors by calling a halt. I may be compelled to lead the

troops to further success, or they would rush into the city over all obstacles without me. But, if after carrying some principal outwork or winning other decided advantage, the enemy should desire some short interval for deliberation, let him [the enemy] send a flag to demand a truce for that purpose and, if possible, I shall halt the troops.[86]

Brigadier General Franklin Pierce, a former U.S. senator from New Hampshire and future president, arrived in Puebla in the first week of August with about 2,500 men. Also with Pierce was the garrison from Jalapa, which had come up with this last expected group of reinforcements in accordance with Scott's orders in early June. Now Scott had about 11,000 men at Puebla who were ready for duty, not including about 3,000 on the sick rolls.[87]

This concentration of forces, which Scott likened to Cortez' famous decision to burn his ships at Vera Cruz and march inland, perhaps provided the margin of victory in the battles that were soon fought in the Valley of Mexico. But Scott achieved this concentration by abandoning the bandit-infested road from Vera Cruz to Puebla and further constricting the already inadequate communications between the army and Washington.

With the arrival of reinforcements with General Pierce, there was no longer any reason to delay the march to the Valley of Mexico.

SEVEN

Too Much Blood Has Been Shed

The movement of Scott's army toward the Mexican capital, which had been suspended for nearly four months, was resumed on August 7, 1847, with the departure of General Twiggs' division. Trist left Puebla the next morning with Quitman's division. Worth's division departed on the ninth, and Pillow's division followed on the tenth.

To reach the Mexican capital, the army had to cross the Continental Divide. Twenty miles beyond Puebla the ascent became difficult and the surroundings almost alpine. After a few more miles of climbing, the columns reached the pass at Rio Frio at about 10,500 feet. "The whole route," Trist wrote to Buchanan, "presents a series of natural defenses which would have amply sufficed our countrymen to cut to pieces an army of one hundred thousand men." But the American army found only abandoned Mexican earthworks. "The enemy, after expending great labor fortifying a long chain of heights forming the pass of Rio Frio, had left them unoccupied."[1]

As the mountain mists parted, the marchers glimpsed the panorama of the great Valley of Mexico below. Cadmus Wilcox, aide to General Quitman, described it as "a great garden, dotted with bright lakes, fields of emerald, and the white domes and glittering spires of the villages that environ the capital." To the south were six large volcanoes, dominated by snow-capped Popocatépetl.[2] Soon the road turned down, and the wagon drivers and artillerymen began to brake their wheels. On August 11, Trist arrived at Ayolta, about twenty miles from the Mexican capital. The army paused nearby for several days while Scott decided on the best way to approach the city.

During the next several weeks, Trist lived at army headquarters and was always near Scott. Three years at West Point had prepared him for a role as an intelligent observer and defender of Scott's military decisions. Since the

SEVEN / *Too Much Blood Has Been Shed*

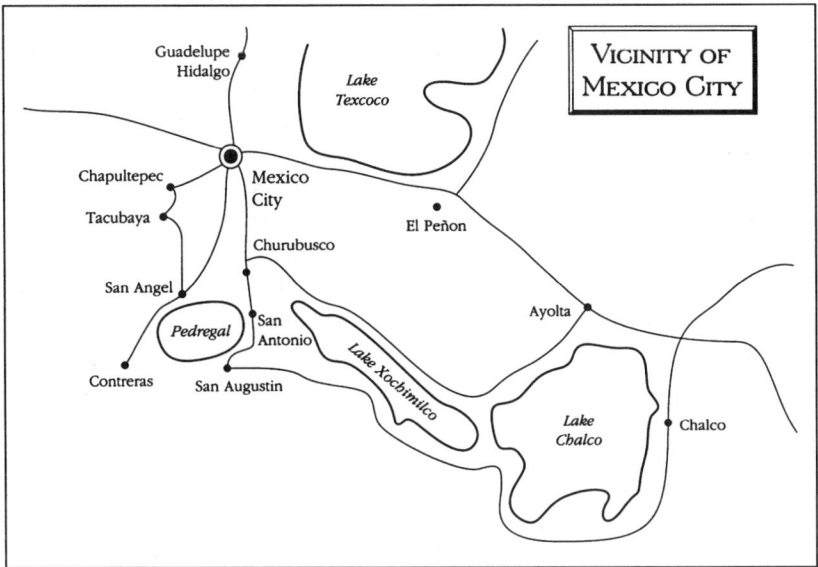

only goal of Scott's campaign was "to conquer a peace," many of his decisions were based on diplomatic and political considerations. Trist participated in these decisions as an informal diplomatic-political adviser to the commanding general.

The choice of a route to the capital was highly influenced by the hope of Scott and Trist that their approach would lead to peace negotiations, not further bloodshed. In that era the city was surrounded by lakes and marshes. It was reached by a few main roads, several of which ran over causeways through the marshes. Immediately in front of Scott's army, on the direct road between Ayolta and the capital, lay the fortress of El Peñon. Trist rode with Scott to a hill beyond Ayolta where they could see the fortress and a part of the city, including the cathedral. Scott's impression of the difficulty of attacking the fortress was confirmed by reconnaissance that day and the next by Captain Robert E. Lee and two other engineer officers. Scott did not know that Santa Anna was waiting for him at El Peñon with more than 5,000 men and had large concentrations nearby at other key points.

Aside from the direct route past the fortress, there were three other possible routes. One involved marching thirty miles around the end of Lake Texcoco. Lt. Ulysses S. Grant thought this northern route would avoid fortified positions and bad terrain until the army reached the least fortified of the city's gates. Although it might have been the best route for a direct attack on the capital, Scott hoped that would not be necessary.

Thornton had suggested that the best place from which to conduct peace negotiations would be the comfortable village of Tacubaya about three miles south of the capital, where Macintosh and other British residents lived. If it proved necessary, Tacubaya would also be a good base for an attack on the capital. One approach to Tacubaya led along the northern shore of Lake Xochimilco to the town of Mexicalzingo.[3] At first Scott favored that route, but reconnaissance by Captain Lee and other engineers indicated that a route south of Lake Chalco would be practical for the 1000-wagon supply train and heavy artillery. Scott chose this route. On August 18 his headquarters was established at San Agustin, a village about eight miles south of the capital that ordinarily provided various forms of gambling for the capital's elite.

"The only road to the city," Trist wrote to Buchanan, "consisted of a causeway, flanked on either side by flooded lands, on the firmest spots of which a man would have been ankle deep in mud and consequently impractical for cavalry or artillery, and intersected by a series of redoubts and batteries of great strength. The first of these was the Hacienda of San Antonio."[4]

Like El Peñon, San Antonio was too strongly defended for a frontal attack. At first, flanking movements seemed to be precluded by the marshes of Lake Xochimilco on the right and by a rugged and apparently impassable lava field, the Pedregal, on the left. But two engineer officers, Captain Robert E. Lee and Lieutenant P. G. Beauregard, scouted the area on the eighteenth and reported that a road could be cut through the Pedregal to outflank San Antonio. Scott agreed and sent Pillow's division to build the road with support by Twiggs' division.

The previous day General Valencia had moved south from the capital and taken up a defensive position on a commanding ridge west of the Pedregal near the village of Contreras. Santa Anna thought Valencia was too far from the capital and ordered him back to a defensive position north of the Pedregal. Valencia, hoping for his own glorious victory over the Americans, ignored the order.

About 3 P.M. on August 19, men of Pillow's division working in the lava field came under fire from units of Valencia's army. Pillow sent Riley's and Cadwalader's brigades to cut off Valencia's route of retreat and planned a frontal attack on Valencia at dawn by Persifor Smith's brigade. Scott, who arrived on the scene at 4 P.M., approved these plans and returned to his headquarters at San Agustin.

By dark, Santa Anna had arrived with several thousand men and posted them on heights north of the Pedregal. Nightfall brought a heavy rain. Not long after dark, Pillow lost his way in the Pedregal, returning eventually to San Agustin; effective command of the three American brigades fell to the senior brigade commander, Brigadier General Persifor Smith. He decided that the frontal assault on Valencia's camp planned by Pillow was not feasible

SEVEN / *Too Much Blood Has Been Shed*

and brought his brigade to join Riley's and Cadwalader's brigades in a wooded valley west of the ridge occupied by Valencia. One of the engineers discovered a difficult but usable route through a ravine to the rear of Valencia's camp, and Smith issued orders for an surprise attack through the ravine at dawn.

Captain Lee volunteered to carry word of Smith's decision to Scott through the boulders and chasms of the Pedregal. On the way he met Shield's brigade and directed it to Smith's position. Trist was with Scott when the drenched and exhausted Lee arrived at Scott's headquarters at San Agustin just before midnight: "Having crossed the Pedregal during daylight he had by a sort of miracle made his way back notwithstanding the intense darkness.... After taking some nourishment, he again went forth into the rain and darkness ... to cross the Pedregal for the third time that day."[6] Lee accompanied General Twiggs, who had also become separated from his troops and was sent by Scott with available units to make a demonstration in Valencia's front while Smith began to attack his rear. Scott later described Robert E. Lee's trips through the rainswept lava field that night as "the greatest feat of physical and moral courage" of the campaign.[7]

During the night the three brigades commanded by Persifor Smith stumbled into position through the pitch blackness. At 5 A.M. on August 20, the demonstration organized by Twiggs and Lee distracted Valencia's men while Smith's brigades attacked the rear of the camp with a volley and bayonet charge. Demoralized by the surprise attack, the Mexicans soon broke and ran, passing through a withering fire from General Shields' men as they dashed down the road toward the capital. By mid-morning 700 Mexicans had been killed and 843 had surrendered. In this engagement, known in America as the battle of Contreras, the Americans captured 700 pack mules, 22 artillery pieces, and large quantities of ammunition and small arms.[8]

Santa Anna and most of his troops retreated that morning to the junction of the San Antonio and Mexicalzingo roads at Churubusco, which General Rincon was ordered to hold as long as possible to protect the withdrawal of the Mexican force from San Antonio. General Worth sent a part of his division through the eastern edge of the Pedregal to outflank San Antonio, but most of the Mexican defenders escaped to Churubusco.

There was no sign of a flag of truce or a request for peace talks. "I had considered, from early that morning," Scott wrote later, "the informal arrangement discussed in the council at Puebla as having ceased to be binding in any degree ... as we did not meet any flag covering propositions of peace after entering the basin and particularly after the battle of Contreras. Hence not a moment was lost in advancing to the next points of attack — the rear of San Antonio and Churubusco."[9]

Scott ordered an assault against the fortified convent of Churubusco, which controlled a crucial bridge on the road to the capital. This time the battle was not so one-sided, and General Rincon's troops beat off two American attacks. Eventually the Americans outflanked some of the Mexican defenses, captured the bridge, and scaled the parapet around the convent. The Mexicans in the convent surrendered in midafternoon. The Americans captured 1,259 prisoners, including three generals.

It would be asserted that fall that the Americans could have taken the Mexican capital on the evening of August 20 if Scott had allowed them to do so. But there are very substantial reasons for doubting that it could have been done and that it should have been attempted. When the Mexicans surrendered at Churubusco at 3 P.M. on the twentieth, the American troops were hungry and exhausted. They had marched and maneuvered since the morning of the previous day, crossed very rugged terrain during the night in a driving rain, and fought major battles at dawn and again at midday. "Our troops," Scott commented later, "had then been ... very generally about 28 hours without subsistence as well as without sleep."[10] Trist also listed "the condition of the troops, who were in a state imperatively demanding food and rest" among the reasons why the well-prepared defenses of the Mexican capital were not stormed that evening.[11]

Both of the battles of August 19–20 had been fought at locations well outside the prepared defenses of the capital. But on the evening of the twentieth the Americans came near three major fortresses that commanded the approach to the city. In September, Scott would consider it necessary to fight two bloody battles to capture these forts before attempting to enter the city. The Mexican forces involved in the two August battles were only about a third to a half of the total Mexican forces near the capital, which had been estimated at around 30,000.[12]

Scott still hoped for an indication of Mexican interest in peace negotiations and for an armistice that would avoid further American and Mexican casualties. Of the total American force deployed of about 8,500, the American losses in the battles of August 19–20 were 137 killed, 877 wounded, and 38 missing.[13] While these casualties were only a fraction of the losses suffered by the Mexicans, they were twice as large as the American losses at Cerro Gordo, the only other major engagement of Scott's campaign. "The slaughter of our men is greater than ever before," Lt. Ulysses S. Grant wrote home, "and worse than death is the awful suffering of the torn and wounded on both sides."[14]

The commanding general also thought that an attack on the city that night might end in pillage and atrocities. It would be the first American

SEVEN / *Too Much Blood Has Been Shed* 113

attack on an enemy capital, and no one knew how the green troops would behave.[15] Scott's worry about atrocities was not unfounded. An attempt on October 9 by American troops fresh from the United States to surprise Santa Anna at Huamantla ended in a night of drinking, looting, shooting, and rape.[16]

Scott's anxiety was shared by Santa Anna and by the British merchants in the capital. Late in the afternoon of the twentieth, Santa Anna and his cabinet agreed that they should appeal to the Spanish minister and the British consul, Macintosh, for help in preventing an American attack.[17] The Spanish minister demurred, but Macintosh was eager to help. Soon after dark he drove out with Thornton to Scott's headquarters at San Agustin. Publicly, their mission was to insure the safety of the British residents in the capital; in fact, they urged Scott to seek an armistice and peace negotiations. But Scott refused to withhold his attack unless the Mexicans took the initiative and requested an armistice.

"My instructions ... and those under which Scott acted," Trist commented later, "contained not even the remotest reference to an armistice." They knew that the president had strongly disapproved of Taylor's armistice after the battle of Monterrey. But there was also nothing in their instructions that specified that the capture of the Mexican capital was an objective of the campaign. "Throughout," Trist stated, "I have proceeded on the assumption that Peace is the sole end of which hostilities are waged against Mexico. This conviction had constantly governed General Scott likewise."[18] Scott wrote in his memoirs that he had planned "to summon the city to surrender, in the expectation that this summons would bring an offer to negotiate and ... the proposal of an armistice."[19] Scott wrote a draft of a summons to surrender at San Agustin on the night of the twentieth, intending to use it as circumstances permitted the next day.[20]

The next morning, August 21, Scott and Trist were moving toward Tacubaya. At Coyoacan they met a fine carriage containing a Mexican general, Ignacio Mora y Villamil, chief of engineers of the Mexican Army, and Señor Arrangoiz, the former Mexican consul in New Orleans. The Mexicans descended from the carriage, Scott and Trist also dismounted, and they conferred in the shade of a large tree. General Mora presented a packet containing a reply from Santa Anna's foreign minister, General Ramon Pacheco, to the secretary of state's April note proposing negotiations. "The chief of the United Mexican States," Pacheco wrote, "has resolved to listen to the proposals which Mr. Nicholas Trist ... may have to make, provided they be advantageous to both nations and safeguard the honor of the Mexican republic."[21] The note suggested an agreement to conclude a treaty "within a period of a year."

The packet also included official and private notes from Bankhead to Trist. In the private note, the British minister said he didn't understand the reference to a year of negotiations but thought this could be resolved when Trist sat down with the Mexican negotiators. General Mora suggested an immediate truce "to bury the dead" and promised that if Scott would agree to halt the army, the gunners of the fortress of Chapultepec would be ordered not to fire on the Americans as they entered Tacubaya.[22]

These confusing communications were hardly the clearcut Mexican request for peace negotiations which Scott had demanded. Subsequent misunderstanding of the origin of the armistice would have been avoided if Scott or Trist had replied to Pacheco's note in a manner that clearly acknowledged that the Mexican government had finally taken the important first step toward peace negotiations. Such a response would have demonstrated that Scott had had no choice but to agree to an armistice and negotiations or accept the dreadful responsibility for the bloodbath that would have followed a refusal to negotiate.

But Scott could not tarry for long under the tree at Coyoacan that morning. His army was in motion, and the enemy's situation and real intentions were shrouded in uncertainty. Scott decided to send Santa Anna the note he had drafted the night before, omitting only the summons to surrender.[23] It contained no reference to Pacheco's note:

> Too much blood has already been shed in this unnatural war between the two great republics on this continent. It is time that the differences between them should be amicably and honorably settled and it is known to your Excellency that a Commissioner on the part of the United States, clothed with full powers to that end, is with this Army to enable the two republics to enter on negotiations. I am willing to sign, on reasonable terms, a short armistice.[24]

That afternoon General Mora brought Scott's note to Santa Anna. He was delighted to discover that the note gave the impression that Scott had taken the initiative in proposing an armistice for negotiations. He rushed back a skillfully worded reply that night that also ignored the Pacheco note of the previous evening and left the impression that the Mexicans were agreeing to a unilateral request from General Scott for an armistice. This August 21 note was signed by Santa Anna's minister of war, General Alcorta. It acknowledged Scott's note "in which the conclusion of an armistice is proposed for the purpose of preventing the shedding of more blood" and stated that the proposal had been accepted by Santa Anna.[25] This Mexican version of the origins of the armistice reached President Polk in Washington before reports on the armistice from either Scott or Trist, and it contributed to the president's negative reaction to the armistice and to the negotiations that followed.

SEVEN / *Too Much Blood Has Been Shed* 115

Neither Scott nor Trist realized that the exchange of notes with Santa Anna on the twenty-first left the impression that Scott had taken the first step toward the armistice. Trist forwarded a copy of the Pacheco note of August 20 with a dispatch to Buchanan on August 22, but made no direct reference to the Mexican note.[26] Unfortunately, that dispatch did not reach the president until long after he received the Mexican version of the armistice. The impression of a unilateral decision by Scott to halt the army was strengthened by the wording of Scott's August 28 report to the secretary of war in which he also failed to mention the Mexican peace initiative on the night of August 20.[27] Scott stated that he and Trist had feared that an attack on the capital would "scatter the elements of peace, arouse a spirit of national desperation, thus indefinitely postponing the hoped accommodation.... Willing to leave something to this republic ... on which to rest her pride ... I halted our victorious corps at the gates of the city."[28]

By the time Scott received the second Mexican note, he had established his headquarters at Tacubaya. The village, on the side and crest of a rugged hill, was described by one American officer as "an incongruous mixture of palaces, luxurious gardens, ruins, hovels, and squalid poverty."[29] At first Scott occupied the summer palace of the last Spanish archbishop, a handsome building with a beautiful rose garden, a large grove of olive trees, and a good view of the city, including Chapultepec. Later the army headquarters was moved to a more modest and less exposed building.

Three American generals who were lawyers in civilian life—Quitman, Smith, and Pierce—met with Mexican generals Mora and Quijana at Macintosh's attractive house in Tacubaya. After an all-night session on August 22–23, an armistice agreement was reached. Hostilities would be suspended while the Mexican government was engaged in peace negotiations with Trist, but the armistice could be terminated by either party on 48 hours notice. During the armistice the troops of both countries would remain where they were and no preparations for the resumption of hostilities were to be made on either side. The Americans would allow provisions for the capital to pass through their lines, and the Mexicans would allow the Americans to purchase supplies in the city and countryside.[30]

From the beginning, there was much opposition to the armistice in the American army. Some came from officers and men who thought they were being deprived of the glory of capturing "the halls of Montezuma." Many in the army feared that Santa Anna was not negotiating in good faith and would use the armistice to regroup his forces for the ultimate defense of the city.[31] But several officers wrote home of their belief that Santa Anna was sincerely interested in peace.[32]

EIGHT

The Painful Necessity

Santa Anna appointed two generals and two civilian lawyers as commissioners to meet with Trist. General Herrera, the former president of Mexico, was considered the head of the peace party. General Mora, who had brought the peace message on August 21, was an engineer qualified to deal with boundary questions and a strong advocate of a peace treaty. Don Jose Bernardo Couto was an able lawyer specializing in civil and constitutional law; Trist regarded him as "the most eminent lawyer of the republic ... no less noted for proverbial integrity."[1] Don Miguel Atristain had been an agent for Manning & Macintosh and was probably added to the commission at Macintosh's suggestion.[2]

Trist's first meeting with the Mexican commissioners was on Friday afternoon, August 27, at the inconvenient village of Atzcapuzalco eight miles from Tacubaya. At Scott's suggestion, he was accompanied to the first three meetings by Major Abraham Van Buren, son of the former president. During the first meeting, Trist discovered that the initial authority of the Mexican commissioners was limited to receiving his proposals for transmission to the Santa Anna. In order to save time, Trist did not insist on the commissioners receiving full powers to negotiate before he informed them of the U.S. proposals. He gave the commissioners a copy of the draft treaty he had brought to Mexico.[3] They met again the next day at the house of Señor Alfaro, only two miles from Tacubaya. Trist was told that the government was considering the U.S. proposals and that they would meet him again on Monday with full powers to negotiate. But this third meeting was delayed until Wednesday, September 1.

After reading the draft treaty brought by Trist, the Mexican commissioners concluded that the gap between the Mexican and American positions was too wide to be bridged. They requested in writing that the government relieve them of the responsibility for negotiations. The commissioners were persuaded to continue during a long meeting with Santa Anna, which was

EIGHT / *The Painful Necessity*   117

followed by a letter from foreign minister Pacheco stating that the government had placed "in your hands the honor and interests of our country."[4]

Meanwhile, there was growing tension between the American army and the Mexican population. On the morning of the twenty-seventh, just before Trist's first meeting with the Mexicans, one American was killed and several were wounded when a mob stoned an American wagon train sent into the capital to obtain supplies as authorized by the armistice agreement.[5] The difficulties in obtaining supplies continued over the next several days. Moreover, there were indications that the Mexicans were ignoring the provision of the armistice agreement which prohibited military preparations by either side.[6]

In meetings with Trist on Wednesday and Thursday, September 1 and 2, the Mexican commissioners insisted that any treaty which would have any chance of ratification by the Mexican Congress must include the Nueces river as the eastern part of the boundary, rather than the Rio Grande. Trist became convinced that "it is with them a sine qua non which they cannot abandon ... and no treaty is to be hoped for except on this basis."[7] He discovered later that Santa Anna had entered the negotiation with the impression that Trist would not insist on the Rio Grande. This was based on an erroneous conclusion drawn by Mr. Turnbull, the English merchant who visited Trist in Puebla, from a remark by Trist that the negotiators would not find the American terms as bad as they feared.[8]

Next in importance to the Mexicans was retaining New Mexico. They proposed a boundary running along the latitude of 36°30' from the Pacific near Monterrey Bay to a point northeast of Sante Fe, and then south and east to the Nueces. With such a boundary, Mexico would have retained most of present New Mexico and Arizona and all of southern California. Later in the September 2 meeting, however, General Mora raised the possibility that if Trist would agree to the Nueces as the eastern part of the boundary, the commissioners might obtain permission to relinquish New Mexico. Trist reported that "the conference ... resulted in my saying that if they would submit a formal proposition to establish [the Nueces] as the boundary, I would transmit it to Washington and would propose to General Scott to consent to the continuation of the armistice until the answer of our Government could be obtained."[9]

Trist's only recorded comments on the U.S. claim to the disputed area between the Rio Grande and the Nueces, made after the August-September negotiations, conceded that the area was never a part of Texas and that the boundary could only be settled by negotiation.[10] Trist thought the disputed area was of much less importance to the United States than New Mexico, which would provide the essential route to California, and that the compromise border suggested by Herrera would be a good deal for the United States.

But Trist told the commissioners that there was very little chance that such a proposal would be accepted by the president. He commented later that he had "expected ... that the answer from Washington would be a peremptory refusal ... [with] the effect of conclusively satisfying them that the determination of our government was unchangeable."[11]

Trist did not realize how worried the president was about Whig criticism of the origins of the war when the new Congress, with a Whig majority in the House, convened in December. The negotiator did not anticipate that his mere willingness to forward a boundary proposal including the Nueces would be considered an admission that the U.S. claim to the Rio Grande was not well founded. Trist's strategy nearly lost him the chance to complete his mission in Mexico, but it ultimately had the intended effect. By the time of the second round of negotiations in January 1848, the Mexicans knew Polk had angrily rejected the idea of a compromise including the Nueces and they realized there was no alternative to acceptance of the Rio Grande as the eastern boundary.

That fall Polk asserted that the prolongation of the armistice while a Nueces-New Mexico compromise was referred to Washington would have afforded the Mexicans an opportunity to prepare for further resistance. But Trist believed a prolonged armistice would have provided military advantages to the United States because of the arrival of additional reinforcements, the recovery of the sick and wounded, dryer roads in the fall, and the inability of the Mexicans to supply a large army around the capital for an extended period. Trist thought that the best judge of the military advantages for the Americans was Santa Anna, who "pronounced my offer to be not a *diplomatic* trick on my part but a *military* trick originating with General Scott."[12]

Santa Anna feared military defeat if the Americans attacked and political defeat if he made concessions to the Americans. Although he is usually portrayed as a dictator, Santa Anna's power was actually quite limited in the summer of 1847. Trist wrote Buchanan of his conviction, after long talks with Macintosh and Thornton, that Santa Anna would "promote, to the utmost of his ability, the negotiation of a treaty."[13] But he could count upon the support of only a very small minority in the Mexican Congress: "Nothing which he can do will receive its sanction, the factions which compose it being resolutely bent upon his destruction." His enemies feared that a peace settlement with the United States, by giving Santa Anna control over the millions paid for the ceded territories, would enable him to consolidate his power.[14] Justin Smith, author of the most comprehensive study of the Mexican war,

EIGHT / *The Painful Necessity*   119

wrote that there is "superabundant" evidence that Santa Anna acted sincerely in the negotiations with Trist, "as sincerely as the drowning man who clutches at a plank."[15]

Eight members and the president of the Mexican Congress met in Toluca with General Pacheco, Santa Anna's foreign minister, and adopted a resolution reaffirming that any peace agreement not ratified by Congress would be an act of treason under the law of April 20.[16] General Rejon, foreign minister in 1844 and 1846, appealed to Santa Anna to continue the war.[17] The arrival in Vera Cruz of the exiled former president, General Paredes, on a British mail steamer on August 15 renewed fears of a monarchist revolution supported by the British.

In a meeting with Santa Anna and his cabinet on Friday, September 3, the Mexican commissioners advised that Trist's proposals be accepted. Most of the ministers concurred, but the proposals were strongly opposed by the foreign minister, Pacheco, who was backed by General Tornel.[18] A prominent *monarquista*, Tornel had helped Paredes overthrow the moderate Herrera government in 1845. As minister of war in 1846, Tornel had convinced Paredes to approve the order for the Mexican attack across the Rio Grande that began the war.[19]

Trist learned later that on Saturday night, September 4, "Santa Anna was still undecided whether he would or would not give the commissioners ... a carte blanche to negotiate with me such a treaty as they might deem proper."[20] Bankhead wrote to the British Foreign Office that "Santa Anna was sincerely desirous of concluding a peace with the United States, but he was overruled ... by two persons who labored for the sake of personal interests and ambition to overthrow the President's good intentions: General Tornel and Señor Pacheco."[21] In the end, Santa Anna concluded that it would cost him the presidency of Mexico to accept the peace terms Trist had brought to Mexico. Trist reported that Santa Anna "could not bring himself to take the plunge into his Rubicon ... and allowed himself to be carried along by a flood of circumstances ... staking all upon a battle everyone felt sure he would lose."[22]

Trist's final meeting with the Mexican commissioners that summer was on Monday, September 6. He arrived at the scheduled hour, 10 A.M., but the Mexicans did not show up until 1 P.M. They produced rough drafts of two papers. One was a reply by the commissioners to Trist's proposals. They noted that the draft treaty presented by Trist involved the cession by Mexico of Texas, the area between the Nueces and the Rio Grande, New Mexico, and both upper and lower California. The Mexican government had already indicated its willingness, with proper indemnity, to agree to the cession of

Texas and had thus "done away with the cause of the war." Mexico was also willing to cede northern California above the 37th parallel (i.e., San Francisco and beyond) which included "an excellent coast, fertile land, and possible minerals that have not yet been touched."[23] The reference to minerals raises the intriguing question whether the Mexicans had some knowledge in 1847 of the gold that would be discovered the following year in California just north of the 37th parallel.

But Mexico was unwilling to accept the other cessions proposed by Trist. "The zone with the Bravo [Rio Grande] at its back makes a national boundary for Mexico both in a military and commercial sense, and no people ... could agree to give up their boundaries." Trist's offer to submit to Washington a Nueces/New Mexico compromise was also rejected. "Sentiments of honor and delicacy ... prevent our Government from agreeing to the dismemberment of New Mexico."[24]

The second Mexican document was a counter-draft of a treaty between the United States and Mexico. It specified a U.S.-Mexican boundary which included the Nueces from the Gulf to its source, the eastern and northern boundaries of New Mexico (not the southern and western boundaries of New Mexico proposed by Trist), and the 37th parallel to the Pacific.

Both the September 6 note and the draft treaty were intended mainly for domestic political purposes in Mexico. Santa Anna wanted to gain all possible political advantage by rejecting the American demands. But these tactics also had important diplomatic effects. Santa Anna rushed to print a 36-page collection of documents in Spanish on the negotiations with Trist. It did not include the Pacheco note of August 20 offering negotiations, but opened with Scott's August 21 note suggesting an armistice.[25] This publication reached Polk before Trist's report on the negotiations. It convinced the president that Scott had initiated the armistice, that the Mexicans had not negotiated in good faith, and that he should recall Trist from his peace mission in Mexico.

The August-September negotiations were the result of a persistent effort by Scott and Trist to achieve a peace treaty — the only objective of the war proclaimed by the president — as quickly as possible with a minimum of bloodshed. Had they been successful, no one would have questioned the effort or the timing. Because they were unsuccessful and more lives were lost in subsequent battles, the August-September negotiations have been dismissed by many historians as a useless and misguided effort. For example, in 1974 K. Jack Bauer used 438 pages to describe the war but gave only 10 lines to the effort in the summer of 1847 to end it.[26]

Trist told the commissioners during the September 6 meeting that their responses that day meant the end of the negotiations. He confirmed this position in a polite note the next day:

EIGHT / *The Painful Necessity* 121

> The authority with which he is clothed being limited ... to the conclusion of a treaty upon the basis of the ultimatum presented by him on the 2nd instant, the undersigned finds himself ... under the painful necessity of recognizing the absolute irreconcilableness which exists between the views of the two governments ... and of considering these final instructions to their Excellencies as putting an end to the negotiation which he has had the honor to conduct with them.[27]

The negotiations had failed, but Trist had earned the respect of the Mexican negotiators. He wrote his wife that he had taken "a most cordial leave" of the commissioners.[28] "In all our relations with Mr. Trist," they stated in their report, "we found ample motives to appreciate his noble character and if at any time the work of peace is to be consummated, it will be done by negotiators adorned by the same estimable gifts which in our judgment distinguished him."[29] The respect of the Mexican negotiators Trist had earned that summer would prove invaluable four months later when there was another chance for peace. But immediately ahead lay the resumption of hostilities.

As soon as Santa Anna decided to reject the American peace proposals, he gave orders to strengthen the defenses of the city and block further American purchases of supplies. Both measures clearly violated the armistice agreement. Shortly after Trist informed General Scott of the failure of the negotiations, Scott notified Santa Anna that unless satisfactory assurances of Mexican compliance with the armistice agreement were received by noon the next day he would consider that the armistice had been terminated. Santa Anna responded that he was willing to rely on a military resolution of the conflict. He also issued a proclamation to the inhabitants of the city promising to "preserve your altars from infamous violation and your daughters and wives from the extremity of insult."[30]

Between the Americans at Tacubaya and the capital lay three strong fortresses — Molino del Rey, Casa de Mata, and Chapultepec. Molino del Rey was a 200-yard long pile of stone buildings; it had formerly been a foundry, and Scott had received reports that cannon were being forged there. Near it was a fort which contained the Casa de Mata, a large building used for the storage of powder. On a height above these buildings was the castle-fortress of Chapultepec, which housed the national military academy. Since artillery at these strongpoints could fire on troops advancing to the gates of the city, Scott believed that he must capture these fortresses before attempting to enter the city.

At dawn on September 8, only 36 hours after Trist's last meeting with the Mexicans, Scott began his attack on Molino del Rey. The initial attack by General Worth's division was driven back by strong Mexican artillery fire after heavy losses. American guns were brought into action, the American attack persisted, and the defenders were driven from the Molino buildings. The Americans found only molds for the casting of cannon, but no evidence of their recent use. The Casa de Mata caught on fire and the powder blew up; the other buildings were destroyed at Scott's orders. The American losses were 116 killed, 665 wounded, and 18 missing. About 2,000 Mexicans were killed or wounded, and 685 Mexicans were taken as prisoners.[31]

The attack on Molino del Rey was Scott's first major mistake of the campaign. Kendall of the *Picayune* blamed Macintosh for giving Scott the false information that the Molino was a cannon factory.[32] Trist was with Scott during the battle but left no record of his reactions.

The elimination of Molino del Rey and Casa de Mata left only the fortress of Chapultepec. Several officers, including Captain Robert E. Lee, thought the capture of these two fortresses should be followed by an attack on the southern gate of the city, bypassing Chapultepec. Scott, however, stuck with his original plan to attack Chapultepec and then the western gates.[33] But he kept a major force near the southern gates, reinforced it by daylight under the eyes of the Mexicans, and then withdrew the troops by night. Santa Anna was deceived and sent major units to the southern gates.

Scott began a bombardment of Chapultepec on the twelfth. Trist watched from the roof of the archbishop's palace in Tacubaya. The bombardment failed to drive the Mexicans out of the fortress, and Scott sent in an assault force on the morning of the thirteenth. At first the attack faltered, but reinforcements arrived and a tide of Americans stormed over the parapet and through the buildings. An hour and a half after the battle began, the Mexican defenders surrendered and the Stars and Stripes was raised over the castle. Kendall reported in the *Picayune* that Trist rode to the crest of the hill soon after it was captured. He was recognized by an Irish-born officer who exclaimed, "I say, sir, its a beautiful treety we've made wid 'em today, sir!"[34]

While a part of Scott's force was taking Chapultepec, other units were storming across the causeways toward the western gates of the city. As soon as the fortress was secured, most of the assaulting units also headed for the gates. By nightfall, General Quitman's division had captured the gate of Belen and several defensive positions inside the city. General Worth's division had occupied the suburb outside the San Cosme gate and was poised to enter the city in the morning.

The total American casualties during the two-day battle — which Scott had hoped to avoid through peace negotiations — were 246 killed, 1,368 wounded, and 47 missing, bringing total U.S. casualties in the Valley of

EIGHT / *The Painful Necessity* 123

Mexico to 2,703. But, as Scott estimated later, Mexican losses were about 7,000 killed and wounded, plus 3,730 prisoners, including 13 generals, 3 of whom were former presidents of the republic.[35]

That evening Santa Anna met with his remaining senior generals. They agreed that the army was completely demoralized by the day's events and that it should evacuate the city. Santa Anna fled north to Guadalupe Hidalgo at 9 P.M., and the retreat of the army began at midnight. Several hours later a delegation from the city council came out to inform Scott that the federal government and the army had fled from the capital.

Early the next morning, September 14, Worth and Quitman occupied the city. At 9 A.M. General-in-chief Winfield Scott, dressed in his most splendid uniform, rode into the vast plaza in front of the cathedral and the National Palace. Nicholas Trist was at his side. The American flag had just been raised over the Palace. Most of the artist's renderings of the scene show a grand parade of troops in precise formations. In fact, Trist recalled that the men of the rifle regiments that had occupied the plaza were taking their ease until they spotted Scott: "As the general-in-chief drew near, they all stood up to greet him with their cheers — sounds which ... filled the air with a music such as it has fallen the lot of but few to hear, and the memory of which can never fade from my heart."[36]

The war was over, although they did not know it then, but peace was not yet within their grasp.

With his withdrawal from the Mexican capital on the night of September 13, 1847, Antonio Lopez de Santa Anna ceased to be a major player in the conflict between the United States and Mexico. In 1850 Brantz Mayer, who had observed Santa Anna at close range while serving as secretary of the U.S. Legation in Mexico in the early 1840s, wrote this evaluation of Santa Anna's role in Mexico:

> Santa Anna ... possessed a willful, observant, patient intellect, which had received very little culture; but constant intercourse with all classes of men made him perfectly familiar with the strengths and weakness of his countrymen.... Believing most men corrupt or corruptible, he was constantly busy in contriving expedients to control or win them.... He seemed to cherish the idea that his country could not be virtuously governed. Ambitious and avaricious, he sought for power not only to gratify his individual lust of personal glory, but as a means of enriching himself and purchasing the instruments who might sustain his authority. Accordingly he rarely distinguished the public treasure from his private funds. Soldier as he was by profession, he was slightly skilled in the duties of a commander in the field, and never won a great battle except through the

> blunders of his opponents.... No one excelled him in ingenuity, eloquence, bombast, gasconade, or dialectic skill.... He never was popular or relied for success on the democratic sentiment of his country. He ascertained at an early day that the people would not favor his aspirations, and, abandoning federalism, he threw himself into the embrace of the centralists. The army and the church establishment — combined for mutual protection under his auspices — were the only two elements of his political strength; and as long as he wielded their mingled power, he was enabled to do more than any other Mexican in thoroughly demoralizing his country.[37]

Although he was the dominant figure in Mexico for considerable periods before and after the war with the United States and was president of Mexico during most of the war period, Santa Anna was in exile abroad when the war began and again when it ended. He bore no responsibility for starting the war and refused to accept responsibility for ending it on James K. Polk's terms. When he fled from the capital on the night of September 14, he abandoned the leadership of a thoroughly demoralized and disorganized country.

It would be three months before new civilian leaders in Mexico would reluctantly conclude that acceptance of Polk's peace terms was the least unattractive of their available options. Before then Polk, totally misjudging the situation in Mexico, would recall his envoy and set the American nation on the road to entrapment in a quagmire in Mexico.

NINE

Mr. Trist Is Recalled

For the president and the cabinet, the six months between Trist's departure from Washington in mid–April and the arrival in mid–October of the news of the capture of the Mexican capital were months of anxious waiting. During most of this period, there was very little news from Mexico. When dispatches and news reports did arrive, they only created new anxieties concerning events in Mexico since they had been written.

Although Polk had hoped to keep Trist's mission a secret, the fact that he had been sent to Mexico was published in newspapers only a week after he left Washington. But the public remained in the dark about the nature of Trist's mission. The administration paper, the *Union*, wrote on June 3 that "the objects of Mr. Trist's visit to Mexico are known to no persons in the U.S. beyond the President, members of his cabinet, and one confidential clerk in the State Department." Even the secretary of state hardly knew what to expect from the Trist mission. "I shall not be astonished to hear any day that a treaty of peace has been concluded," Buchanan wrote to John C. Fremont on June 11, "and I shall not be much disappointed should the war continue for years to come."[1]

During the first few weeks Trist was in Mexico, the army was relatively close to the Mexican coast and dispatches from Scott and Trist reached Washington in less than a month. By mid–June the president had received dispatches from both Trist and Scott which described their feuding in May. Polk was furious at Scott for impeding the peace mission and directed Marcy to prepare a dispatch to Scott "rebuking him for his insubordinate course."[2] Marcy wrote Scott that the president feared that "your course may obstruct the measures he has taken to procure a peace" and stressed that cooperation between Scott and Trist was required by duty, the public good, and the cause of humanity.[3] Buchanan informed Trist that the president wished him to visit Scott and show him his instructions and the draft treaty. He added that "while ... our minister of peace is at the headquarters of the Commanding General, this is not the time for personal altercations."[4]

After copies of Trist's May 9 and 30 letters to Scott reached Washington in late June, Buchanan wrote Trist of the president's "deep mortification" over the feud between Trist and Scott. Polk and his cabinet thought that after the American victory at Cerro Gordo, "the golden moment for effecting a peace" had been lost because of Scott's failure to forward Buchanan's April letter to the Mexicans.[5] Moreover, as Buchanan added in a personal note to Trist, the quarrel had been the basis for "much Whig abuse and misrepresentation."[6]

Between mid–July and mid–September there was almost no news from Mexico, and communications remained very limited until late fall. When Scott's army marched toward the Mexican capital in early August, the road back to Vera Cruz was left to the bandits who had dominated the route for many years. Even in peacetime, no one had traveled along the road without a large escort. Scott was short of cavalry and could not spare large escorts in August and early September to carry dispatches down to the coast. After the capture of the Mexican capital in mid–September, the road to the coast was blocked for more than a month by Santa Anna's siege of Puebla and by the heavy fall rains which made the road almost impassable. It was November 1 before the first army wagon train could be sent down to Vera Cruz and another month before posts along the route could be regarrisoned.

For four months, August through November, Scott and Trist could send dispatches to Vera Cruz by the monthly British diplomatic courier, by other foreigners who traveled to the coast from time to time, by the Mexican and Indian messengers recruited by war correspondents to carry their news stories to the coast for dispatch to New Orleans, and, after November 1, by an occasional wagon train. The letters carried by some of these couriers were stolen by bandits; some of them would take only small pieces of paper which could be concealed on their persons. Never knowing whether or when a dispatch would arrive in Vera Cruz, Scott and Trist usually sent duplicates by the next available courier. Some of the duplicates reached Washington even though the originals were lost. All in all, communication between the army and Washington was extraordinarily uncertain and exceedingly slow. Trist's late July dispatches from Puebla were seven weeks on their way to Washington, and two important late August reports arrived in Washington eight weeks after they were written.

By the end of the summer, Polk's patience was wearing thin. There had been no official reports from Mexico since the arrival in mid–July of dispatches written by Scott and Trist in Puebla in early June when they were still feuding. Several rumors concerning developments in Mexico had proved false: On July 30, Polk heard that the Mexicans had appointed commissioners to meet Trist eight leagues beyond Puebla, but there was no substantiation.

NINE / *Mr. Trist Is Recalled*

The Baltimore *Sun* printed on August 10 a report that Scott was in the Mexican capital, but retracted it a week later when information arrived that Scott had still been in Puebla as late as July 30.

On September 7, Polk told the cabinet that because the war was lasting longer and costing much more than had been expected, he was now inclined to change Trist's instructions to reduce the payment to the Mexicans and insist on more territory. The cabinet agreed that the payment should be reduced, probably from the $30 million maximum to $15 million, and they discussed lowering the western segment of the border to 31° or 31°30' instead of the 32° in Trist's instructions as modified on July 19.[7] If implemented, such a change would have eliminated the need for the Gadsden Purchase in 1853 but would not have greatly increased the amount of territory acquired from Mexico.

Polk recorded that during the September 7 meeting, Attorney General Nathan Clifford said that "if the army took possession of the city of Mexico and the Mexicans still refused to make peace ... Mr. Trist should be recalled.... Mexico and the world should be informed that we had no further propositions of peace to make and that we should prosecute the war with the whole energy of the nation and over-run and subdue the whole country, until Mexico herself has sued for peace." The secretary of the treasury, Robert Walker, concurred. Polk agreed with Clifford's views except regarding the recall of Trist: "I thought we should keep our minister with the headquarters of the army ready to receive any propositions or overtures of peace which the Mexicans might have to make."[8]

The first reports of American victories near the Mexican capital reached Washington on September 11. The news of the August 19–20 battles had been rushed down to the coast by relays of dispatch riders arranged by Freaner of the New Orleans *Delta* and Kendall of the New Orleans *Picayune*, and copies of these papers were speeded to Washington. On the night of September 14, Polk received the New Orleans papers and Trist's dispatch of August 29, which Trist had asked Freaner to send with his news stories. But the unusually quick arrival of this single dispatch only contributed to the president's misunderstanding of events in Mexico. It described Trist's first inconclusive meeting with the Mexican negotiators, but contained no information on the origins of the armistice or on the outcome of the negotiations. Trist's previous dispatch of August 22, which included a copy of the August 20 Mexican note requesting negotiations, did not arrive in Washington until five weeks later. But the August 29 dispatch contained a copy of Scott's August 21 note proposing an armistice, and it convinced the president that the armistice resulted from Scott's initiative.[9]

Polk thought Scott should have pressed for immediate acceptance of the U.S. peace terms during a short armistice; if the Mexicans rejected his ultimatum, Scott should have "taken possession of the city." This reaction, before he had any idea of the results of the negotiations, supports other indications that Polk never intended a negotiated settlement.[10]

Polk's negative response was buttressed by a letter from General Pillow and by dispatches from Kendall to the *Picayune*. In a dispatch reprinted by the *Union* in Washington on September 18, Kendall was highly critical of the armistice. "There are many who believe that General Scott has been compelled to adopt this policy ... by Mr. Trist and his instructions.... The whole affair looks like one of Santa Anna's old tricks to gain time and plan some new scheme of trickery." Kendall had been with the "Sante Fe Pioneers" captured by the Mexicans in 1842, and his extreme suspicion of every Mexican move was derived in part from his hardships as a prisoner in Mexico.

Kendall's comments contributed to the belief of the president and the secretary of war that a protracted armistice would give the Mexicans a military advantage in any subsequent battle, a belief Trist would later challenge.[11] "I fear the negotiators have got to writing," Marcy wrote to a friend. "If so, all is over. The Mexicans are the most famous people in the world for protracting business and both Trist and Scott are interminable writers. When they begin, they never know where to stop."[12]

By September 25 the president was "waiting with great anxiety for the next arrival from Mexico." It came a week later, on October 2, but was not from Scott or Trist. It was the 36-page pamphlet published by the Mexican government on September 8, containing what appeared to be a complete collection of the documents of the peace negotiations in August and early September. But it omitted the Mexican request for negotiations on August 20 and began with Scott's August 21 note suggesting an armistice for the purpose of negotiations. The Mexican publication also contained the Mexican counter-draft of a peace treaty.[13]

When it arrived, Polk was still "feeble" from an attack of "bilious intermittent fever"—apparently the chronic diarrhea that plagued him from time to time during his presidential term. It had kept him in bed for most of the preceding week.[14] His feeble condition enhanced his tendency to make snap decisions with incomplete information and inadequate consideration of the consequences. Incensed by the Mexican rejection of his peace terms, he decided immediately to terminate Trist's mission to Mexico. It did not occur to him to withhold the recall order until he received Trist's report on the negotiations. The cabinet concurred with the decision during a meeting in Polk's bedroom on October 5. He did not leave his room for several more days and still felt weak and fatigued as late as October 10.

NINE / *Mr. Trist Is Recalled*

Polk explained the decision to recall Trist in his diary on October 5:

> Mr. Trist is recalled because his remaining longer with the army could not, probably, accomplish the objects of his mission and because his remaining longer ... probably would impress the Mexican government with the belief that the U.S. were so anxious for peace that they would ultimately conclude one on Mexican terms. Mexico must now first sue for peace, and when she does we will hear her propositions.[15]

The reasons for the president's decision were amplified in Buchanan's October 6 letter notifying Trist of his recall:

> The counter draft of the Mexican government ... proves conclusively that they were insincere in appointing commissioners ... and that the armistice and subsequent negotiations were merely intended to gain time.... They must have known that the Government of the United States never would surrender either the territory between the Nueces and the Rio Grande or New Mexico or any portion of upper California.... The President, believing that your continued presence with the army can be productive of no good, but may do much harm by encouraging the delusive hopes and false impressions of the Mexicans, has directed me to recall you from your mission and to instruct you to return to the United States by the first safe opportunity. He has determined not to make another offer to treat with the Mexican government, though he will always be ready to receive and consider their proposals. They must now sue for peace. What terms the President may be willing to grant them will depend upon the future events of the war and the amount of the precious blood of our fellow citizens and the treasure which shall in the meantime be expended. Should the Mexican government desire hereafter to open negotiations or to propose terms of peace, their overtures will be immediately transmitted to Washington by the commanding General, where they will receive the prompt consideration of the President.[16]

Trist was left with virtually no discretion. If negotiations were under way when he received the recall instructions, they must be "immediately suspended." Although he was authorized to bring with him any new Mexican proposals, he was not authorized to delay his return in order to receive such proposals.[17]

The decision to recall Trist was not based on dissatisfaction, at the time of the decision, with Trist's handling of the negotiations. Polk knew only that the Mexicans had rejected the terms Trist brought to Mexico and had proposed terms the United States could not accept. Although the Mexican documents indicated that Trist had offered to refer to his government a Nueces/New Mexico compromise if proposed by the Mexicans, Polk and Buchanan did not believe that Trist had made such an offer.[18]

Polk had heard a rumor that Scott had captured the Mexican capital but had no details of the battles of September 8 and 13 that led to the fall of the capital and no inkling of the removal of Santa Anna as president and the formation of a new government. In recalling Trist, Polk was refusing to continue negotiations with an undefeated Mexican regime still headed by Santa Anna. When the recall order arrived in Mexico, Trist was about to open new negotiations with a new civilian government in Queretaro. It was these circumstances which led Trist to state in December that "the determination of my government to withdraw the offer to negotiate ... has been taken with a reference to a supposed state of things in this country entirely the reverse of that which actually exists."[19]

The Polk administration's response to the failure of the August-September negotiations was to prepare to continue the war for as long as necessary. After earlier refusals to negotiate, the Mexicans had received Polk's olive branch but had rejected his peace terms. Now it was again time to brandish the sword.

The cabinet adopted essentially the aggressive position Clifford had recommended on September 7. In a personal note with the official recall order, Buchanan wrote Trist that "the spirit of the country is now thoroughly aroused and the war will be prosecuted with the utmost vigor."[20] Marcy wrote Scott that "we must take the best measures ... to beget a disposition in the people of Mexico to come to an adjustment on fair and honorable terms.... The people of Mexico ... are no less parties to the war than the Mexican army and ... must be made to feel its evils."[21]

Marcy notified Scott that about 15,000 additional men were en route to him. "With this augmentation of strength it is hoped that you will be able ... to carry out further aggressive operations, to achieve new conquests, to disperse the remaining army of the enemy, and prevent the organization of another." He expressed confidence that Scott would conduct these operations "in the most effective way to bring about the main and ultimate objective of the war: namely, to induce the rulers and people of Mexico to desire and consent to such terms of peace as we have the right to ask and expect." But Scott was given no guidance as to the type of operations that might achieve these objectives. He was told that Trist had been recalled and that he should forward immediately any new peace propositions he received after Trist left, but "it is not expected that your movements or measures for carrying out hostilities will be thereby relaxed or in anywise changed."[22]

Two weeks after Polk's decision to recall Trist, the president began to discover the real situation in Mexico that fall. On October 20 newspapers were received with a full, if still unofficial, account of the capture of the

Mexican capital. The next day the State Department received four dispatches from Trist written between August 22 and September 28. They reported on the August-September negotiations, the fall of Santa Anna, and the formation of a new government. The latest dispatch contained Trist's judgment that "the most powerful effort which this country is capable of is now making in favor of peace."[23] But the new situation unfolding in Mexico was overshadowed by the anger of the president and secretary of state over Trist's offer to submit to his government a Nueces/New Mexico boundary compromise.

Their reaction was dictated mainly by domestic politics. Throughout the previous year and a half, the opposition Whigs had reiterated their claim that Polk had provoked the war with Mexico by sending Taylor to occupy the disputed zone between the Nueces and the Rio Grande. These attacks had contributed to the election of a Whig majority in the House of Representatives in the fall of 1846. The "lame-duck" second session of the previous 29th Congress had ended in March, and Polk expected a new round of Whig attacks when the new 30th Congress with a Whig-controlled House began its first session in December. It was therefore essential from a political standpoint that Polk maintain the position that the area between the Nueces and the Rio Grande had been a part of Texas — and thus a part of the United States — and that the Mexican forces that crossed the Rio Grande in the spring of 1846 had invaded the United States. Trist's willingness to refer to his government a Nueces/New Mexico compromise proposal suggested that the U.S. claim to the area between the rivers was not well founded or that the area was of marginal importance and might be traded for New Mexico. Polk was furious with Trist for even considering the Mexican commissioners' tentative proposal, even though it was ultimately rejected by the Mexican government.

Polk's narrow conception of Trist's assignment in Mexico was indicated by his comment that Trist had "departed from ... the simple duty with which he was charged, which was to submit and enforce the ultimatum of his government."[24] In Polk's view a peace was to be conquered, not negotiated. Buchanan wrote Trist on October 25, outlining all the reasons why the administration could not consider alienating any of the soil of Texas.[25] But the strongest reason for Polk's outrage was stated by Buchanan in an accompanying private letter: "You have placed us in an awkward position, and the President feels it deeply. To propose to consult the Government whether they would abandon that portion of our country where Mexico attacked our forces and on our right to which the Whigs have raised such an unfounded clamor, will be a fruitful case of appeal against us in the next Congress."[26]

On October 7, nearly two months before his annual message to Congress was due, Polk began drafting paragraphs for the message regarding the

Mexican war. He worked on the message on at least six days in October. Although he made various changes in November and early December, the Mexican portion of the message continued to reflect the president's mood and conclusions at the time he recalled Trist in early October.

While Polk was preoccupied with preparing the defense of his past actions, the arrival on October 20 of news of the fall of the Mexican capital stimulated many newspapers to comment on U.S. options in Mexico. A number of these suggested that the solution to the Mexican problem lay in annexing all of Mexico to the United States.

The New York *Sun* had suggested the "all Mexico" idea in May, not long after the return of its editor, Moses Beach, from his counterproductive mission in Mexico. By stressing that the Mexican lands were not appropriate for plantations operated by slaves, the *Sun* made the annexation idea acceptable and intriguing to antislavery groups in the North who had previously regarded the war as a Southern plot to add more slave states.[27] In August the *National Era* in Washington proposed that individual Mexican states be invited to join the American Union;[28] this idea was also proposed later by the *National Whig* in Washington.

Support for the "all Mexico" idea was strongest in the "penny press" of Northeastern cities with large Catholic and immigrant populations. The *Sun* in New York led a fall parade of "all Mexico" editorials, proclaiming that annexation would offer the Mexicans "a position infinitely above any they have occupied." In Boston, the *Times* thought annexation would be "a work worthy of a great people." The *Public Ledger* in Philadelphia wrote that "our Yankee young fellows and the pretty senoritas will do the rest of the annexation and Mexico will soon be Anglo-Saxonized."[29] The Baltimore *Sun* thought the annexation of all of Mexico would be an achievement of "moral grandeur" and an "act of benevolence" benefiting the Mexicans.[30]

Polk was not willing to consider the annexation of all of Mexico, but he did not reject the possibility of annexing additional territory below the Rio Grande. He told the cabinet on November 9 that "we should continue the prosecution of the war with an increased force, hold all the country we had conquered or might conquer, and levy contributions upon the enemy to support the war, until a just peace was obtained." Such a peace would have to be based on "indemnity in territory." The United States must get California and New Mexico: "if Mexico protracted the war, additional territory must be acquired."[31]

Scott's report on the capture of the Mexican capital arrived in Washington on November 12, nearly two months after the event. The secretary of war sent Scott a warm letter conveying "the highest commendation of the

President" and indicating that "these wonderful achievements are the theme of praise and admiration throughout the nation."[32] But Marcy's letter contained no indication that the government in Washington perceived the need for any new instructions to fit the changed situation in Mexico. Over the next several weeks, the State Department received four midfall dispatches from Trist that clearly indicated that a new movement toward peace was taking place in Mexico. But these had been written before Trist received the recall order; he was supposed to be on his way home, so there was no need for further efforts to communicate with him. During the initial three months of the first American military occupation of an enemy capital, the general commanding the occupation forces and the State Department representative with the army received no instructions from their superiors in Washington that were specifically relevant to the unprecedented situation in which they found themselves.

On November 18, Polk received dispatches from Trist written on September 27 and October 1, with early accounts of the effort to organize a new Mexican government.[33] They did not convince Polk that there was much chance that the new government would accept his peace terms. On the same day, Polk told Buchanan to draft a paragraph for the annual message to the effect "that failing to obtain a peace, we should continue to occupy with our own troops and encourage and protect the friends of peace in Mexico to establish a Republican Government able and willing to make peace."[34] On November 20, Polk revised Buchanan's draft paragraph to state that if such a government could not make peace, "we should take the measure of our indemnity into our own hands and dictate our own terms to Mexico."[35]

On December 2, just before his annual message was due, Polk received two late October dispatches from Trist.[36] His October 25 dispatch reviewed the factional divisions among members of the current Mexican Congress which was assembling in Queretaro. Although his October 31 dispatch indicated that negotiations might be possible later that fall, he asked for permission to return to the U.S. if negotiations were deferred until authorized by a new Congress scheduled to assemble in January. These dispatches did not provide much basis for optimism concerning the prospects for peace. Ironically, the day Trist wrote the second dispatch the Mexican foreign minister wrote him from Queretaro that commissioners were being appointed to begin new negotiations, but Polk did not hear about this development until after his annual message to Congress.

Polk's third annual message, sent to the new Congress on December 7, contained no indication that the political situation in Mexico was fundamentally different than it had been in earlier periods in which the Mexican government had been headed by Paredes and Santa Anna.

> The terms of the treaty proposed by the Mexican commissioners were totally inadmissible.... They must have known that their ultimatum could never be accepted.... Believing that his continued presence with the army could be productive of no good, I determined to recall our commissioner.... I shall not deem it proper to make any further overtures of peace, but shall be ready at all times to receive and consider any proposals. We should press forward our military operations.... The national honor, no less than the public interest, require that the war should be prosecuted with increased energy and power until a just and satisfactory peace can be obtained.[37]

Although the United States had been at war with Mexico for eighteen months and had captured the Mexican capital, the secretive president gave the Congress and American people no indication of the terms of a peace treaty he would regard as "just and satisfactory." But he noted that the additional war expenses since his initial, and still secret, peace terms in April "must influence the terms of peace which it may be deemed proper hereafter to accept."

The president denied that the annexation of all of Mexico was the goal of his war policy: "It has ever been my desire that she should maintain her nationality, and, under a good government adapted to her condition, be a free, independent, and prosperous nation." He also rejected the idea that the United States should "retire to a designated line and simply hold and defend it" without a peace treaty, since a large army would have to be kept in the border zone to cope with guerrilla warfare by the Mexicans.

Polk thought a satisfactory peace might be obtained only if the American commander in Mexico gave "encouragement and assurances of protection" to the friends of peace, helping them establish and maintain a government "able and willing to conclude a peace which would be just to them and secure to us the indemnity we demand." There were several other indications in the message that the president did not expect an early peace treaty and that he thought a U.S. military occupation in central Mexico would be necessary for a substantial period. (Two weeks after the message, the cabinet unanimously decided that a peace treaty with a government established under the protective wing of the American army should stipulate "that a sufficient portion of our army should remain in Mexico for a year after peace was concluded to afford the desired protection."[38]) Although Polk expected guerrilla warfare in the border zone if the United States withdrew without a treaty, there was nothing in the message on the prospects of guerrilla warfare waged by Mexicans who did not support a government

NINE / *Mr. Trist Is Recalled*

established with the support of the American army or on the likelihood of a revolution against that puppet government as soon as American military protection was withdrawn.

If a pro–peace government were formed with U.S. support, Polk proclaimed in the message, the war would prove to be an enduring blessing to Mexico. "After finding her torn and distracted by factions and ruled by military usurpers, we should then leave her with a republican government in the enjoyment of real independence and domestic peace and prosperity, performing all her relative duties in the great family of nations and promoting her own happiness by wise laws and their faithful execution." This naive declaration demonstrates that Polk was thinking of an extended occupation in Mexico with "reorientation" and "democratization" goals similar to those of the long-term U.S. military occupations in Germany and Japan after World War II.

On the other hand, if efforts to establish a Mexican government willing to make peace proved fruitless, the United States "must continue to occupy her country with our troops, taking the full measure of indemnity into our own hands, and must enforce the terms which our honor demands."

Similar ideas had been presented in an editorial on "Occupation of Mexico" in the November issue of a Democratic journal, *The United States Magazine and Democratic Review*, whose editor had coined the term *Manifest Destiny* two years earlier.

> An American army should occupy the country ... until such time as a system of entire free trade, scrupulous administration of justice, and undoubted security to property shall have developed to the fullest extent [and] the United States troops may be withdrawn.... All that is required is a firm and liberal government.... Such a government ... supported by a column of United States troops ... should attack and crush every Mexican force and suppress ... every insurrectionary movement or organized hostility. By these means ten years would not elapse before the ... civil government of Mexico [had] sufficient strength to maintain itself against the rise of any new military interest.... The soldiers succeeding each other for short terms would most of them, as they were discharged, remain in the country, and gradually infusing vigor into the race, regenerate the whole nation.

In 1847, Americans had no experience with the military occupation of enemy countries. They did not begin to understand the manifold political, military, manpower, financial, and other problems that would inevitably have been associated with an extended military occupation of heavily populated Mexican areas, whether the objective of the occupation was an eventual peace treaty or the annexation of those areas by the United States.

Thanks to Nicholas Trist, the United States avoided entrapment in this Mexican quagmire. A few days before Polk's message, Trist reached a fateful decision that would lead to a treaty ending the war and providing for the prompt removal of American troops from Mexico.

TEN

I Will Make a Treaty

After the capture of the Mexican capital on September 14, 1847, Trist waited there for two months for new peace initiatives from the Mexicans or new instructions from his government in Washington.

The Mexican Constitution of 1824 provided that if the office of president of the Republic became vacant, it could be filled by the president of the Supreme Court. That office was also vacant. Manuel de la Peña y Peña, a prominent lawyer, law professor, and judge, was now the eldest justice of the Supreme Court. Peña had previously served as minister of the interior, senator, and foreign minister. Now he was persuaded by moderate political leaders to assume the provisional presidency of Mexico.[1]

Trist reported on September 27 that "the most powerful effort which this country is capable of, is now making in favor of peace" and that Peña was on his way to Queretaro, 140 miles north of the capital, where the Congress was to meet on October 5.[2] But the arrival of members of Congress was delayed by the inability of impoverished provincial governments to pay their traveling expenses, by the reluctance of some members to become involved with negotiations with the American invaders, and by the general confusion in the country.[3]

Santa Anna was responsible for much of the confusion. Although he resigned as president on September 14, he continued to command the army. In late September he led about 8,000 men over the mountains and attempted to retake Puebla. Relief of the small American garrison in Puebla by troops from the capital was prevented by heavy fall rains that made the mountain road impassable for wagons and artillery. Santa Anna's siege was raised in early October when about 3,000 American reinforcements under Brigadier General Joseph Lane reached Puebla from the coast. On October 7 Peña's government removed Santa Anna from the command of the army.[4]

As a result of the rains and the siege of Puebla, the road from the capital to Vera Cruz remained closed for several weeks after the capture of the capital; very little news from the United States reached the capital until the second half of October. Even then the road was still infested with bandits. Communication with the coast was sporadic and uncertain until December, when Scott was able to establish several posts along the road with newly arrived reinforcements.

During the early weeks of the first American military occupation of an enemy capital, the senior officers of the army concentrated on the allocation of credit for the capture of the city. This process led to two major feuds between generals. The first was between General Scott and Major General Gideon Pillow, the close friend of President Polk.

In early October, Scott received Pillow's report on his division's action on August 19 and 20. After ordering a frontal attack at dawn, Pillow had lost his way in the rainswept lava field during the night of August 19–20 and was not present when units of his division attacked near Contreras. Moreover, his original plan for a frontal attack was replaced, with the approval of General Scott, with a surprise attack through a ravine. Despite these well-known facts, Pillow claimed in his report that he had planned the main movements of the American forces, and he took most of the credit for the American success. A similar pattern emerged in Pillow's reports on the September battles. Scott wrote him that he perceived an effort on his part "to leave General S entirely out of the operations" and "to make you control the operations of the whole army."[5] But Pillow refused to revise his reports.

Newspapers brought to Scott's headquarters by the British courier on October 19 included a letter signed "Leonidas" in the September 25 New Orleans *Delta* that gave General Pillow most of the credit for the American victories in August. It also claimed that the armistice after these battles had been merely a trick by Santa Anna to gain time to strengthen his fortifications. The "Leonidas" letter implied that the central objective of the campaign in central Mexico had been the capture of the capital and that Scott should not have allowed the possibility of peace to interfere with the achievement of this paramount military objective.

Pillow denied responsibility for the letter, but Trist was among many in the army who thought that Pillow had written it or encouraged someone else to do so. Later Trist and Scott heard about a letter from Mexico signed "Veritas" that had been published on October 23 in the *Union* in Washington. It positively dripped with praise for Pillow and indicated that his role at Contreras in August had "won him the applause and admiration of the whole army."[6] Trist was sure that the administration paper would not print such puffery for Pillow unless the president was eager to play down Scott's role in the battles.

TEN / *I Will Make a Treaty*

Trist saw these highly distorted reports and letters as proof of a political plot by Pillow and Polk to limit the credit given Scott by the public for the August and September victories and thus to reduce his chances for a Whig nomination for president in 1848. Having made his peace with Scott in the summer after feuding with the general in the spring, Trist was now 100 percent on Scott's side.

A second feud erupted during the same period between Scott and Brigadier General William Worth. The ambitious and egotistic career officer thought Scott's reports had given him too little credit for his roles at Cerro Gordo and in the capture of Mexico City. He also resented Scott's cancellations of an order issued by Worth in Puebla allowing Mexican laws to continue in force and of Worth's "Poison Circular" that alerted his troops to the alleged danger that Mexicans would attempt to poison the Americans.

The two feuds became intertwined after Scott issued a general order republishing the president's January 1847 prohibition of the writing of accounts of battles for publication until after the completion of the campaign. Worth, who may have been implicated in the "Leonidas" letter, thought the order was directed against him. Following a bitter exchange of letters with Scott, he sent a very intemperate letter through channels to the president accusing Scott of conduct unbecoming an officer. Scott responded by placing Worth under arrest.[7]

Pillow responded to the general order with an insulting letter to Scott's adjutant and a letter to the secretary of war requesting a hearing on the charge that he had written the "Leonidas" letter. Since the letter to Marcy bypassed Scott in violation of regulations, Scott also brought charges against Pillow, who responded with a long and bitter complaint to his friend, James K. Polk.[8] Pillow's letter also described Trist's strong support for Scott, and it contributed significantly to Polk's negative assessment of Trist's performance in Mexico.

During the midfall period in which he became convinced of a plot by Pillow and Polk against Scott, Trist was also increasingly disturbed by the indications that most officers of the army were cool or hostile to peace negotiations and that many supported a permanent American occupation of much or all of Mexico. Later, Trist would become convinced that the plot against Scott was part of a broader scheme to pave the way for the annexation of all of Mexico.

Brigadier General Worth was an outspoken annexationist. "Our race is finally destined to overrun the whole continent," he wrote the secretary of war. "It is our decided policy to hold the whole of Mexico ... by occupation, permanent conquest, and future annexation." Worth thought Mexico should be divided into territories, each administered by a U.S. civil governor assisted by a military officer.[9] Major General Quitman, the highest ranking of the volunteer generals and a leader of the ardent Mississippi expansionists, thought the annexation of southern Mexico would give the United States the "power to tax the commerce of the world" using a transit route from the Atlantic to the Pacific across the Isthmus of Tehuantepec.[10]

Many others in the army supported an expanded occupation, at least in northern Mexico. Brigadier General James Shields of Illinois, previously commissioner of the Land Office in Washington, had written Buchanan in March that the United States should annex all of the Mexican territory north of the Sierra Madre mountains.[11] Brigadier General Persifor Smith, a former Louisiana judge, thought the United States should withdraw from central Mexico but keep the other Mexican territories it had conquered.[12] The editor of the *Delta* in New Orleans, after talking with a number of American officers who had left the Mexican capital on November 1, wrote that "there is a prevalent, almost unanimous opinion in the army in favor of occupation of the country."[13]

Newspapers arriving from the United States in late October indicated a growing sentiment in the United States for continuing the war and occupying more Mexican territory. "We must offer the olive branch no longer," wrote the administration paper, the *Union*. "The war must be resumed at once, with new vigor. Its burdens must be thrown on the conquered. By such a course alone can we hope to secure a peace."[14] The *North American*, an American paper established in the Mexican capital, reported on November 5 that "all parties in the United States are in favor of a continuation of the war, and the project for a formal occupation of Mexico has become the general topic of the day." The U.S. newspapers also contained indications that the cabinet in Washington had been talking about new and tougher peace terms that Trist was sure would be even more unacceptable to the Mexicans than those he had brought to Mexico.[15]

"Among all those in Mexico," Trist wrote in 1848, "there was ... but one exception to the ... universal belief that a treaty of peace had become an impossibility.... That one exception was myself."[16] On October 20 he wrote Louis de la Rosa, Peña's foreign minister, "The full powers which it would have been ... so great a happiness to use ... stand unrevoked, and so long as this shall be the case the undersigned will continue anxiously to cherish the wish that they may not have been conferred in vain."[17]

A quorum was achieved in the Mexican Congress on November 5, but progress towards peace was impeded by the conflict between the three main factions in the Congress. The conservative *Monarquistas*, supported by the church and the army, hoped for the establishment of a monarchy in Mexico.

TEN / *I Will Make a Treaty*

The *Puros*, radical democrats who admired the U.S. constitution, opposed the power and position of the church and army in Mexico and supported the annexation of Mexico by the United States. The *Moderados* were the "peace party." They were moderate republicans who supported the Mexican Constitution of 1824, desired the continuation of Mexico as an independent republic, and opposed both extremes — monarchy and annexation.

On November 11 the Moderados in the Congress won a crucial vote and General Pedro Anaya was elected provisional president of Mexico to serve until a newly elected Congress met in January. Anaya appointed Peña as foreign minister and General Mora, whom Trist described as an "avowed Apostle of Peace," as minister of war. For a few days, Trist was cheered by these "brightening prospects."

On the morning of November 16, the *American Star* carried a story of "Mr. Trist's Recall" from the *Union* in Washington: "Orders have been sent to recall Mr. Trist.... No other agent will be sent, and no propositions made by the U.S. for peace." At 3:30 that afternoon, Trist received Secretary Buchanan's October 6 letter ordering him to return to the United States.

Trist was appalled by the order, which he realized was based on a monumental misconception by the president of the situation in Mexico. During a sleepless night, Trist wrestled with the idea of ignoring the order, at least until he received fresh instructions written after the president learned of the capture of the capital, the fall of Santa Anna, and the formation of the new government in Queretaro. But sober reflection the next morning led to the conclusion that he must obey the orders of the president.

The news of his recall was devastating to the peace party and elating to their opponents. "By both parties the peace men were considered as floored; this was the coup de grace for them," he commented later.[18] Thornton, British chargé d'affaires since Bankhead's illness forced him to leave for England on October 11, was going to Queretaro to represent his government at the temporary Mexican capital. Trist asked Thornton to convey the news of his recall unofficially to Peña. A few minutes after Thornton arrived at the temporary capital on November 21, Peña called on him with a draft message notifying Trist of the appointment of commissioners to resume peace negotiations. Peña was "thunderstruck" at the news of Trist's recall.[19]

Thornton may have suggested Peña's response, which was to ignore the unofficial news of Trist's recall and send him the already-drafted letter concerning the appointment of commissioners. Peña's letter stated that the two previous civilian commissioners — Couto and Atristain — would serve again. General Herrera was ill and General Mora was now minister of war, so they would be replaced by Luis Gonzaga Cuevas and General Manual Rincon.[20]

Cuevas has served as Mexican foreign minister in 1837 and in 1845. Trist thought both new commissioners were "men of the highest standing ... and conspicuous among the leaders of the peace party."[21]

A note from Thornton arrived with Peña's letter:

> I leave it to your ... charity for this unhappy nation, to lend a hand toward the preservation of her nationality. I look upon this as the last chance for either party of making peace. Already Mexicans are beginning to perceive that you are not such barbarians as they supposed, and the opinion must every day increase that your presence will ensure them more safety for personal and property than they have ever enjoyed under their own government.... The circumstances of your recall, especially at the moment when commissioners have been named, will give additional strength to the enemies of peace, and I will look upon it that hope of it goes with you.[22]

But Trist believed that he had no choice but to notify Peña officially that he had been recalled. "The undersigned regrets ... that the powers conferred upon him ... have been revoked," he wrote on November 24. "[He] still cherishes ... the hope that the signature of the treaty, which has been reserved for another hand than his, is destined to take place at an early day."[23] At Peña's request, the Mexican commissioners pleaded with Trist to remain in Mexico and continue the negotiations.[24] They tried various arguments, with no immediate result.

As Trist awaited the departure of the next wagon train to the coast, however, more evidence piled up that the alternatives to an early peace were a prolonged war, a protracted occupation, and, perhaps, the ultimate absorption of much or all of Mexico into the United States.

On November 18 a large mail arrived, including New Orleans papers up to November 2 and Washington papers as late as October 19. Articles reprinted or quoted by the *North American* and the *American Star* reiterated that no new representative would be sent to Mexico and that if Mexico wanted peace, she would have to sue for it. An October 11 letter from Washington said "the conclusion come to by the Administration is to take possession of a certain line, and to reduce everything north of it to complete subjection." The letter referred to the "rigorous war we are about to begin." The *Union* in Washington said Scott would have 25,000 or 30,000 men when all the planned reinforcements reached him. These reports convinced the *American Star* that "the military occupation of the country has been fully decided upon by the Administration." No such decision had been reached in Washington, but these exaggerated accounts of administration plans for a renewed war and an expanded occupation clearly contributed to the decision Nicholas Trist reached in early December.

TEN / *I Will Make a Treaty*

The November 23 issue of the *North American* quoted a report in the New York *Herald* of October 19 that the cabinet was discussing the question whether "the nationality of Mexico should be annihilated." The *Herald* strongly supported annexation of all of Mexico. "A force must be poured into the country sufficiently powerful to overawe resistance. Every state government must be overthrown and new governments ... erected.... It is a glorious prospect, this annexation of all of Mexico." Nicholas Trist did not agree that the annexation of all of Mexico was a glorious prospect. He thought that an attempt to annex all of Mexico would involve the United States in very serious problems on several levels.

The first level of problems would be military. Trist, who had completed most of the course at West Point, shared the outlook on the military problems of annexation of his best friends in Mexico, Freaner of the *Delta* and General Scott. Freaner had written to the *Delta* on September 17 that "annexation of this section of the country is totally impracticable and ... those who have been its advocates in the U.S. are ignorant of the difficulties ... and the endless trouble and exasperations it would lead to."[25] On November 26, Freaner wrote that occupation of the entire country would require at least 75,000 men and that it was extremely doubtful that such a force could be raised in the United States or sustained in Mexico for a substantial period.[26] General Scott thought that annexation could only be achieved through a long-term military occupation. "Annexation and military occupation," he wrote to the secretary of war, "would be ... one and the same thing as to the amount of force to be employed by us.... If we would withdraw our troops ... all Mexico ... would again relapse into a permanent state of revolution, beginning with one against annexation."[27]

Second, Trist doubted that the Mexicans could be assimilated into the democratic political system in the United States and was deeply concerned about the very negative impact of the annexation on American government and politics. He had written Jefferson in the 1820s that the former Spanish population of Louisiana was ill-prepared for participation in the American political system, even after two decades under the American flag.[28] He had lived for more than a decade in a Spanish colony and knew well the legacy of Spanish autocracy and corruption that still lay heavy on the people of Mexico after only 26 years of independence from Spain.

"The policy of continued occupation," he wrote Buchanan in October, "would necessarily give rise to ... the inoculation of our race with the virus of Spanish corruption in office."[29] By early December he was convinced that annexation offered "incalculable danger to every good principle, moral as well as political, which is cherished among us."[30] In 1848 he wrote that his reasons for opposing the annexation of all of Mexico could be summed up in one word, corruption.³¹ Some years later he recorded his belief that the lives and money he saved the nation by ending the war were less important than his service in avoiding "the consequences to the vital spirit of our institutions and to our morality as a people" which would have resulted from the annexation of Mexico as a military conquest.³²

Finally, Trist feared that a U.S. attempt to annex much or all of Mexico would raise a host of problems concerning slavery in the former Mexican areas that could threaten the Union itself. Mexico had abolished slavery in 1829, although many Indians in Mexico lived under a form of peonage which was not so different from slavery. In the August-September negotiations, the Mexicans had proposed that the treaty specify that slavery would be excluded from all Mexican territory to be acquired by the United States. While assuring the Mexicans that his views on slavery were not very different than theirs, he explained that a prohibition against slavery in the treaty would be an insuperable barrier to its ratification by the U.S. Senate.³³

Trist had still been in Washington in the summer of 1846 when the Wilmot Proviso prohibiting slavery in territories acquired from Mexico had been proposed and during the following winter when debate on the Proviso had dominated the Congressional session. By the time he left for Mexico, it was clear that the nation faced a major sectional conflict over the admission of slavery into the territories that would be acquired even under the draft treaty Trist brought to Mexico. The annexation of a much larger area or all of Mexico would require the eventual admission to the Union of many additional states, destroying the precarious balance between slave and free states in the Congress and seriously threatening the survival of the Union. The "nullification" controversy in the early 1830s, in which Trist had been an active participant, had indicated how far Southern leaders were willing to go if they thought the South's vital interests were threatened.

This threat to the Union was on his mind on November 27, when Trist sent official and personal messages to the secretary of state urging the prompt appointment of new commissioners to negotiate with the Mexicans. "The complexion of the new Congress which is to meet at Queretaro on the 8th of January is highly favorable," he wrote Buchanan. "This will be the last chance for a treaty. I would recommend ... the immediate appointment of a commission." He also sent a note to his wife: "Say to Mr. B that if he wants peace and wishes to save our Union, to lose not a minute in appointing commissioners."³⁴

As the time to leave approached, Trist became increasingly doubtful that the peace party in Mexico could survive until new commissioners were sent to replace him. He expressed anxiety and frustration in a letter to Thornton:

What is my line of duty to my government and my country, in this extraordinary position in which I find myself? Knowing as I do, that Peace is the earnest wish of both, is it, can it be my duty to allow this last chance for peace to be lost, by conforming to a determination of that government taken with reference to a supposed state of things in this country entirely the reverse of that which actually exists?[35]

Although some accounts of Trist's mission have indicated that Thornton or Scott urged him to remain in Mexico and negotiate a treaty, there is no evidence of a direct effort of this sort by either man. Thornton had been in Queretaro since November 21. His evaluation of the Mexican situation in letters to Trist obviously contributed to Trist's decision, but they contain no suggestion that Trist ignore the president's order and they indicate that Thornton thought Trist's departure was inevitable. Trist was eager to avoid complicating Scott's already difficult relationship with the president by involving the general in the question whether a presidential order should be ignored. He wrote in 1848 that "not a single thought had passed between us, in regard to my doing otherwise than conform to those instructions, fatal as they manifestly were."[36]

Ironically, the idea that the president might submit an acceptable treaty for ratification, even if it was negotiated without authorization, may have come from Polk himself. Shortly before Trist's departure for Mexico in April, Buchanan received a letter from Moses Beach, the New York editor sent to Mexico the previous winter as a confidential agent. Beach reported that he had discussed the main provisions of a treaty with several members of the Mexican Congress, and the self-confident editor implied that he might proceed to negotiate a treaty. Since Beach was mainly in contact with opposition leaders, the idea that he could negotiate a treaty was ridiculous. Nonetheless, Polk recorded in his diary that should Beach make an acceptable treaty, "I will waive his authority to make it and submit it to the Senate for ratification.... It will be a good joke if he should assume the authority and take the whole country by surprise and make a treaty."[37] Buchanan may have shared the "joke" with his deputy, Nicholas Trist.

The only person who contributed directly to the momentous decision Trist reached in early December was his friend James L. Freaner of the New Orleans *Delta*. In a dispatch to the *Delta* on December 1, Freaner expressed the opinion that Trist should remain in Mexico and negotiate a treaty:

> If Mr. Trist is the man I have taken him to be, he will conclude a peace, if the Mexicans are willing to take it on the terms we have offered.... The interests of the United States require it at his hands.... If the opportunity offers to Mr. Trist of negotiating a peace, he should assume the responsibility at all hazards, and the country will sustain him.[38]

A day or two later Freaner came to see Trist, who explained the situation in which he found himself. If he returned to the United States as ordered, "the only possible chance for the restoration of peace must inevitably be destroyed through the utter dissolution of the Mexican government and the consequent triumph of the party ... whose aim it [is] to compel the U.S. to admit the whole of Mexico into the Union."[39] Freaner's response was unequivocal:

> Mr. Trist, make the treaty! It is now in your power to do your country a greater service than any living man can render her. I know our country. I know all classes of people there.... They want peace, sir. They pant for it. They will be grateful for it. Make the treaty, sir. Your country, sir, is entitled to this service from you. Do it, Sir! She will support you in it, instructions or no instructions.[40]

Trist recalled the moment of decision vividly more than twenty years later:

> I stood there as the only man living by whom the work could be done.... It must be done by *me* or remain undone long enough for all chances of its being done to be lost "for an indefinite period." The only doubtful point was as to the *possibility* of its being done. This possibility was universally believed to have received its death blow by my recall. Its resuscitation was, at best, but a slender chance — a forlorn hope. However, the state of my mind ... was such as make it obligatory ... as an act of "solemn duty to my country"... to venture upon the attempt.[41]

On December 3, 1847, Trist informed Commissioner Couto that he was willing to remain in Mexico and negotiate a treaty which was based essentially on the U.S. territorial demands. He gave Couto a memorandum proposing that the border run up the middle of the Rio Grande from the Gulf of Mexico to the 32nd parallel and then along that parallel to the Pacific. Couto immediately wrote Peña in Queretaro:

> Mr. Trist has given us to understand that he is disposed to assume the responsibility of a treaty he can take with him to Washington, where, in his opinion, it will be approved by the Senate.... He has informed us ... that he and General Scott are sincerely desirous of peace, and that a continuance of the war will end by ruining Mexico and by producing grave complications in the internal affairs of the United States.[42]

Trist explained his decision in a letter to Thornton on December 4:

> I am now resolved and committed to carry home with me a Treaty of Peace, if the Mexican government feel strong enough to venture upon making one,

TEN / *I Will Make a Treaty*

on the basis as regards boundary of the *Projet* originally presented by me, modified according to the memorandum which I subsequently gave to one of the commissioners.... If they feel able to make and carry through a treaty on this basis, let them say the word and the treaty shall be made. If they do not feel thus able, let them surrender at once to the *Puros* and dismiss forever all thoughts of a treaty: for it is the last chance that Mexico can have for one equally favorable to her, and indeed for one which any party in this country can accept. I am fully persuaded that its terms would not, by any means, meet the views *now* entertained by my government....

I should not now make the offer but for my clear and perfect conviction on these three points: *First*, that peace is still the desire of my government. *Secondly*, that if the present opportunity for peace is not seized at once, all chances for making a treaty at all will be lost for an indefinite period, probably forever. *Thirdly*, that this is the utmost point to which the Mexican government can by any possibility venture.[43]

That night, Trist also wrote his wife. The letter is deceptively full of plans for his return, until a request that she read Buchanan a coded postscript:

Knowing it to be the very last chance and impressed with the dreadful consequences to our country which cannot fail to attend the loss of that chance, I will make a treaty, if it can be done, on the basis of the Bravo by the 32nd degree, giving 15 million besides the three million cash.[44]

Trist spent the next two days attempting to justify his decision in a very long dispatch to Buchanan. The first third of it consisted of a carefully reasoned explanation of the three points in his December 4 letter to Thornton, beginning with his conviction that "peace is still the desire of my government."

The words of the President as I took leave of him are still fresh in my memory: "Mr. Trist, if you succeed in making a treaty, you will render a great service to your country." ... I have carefully examined the dispatches ... by which I am recalled.... I have found there ... nothing whatever which would at all warrant the supposition that he ... believes any less strongly than he did then that the restoration of peace is highly desirable.... On the contrary, the determination of the President to put an end to the mission ... is expressly placed on the ground of his belief "that your continued presence ... may do much harm by encouraging the delusive hopes and false impressions of the Mexicans." It is, therefore, because of its supposed tendency to prolong the war that the Presidents apprehends that the continuance of this mission "may do much harm." Here, then, is the conclusive proof that ... "peace is still the desire of my government."[45]

Trist was also convinced that peace was the desire of his country. He thought the American public would support the war only as long as the government "shall continue to prosecute hostilities with a view solely to securing a peace.... To suppose the contrary is to suppose the character of the war altogether changed ... and that from being ... a purely defensive war on our part, it has become a war of conquest."[46]

Trist's second point was that "if the present opportunity be not seized at once, all chance of making a treaty at all will be lost for an indefinite period, probably forever." Trist thought the peace party in the Mexican Congress "cannot possibly stand, unless the object for which ... it has formed itself be speedily accomplished. Without this, its destitution of pecuniary resources must become aggravated every day and this cannot continue much longer without sealing its fate." If the present government fell, there would be no Mexican government with which the U.S. government could negotiate. "The military occupation of the country will go on. But to what end? ... The only ... conceivable purpose ... will be ... the conquest of the country ... or the use of our military power in directing and protecting the inhabitants in establishing a government for themselves."[47] He did not dream that the president would propose just such a use of U.S. military power a few days later in his annual message to Congress.

The third point Trist made was "that the boundary proposed by me is the utmost point to which the Mexican government can, by any possibility, venture.... This boundary takes from Mexico about half of her whole territory.... However helpless a nation may feel, there is necessarily a point beyond which she cannot be expected to go under any circumstances in surrendering her territory as the price of peace." This point, he believed, had been reached. "They cannot go further. It would be utterly impossible to obtain the ratification of any such treaty."

Trist now ventured on dangerous ground. Although the president thought the continuation of his mission might "do much harm ... in the way of preventing the restoration of peace," the recall order was actually a blow to the cause of peace. "There is not one single friend to peace here but reeled and staggered under the blow.... Of all this the President knew nothing.... Had he known the truth ... he could not have believed that the continuation of this mission could do 'much harm.'"[48]

Then Trist plunged deeper into the quicksand. A long rebuttal of the president's criticism of the armistice was followed by a lengthy defense of Trist's offer to refer a Nueces/New Mexico compromise boundary proposal to Washington. Had he confined himself to explanations of his decision to remain in Mexico, the logic of his arguments might have persuaded the president that Trist had acted in the best interest of the country and indeed of the president himself. But Trist's emotion and indignation triumphed over his reason. The length of the dispatch also reduced its effectiveness. His most

TEN / *I Will Make a Treaty* 149

important arguments were lost in a flood of verbiage which ran to 66 pages of Trist's fine script and required 36 pages even when printed. Nonetheless, Polk did not miss the paragraphs that stated that he had acted rashly or unwisely, and the December 6 dispatch eliminated any chance that the president would forgive Trist for his insubordination.

The government in Queretaro did not immediately grasp the opportunity to reopen negotiations, and the delay extended through the remaining weeks of December. One reason was the Mexican fear that the U.S. government might reject a treaty negotiated by an envoy who had been recalled. Both Thornton and Scott helped to convince the Mexicans, however, that there was a good chance for the ratification of a treaty similar to the draft Trist had brought to Mexico.[49] The leaders of the provisional government also weren't sure they should begin negotiations without the sanction of the new Mexican Congress due to convene on January 1. But Commissioner Couto, an expert on constitutional law, gave his opinion that congressional confirmation of the appointment of commissioners was not required by the Constitution.

For a while the Mexican government hoped the British might be persuaded to guarantee the execution of the treaty and protect the government against a revolution by those dissatisfied with the treaty terms. On December 11, Percy Doyle, previously first secretary of the British Legation, returned from leave in England and became the ranking British diplomat in Mexico. He explained to Commissioner Atristain that the British government had no intention of intervening in Mexico, eliminating the Mexican government's hope that it might obtain a better deal by waiting for a British guarantee.[50]

Publicly, General Scott's posture was that of a tough military commander preparing for an expanding occupation. A general order on December 15 proclaimed that "this army is about to spread over and to occupy the Republic of Mexico, until the latter shall sue for peace on terms acceptable to the United States."[51] But in his dispatches to the secretary of war, Scott cited both military and diplomatic reasons for delaying new operations.[52] About 8,000 additional men joined his army between mid–September and mid–December, but most of these were used to regarrison Jalapa, establish other posts on the route up from Vera Cruz, and occupy other key points in the Valley of Mexico.

On Christmas Day a special courier arrived with copies of Polk's annual message to Congress. Trist was appalled by the president's statement that it might be necessary for the U.S. Army in Mexico to support the formation of a new Mexican government that would be able and willing to sign a peace treaty. Although the message indicated that the president still wanted a peace treaty, Trist feared that the threat of support for a new and more compliant Mexican government would undermine his incipient negotiations with the existing Mexican government. Moreover, he feared that publication of the message in Mexico would "encourage the Puros to redouble their desperate efforts to prevent the impending treaty."[53] Trist was convinced that the Puros wanted the annexation of all of Mexico by the United States, which would be possible only if there had been no peace treaty between the United States and Mexico.

Plans for the negotiations were kept secret to prevent the enemies of peace from organizing effective opposition. "All that the Puros possess respecting it consists of their own surmises and … superficial indications that *something* is going on," Trist wrote to Buchanan on December 29.[54]

While Trist was writing, Peña was authorizing the commissioners to begin negotiations.

ELEVEN

An Exceedingly Laborious Negotiation

Trist's first meeting with the Mexican commissioners in the new round of negotiations took place on the second day of 1848. General Rincon sent word that he was ill and could not participate, and Trist met with the three civilian commissioners — Couto, Cuevas, and Atristain — throughout the ensuing four weeks.

After Trist and the Mexicans produced their "full powers" from their governments, the Mexicans challenged the American claim to Mexican territory as indemnity for the expenses of the war. They proposed that the indemnity question be submitted to international arbitration, but Trist rejected the idea and told the Mexicans that "we must proceed to business at once and ascertain whether we can agree on the terms of a treaty."[1]

The most important provisions were in Article V, which would establish a new boundary between the United States and Mexico. As in the previous summer, there were three distinct issues concerning the boundaries of Texas, "New Mexico" (including the present states of New Mexico and Arizona), and California.

The boundary between Mexico and Texas, the most difficult issue in the summer negotiations, proved the easiest to resolve in January. In September, Trist had been ready to refer to Washington a compromise boundary which included the Nueces, although he had assured the Mexicans that there was virtually no chance that the president would accept any boundary for Texas other than the Rio Grande. Now in January the Mexicans knew that Trist had been severely reprimanded by the president for even considering a proposal with the Nueces as boundary, and they acknowledged that the border must run through the Rio Grande valley. On January 3 the Mexicans proposed that the boundary run parallel to, but a league north of, the Rio Grande. "As to any other boundary than the middle of the river," Trist replied, "it would be a waste of words to talk about it."[2] The Mexicans acquiesced, and subsequent discussions were based on the assumption that the border would run up the Rio Grande from the Gulf of Mexico to a point near El Paso.

The boundary in the region between the Rio Grande and Colorado rivers, which includes most of the present states of New Mexico and Arizona, presented more difficult problems during the negotiations and later. These problems arose primarily from the lack of accurate geographical information on the region.

Mexican settlements extended northward to El Paso and Santa Fe on the upper Rio Grande and to Tucson in present Arizona, but the area to the north and west of these settlements was well known only to the Comanches, Apaches, and other Indian tribes. After independence, Mexico continued Spanish policies which restricted foreign exploration of the arid region between Santa Fe and California. American traders were allowed to bring wagon trains to Santa Fe over the Santa Fe Trail from Missouri, but travel westward from Santa Fe was both prohibited and impractical. A few mountain men and fur traders from the United States had explored the area, but they were reticent about their illegal travel in Mexican territory and left no precise accounts or maps. A U.S. Army topographical engineer, Lt. William H. Emory, had to rely on fragmentary travel accounts and hearsay evidence to fill in some of the blank areas on the map of the Southwest he compiled in 1844.

The draft treaty accompanying Trist's original instructions in April had specified that the boundary would run up the Rio Grande until it intersected the "southern boundary of New Mexico," proceed along "the southern and western boundaries of New Mexico" until it reached the Gila River, and then follow the Gila down to the Colorado. The boundaries referred to in the draft treaty were those delineated on a map of Mexico published early in 1847 by a New York bookseller, J. Disturnell. The Disturnell map was the best map of Mexico available in the United States at that time; Buchanan gave it to Trist before he left Washington and urged him to "make it a part of the treaty."[3] But it contained important inaccuracies which would lead to a major controversy between the United States and Mexico when an attempt was made to establish the treaty boundary on the ground.

Emory, who accompanied General Kearny on the march from Sante Fe to California in 1846, returned to Washington in July 1847. He told Buchanan that the valley of the Gila River offered a favorable route for a railroad to the Pacific but the tracks would have to cross the river several times. Buchanan concluded that the United States should obtain the whole valley of the Gila, and he wrote Trist on July 19 that he should seek a boundary from the Rio

ELEVEN / *An Exceedingly Laborious Negotiation*　　153

Grande to the Gulf of California along the 32nd parallel.[4] The Disturnell map indicated that this parallel ran south of both El Paso and Tucson and crossed the Gulf of California well below the mouth of the Colorado River.

Buchanan's July 13 letter did not reach Trist until after the late-summer negotiations. In those negotiations he proposed the Gila as the principal element of the boundary in the southwest, in accordance with his original instructions. When negotiations resumed in January, Trist tried to insist on the 32nd parallel as required by his revised instructions, but he reported that "it constituted an insuperable obstacle to the negotiation of a treaty."

The area between the Gila and the 32nd parallel had a substantial Mexican population, including 750 at Tucson and 250 at Tubac. Trist reported that the states of Sonora and Chihuahua "solemnly protested against the transfer of a single foot of their territory.... This was therefore a sine qua non with the Mexican government ... because it would have rendered the ratification of the treaty an impossible thing."[5] Trist saw the "force of reason" in the Mexican arguments. Just as the imperatives of American politics required Polk to insist on the Rio Grande as the southern border of Texas, the imperatives of Mexican politics required Peña to insist on the Gila as the border between Old and New Mexico.

The idea of a border between the Rio Grande and the Colorado along the 32nd parallel was dropped, and Trist reinstated the language in the original draft treaty running the boundary along the southern and western boundaries of Mexico to the Gila and then along that river to the Colorado. This language remained in the final version of the treaty, which also stated that the New Mexico boundaries were those shown on the Disturnell map. As Buchanan had suggested, the map was made a part of the treaty.

Buchanan had warned Trist on July 19 that "we cannot learn that the boundaries of New Mexico have ever been authoritatively ... determined."[6] But Trist thought the lines drawn on the Disturnell map, even if not previously established as borders of New Mexico, were anchored on the Rio Grande in the east and the Gila in the west and could be easily surveyed on the ground. But because of inaccuracies in the Disturnell map, determining the actual boundary was to prove much more difficult than Trist anticipated.

Disturnell's southern boundary of New Mexico ran due west from the Rio Grande along the latitude of 32°22', beginning a few miles north of El Paso. The map accurately reflected the accepted fact that the boundary between the Mexican states of Chihuahua and New Mexico crossed the Rio Grande north of El Paso, leaving that town in Chihuahua.[7] The problem was with the location of El Paso and indeed of the entire upper part of the Rio Grande. Although Colonel Doniphan's expedition had passed through El Paso in 1846, it did not include a topographical engineer who could establish

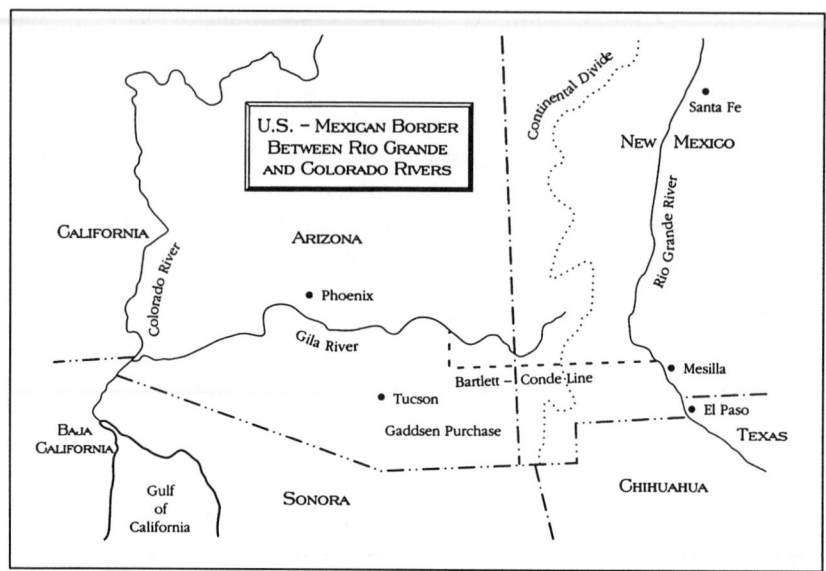

the town's latitude and longitude. In 1851 the joint U.S.-Mexican boundary commission, established pursuant to Trist's treaty, discovered that El Paso was over 100 miles further west and about 35 miles further south than indicated on the Disturnell map.[8] A border running west 8 miles north of El Paso, as indicated on the Disturnell map, was at 31°52' rather than 32°22'.

Moreover, the map showed a western boundary of New Mexico about 175 miles west of the Rio Grande, running due north to the Gila River at a longitude of 109°47'. This western boundary was only guessed by Disturnell. A later historian of the Southwest, Hubert Bancroft, found no evidence than in 1847 any western boundary of New Mexico "had ever been fixed at all, or even thought of."[9] Thus Disturnell's southern boundary of New Mexico ran from a badly misplaced Rio Grande to a nonexistent western boundary of New Mexico.

The first U.S. member of the boundary commission, John Russell Bartlett, agreed in 1851 to a compromise known as the Bartlett-Conde line. It began on the actual Rio Grande at a point 42 miles north of El Paso where the 32°22' line shown on the Disturnell map actually crosses the river; the Bartlett-Conde line ran west from this point for the same distance (175 miles) as Disturnell's southern border of New Mexico. The area to the north of this line is very rugged, with one peak reaching 8400 feet, and did not appear to contain a suitable route for a railroad.

The Bartlett-Conde line would have left in Mexico the Mesilla Valley, which was considered an essential part of the route for a railroad from Texas

ELEVEN / *An Exceedingly Laborious Negotiation*   155

to California. The valley runs west from the Rio Grande to the Continental Divide. Today it contains both the main line of the Southern Pacific Railroad and the El Paso-Tucson segment of the interstate highway (I-10) from Florida to California. Bartlett was subsequently replaced by Major Emory, who in 1847 had called Buchanan's attention to the importance of obtaining the route for a transcontinental railroad. Emory refused to accept the Bartlett-Conde line, and the boundary controversy was not resolved until the United States paid $10 million for additional territory in southern New Mexico and Arizona pursuant to the Gadsden Treaty of 1853.[10]

But Trist knew nothing of these problems in January 1848. So far he had won one round (the Rio Grande) and lost one (the 32nd parallel), although the resulting treaty language was nearly the same as in the draft he had brought to Mexico.

Next came the difficult and important question of the border in California. The draft treaty accompanying Trist's instructions had specified that the western portion of the border would run down the Gila to the Colorado, down the Colorado to the Gulf of California, and down the middle of the Gulf to the Pacific. If Mexico had agreed, it would have ceded both Upper and Lower (Baja) California. Buchanan's April instructions specified, however, that Lower California was not a sine qua non and that Trist should not break off negotiations if he could only obtain New Mexico and Upper California. In this event, the border between the Colorado and the Pacific should follow the division line between upper and lower California shown on Disturnell's map.[11] It ran due west from a point on the Gulf of California some miles south of the mouth of the Colorado to a point on the Pacific considerably south of the bay of San Diego.

These instructions were not very relevant in the late summer negotiations because the Mexicans refused to give up New Mexico or the southern part of the present state of California. They first proposed a border in California at 36°30' that would have divided the present state in the middle near Monterey Bay, and they later included in their counter-draft of a treaty a western border on the 37th parallel which runs just south of San Francisco.[12]

When Buchanan wrote Trist on July 13 that he should seek a western border along the 32nd parallel, he added that if Lower California could not be obtained the border might continue on the 32nd parallel, which reached the Pacific coast just below San Diego. This dispatch was intercepted by the Mexicans and delivered to Trist, opened, at the end of the summer negotiations.[13] The Mexicans thus knew that Trist was not required by his instructions to insist that the United States receive Lower California. The Mexican commissioners admitted that Lower California was worthless and said the United States would be welcome to it if it were a few hundred miles distant from the Mexican coast. But because parts of it were only 50 miles from the Mexican mainland, Mexico was eager to keep it in order to control smuggling.[14]

Trist decided that under these circumstances it was pointless to make further efforts to obtain Lower California. When the January negotiations began, there was a tacit agreement that Lower California would remain Mexican although there was no agreement on the line dividing the two Californias. Trist proposed a line from the mouth of the Colorado to a point south of San Diego. The Mexicans insisted on a land bridge from the Mexican mainland to Lower California and initially proposed a line from the junction of the Gila and Colorado rivers to a point north of San Diego.[15]

The negotiation was complicated by problems on both ends of the California section of the border. On the eastern end, the precise location of the mouth of the Colorado was uncertain. The Disturnell map showed it at about 32°30' and the intersection of the Gila and Colorado at about 33°. But during the fall, Trist heard from Buchanan that when Major Emory passed through the Gila valley with Kearny in 1846, he calculated that the junction of the Gila and Colorado was at only 32°43'.[16] Moreover, Trist discovered that an excellent atlas produced in 1844 by an attaché of the French Legation in Mexico, Eugene de Mofras, showed the mouth of the Colorado at 31°51', or some 40 miles south of the point indicated on the Disturnell map.[17] Trist realized that if the official French map was more accurate than the commercial product of a New York bookseller, as in fact it was, even a border along the 32nd parallel would not give the United States access to the Gulf of California. It thus seemed pointless to continue to press for the 32nd parallel, and he accepted the Mexican proposal that the southern border of California begin at the intersection of the Gila and the Colorado.

This left only the matter of the western end of the border, including the vexing problem of the great bay of San Diego. At first Trist thought the issue might be resolved by finding evidence of the establishment by Spanish or Mexican authorities of a division line between the Californias. He enlisted the help of the Mexican commissioners and several Americans, including Captain Robert E. Lee, but the search was fruitless. "It appears," Trist reported to Buchanan, "that no *line* of division was ever established between the two Californias," although there was evidence that Lower California had always included a land bridge crossing the Colorado from the state of Sonora.[18] This research led Trist "to propose that a division line between the two Californias shall now be *established* as running from the mouth of the Gila to a point on the Pacific one league due south of the

ELEVEN / *An Exceedingly Laborious Negotiation*

southernmost extremity of the port of San Diego."[19] This proposal was accepted by the Mexican commissioners by January 9, but the Mexican government did not accept the loss of San Diego until later in January.

A letter written by Trist's wife in 1864 that was discovered by Robert W. Drexler, author of a concise biography of Trist published in 1991, throws new light on Trist's attitude toward the terms of the treaty. Virginia Trist quoted his repeated comment to family and friends in later years that he was "intensely ashamed" of the treaty terms that were necessary in order to obtain acceptance of the treaty by the American president and Congress.

> This had been my feeling at all our conferences and especially at moments when I had felt it necessary to *insist* upon things which [the Mexicans] were adverse to. Had my course at such moments been governed by my conscience ... and sense of justice ... I should have yielded in every instance. Nothing prevented my doing so but the conviction that the treaty would then be one which there would be no chance of acceptance by my government. My object throughout was ... to make the treaty as little exacting ... upon Mexico as was compatible with its being accepted at home. In this I was governed by two considerations: One was the iniquity of the war, as an abuse of power on our part. The other was that the more disadvantageous the treaty was made to Mexico, the stronger would be the ground of opposition to it in the Mexican Congress by the party who had boasted of its ability to frustrate any peace measures.[20]

Although Trist's dispatches contained only hints of his feelings about the American peace terms, the need to produce a treaty acceptable to the Mexican Congress was clearly stated in a dispatch on January 25. Trist thought the Puros would raise every possible objection to the treaty, in the hope of preventing a negotiated peace. It was therefore necessary that from the Mexican standpoint, the treaty contain as few objectional features as possible and as many positive provisions as practicable.[21]

As a result of delays in the election of some members of the new Mexican Congress, it did not assemble as scheduled on January 8. The interim term of President Anaya expired, and Peña again assumed the provisional presidency, with Rosa again serving as foreign minister. Since the Mexican Congress was not in session during the negotiation of the treaty, it had no direct impact on the negotiations, but the need to provide a treaty acceptable to the Congress was a constant concern of the negotiators.

There had been few opportunities for compromise on the boundary questions, but Trist tried to be more flexible in the second week as the negotiators turned to the nonboundary provisions of the treaty. He encouraged the commissioners to present their suggestions for modifications of the non-boundary provisions of the original U.S. draft. This led to an entirely new Mexican draft, but very little of the Mexican language could be accepted without further revision. Trist reworked each article using as guidance his instructions, the U.S. draft treaty, other U.S. treaties, and his general knowledge of U.S. policies. The remainder of the second week and all of the third week of January were required for working out these revisions. During the drafting process, Trist made a considerable effort to provide a greater correspondence between the English and Spanish versions of the treaty than was common in treaties of that era.[22]

During the first two weeks of January, the negotiations had proceeded in an orderly fashion with only a moderate sense of urgency. When Trist wrote to Buchanan on December 6 explaining his decision to stay in Mexico, he supposed that the negotiations would begin in December and be completed well before a reply to his letter could be received from Washington. But now in the third week of January, it had been six weeks since his decision to stay in Mexico and it would soon be time for a response to arrive from the president. The letters and newspapers which arrived from the United States in January contained many indications that the response of the administration in Washington to these new peace negotiations might be a very hostile one.

Early in the month there had been further indications of the growing public support in the United States for a permanent occupation of Mexico. The *North American* reported on January 10 that "the obliteration of Mexican nationality is certain, destiny has ordained it." Later in the month two communications from the secretary of war strongly suggested official hostility to an immediate peace settlement.

The first on these was a December 14 letter to Scott from Marcy stating that "to deprive the enemy of the means of organizing further resistance to protract the war, it is expedient to subject to our arms other parts of the country." Until he received this letter, Scott had been able to ignore Marcy's October 6 orders to "carry out further aggressive operations" and "achieve new conquests" on the ground that they had been sent before the formation of a new government in Queretaro that hoped for peace. Scott's only move to expand the occupation had been the move of a brigade to the nearby town of Toluca. But the December 14 letter from Marcy, written long after Washington knew of the movement toward peace in Mexico, stressed the administration's view that a peace settlement "cannot be speedily obtained without making the enemy feel that he is to bear a considerable part of the burden of the war."[23]

ELEVEN / *An Exceedingly Laborious Negotiation* 159

The second disturbing communication from Marcy indicated that the president had heard about, and strongly disapproved of, Scott and Trist's July plan to purchase support for a peace treaty in the Mexican Congress. Buchanan's December 21 letter on this subject to Trist did not arrive until later, but by the third week in January, Scott had received a letter from Marcy that left no doubt that the president was totally unsympathetic toward the July effort to purchase support for peace. These two letters raised serious doubts whether Polk still wanted a peace treaty with Mexico, at least on his original terms.[24]

The *North American* reported on January 26 that it had received U.S. newspapers indicating a "full and hearty approval of the war policy of the Administration"; all of the independent newspapers "declare with cheering unanimity that the American government cannot recede, that it must not yield an inch but hold the territory conquered and occupy it." In publishing such reports, the editors of the two American newspapers in the Mexican capital were not inhibited by much information about Trist's peace negotiations. "We know nothing of the reported accommodation," the *North American* wrote on the twenty-seventh. The next day the *American Star* wrote that "the fact that Mr. Trist continues in the capital is indirect evidence that there is good hope that his overtures will be accepted."

Trist faced two grim possibilities, either of which could prevent the signing of a peace treaty. One was that he would look up from his papers one day and find a military officer with specific orders from the president requiring him to terminate the negotiation and return immediately to the United States. This fear was not unfounded, since military orders requiring him to leave Mexico were discussed in the cabinet in Washington in late January and were actually issued in February. The other grim possibility was that Scott would feel compelled to undertake further military operations that would effectively terminate the peace negotiations.

Before the January negotiations began, the Mexican commissioners had sought a promise that the suspension of hostilities would take place upon the *signing* of the treaty.[25] But Trist replied that his instructions provided that a suspension of hostilities could take place only after the *ratification* of the treaty by the Mexican government. In the first days of January, Scott had sent Brigadier General George Cadwalader's brigade to occupy Toluca, a town about 35 miles from the capital. The Mexican commissioners wrote Trist that Cadwalader's expedition had weakened the spirit of accommodation in Queretaro, and they pressed for a commitment from General Scott to suspend further movements while the treaty was being negotiated. Trist explained that Scott "knows my remaining here to be in violation of instructions and he has himself received fresh instructions acquainting him with the will of the President that the war be pushed ... with rigor.... He cannot enter into any agreement ... even if we sign the treaty, without disobeying orders." But when the treaty was ready for signature, Trist promised to "lay it before him, saving that its being signed depends upon his engaging to suspend further movements until he can receive instructions from Washington."[26]

All Scott's actions and correspondence in December and January indicate that he was extremely reluctant to do anything that would reduce the chances of an early peace treaty. Yet the pressures on him to expand the occupation were becoming irresistible. The president, secretary of war, much of the American press, most of the officers of the army in Mexico, and even important Mexican leaders wanted him to occupy more Mexican territory. The arrival on January 21 of Brigadier General Thomas Marshall with 1400 more men added to the pressure for an expanded occupation.[27]

After a talk with Scott on January 23, the British chargé, Percy Doyle, told the Mexican commissioners that Scott would be able to justify further delays only if a peace treaty was imminent.[28] At first Trist thought this veiled threat would convince the hesitating Mexican government that it should authorize the Mexican commissioners to sign the draft treaty.[29]

But Rosa wrote the commissioners on the twenty-sixth that the government insisted on the immediate withdrawal of American forces from the capital, the turnover to Mexico of all custom revenues, and an immediate payment by the United States to enable the government to sustain itself. "The government will never agree to close the negotiations without having here, at Queretaro, under its control, the sum of 300,000 to 400,000 dollars and a positive assurance of receiving 200,000 dollars every month afterwards for a period of three months. Without sums as a large as these to enable it to face the difficulties that will arise upon the signature of the treaty, the government is certain to be overturned within a few days."[30] The next day Rosa informed the commissioners that "the government sorrowfully resigns itself to making peace in order to avoid greater evils, but these evils will not be avoided if the war of invasion is to be succeeded by civil war and the present administration is left without the means to repress sedition."[31]

On the twenty-eighth, Trist tried to resolve the impasse regarding further military operations. He wrote Scott to ask for "a pledge of your word that no more expeditions shall take place for the further occupation of the country until, the treaty having been received in Washington, new instructions from thence shall have reached you." This pledge was essential to sustain the peace party's claim that they were acting to prevent further bloodshed.[32] Trist took the letter to Scott that evening, but the general refused to make the pledge Trist requested.

ELEVEN / *An Exceedingly Laborious Negotiation*   161

Aside from reluctance to take an action violating his orders from the secretary of war and conflicting with the strong public pressure for an expanded occupation, Scott apparently believed that the threat of active military operations—possibly including a drive to Queretaro—might be the only thing that could end the procrastination of the Mexican government. The events of the next two days indicate that on the evening of the twenty-eighth Scott and Trist agreed on a plan to force the Mexican government to sign the treaty.

At 11 P.M. that night, Trist called on Doyle at the British Legation. He told Doyle he had decided to break off negotiations unless the treaty was signed immediately. Doyle reported later to the Foreign Office that Trist felt "it was useless going on from day to day as they were doing, that he did not doubt the good faith of the Mexican commissioners, but felt assured that the general government did not give credit to the statements he had made, and he was determined to break off negotiations at once." But Trist asked Doyle to tell the commissioners confidentially that he would still sign the treaty if the Mexican commissioners were authorized to sign it by the following Tuesday, February 1. "He saw clearly," Doyle wrote, "that they did not give sufficient credit ... to the danger of delay, and he concluded by asking me ... to see the commissioners and convey the above message ... as they would place reliance on what I might say to them respecting the very serious risk they were running."[33]

Trist's ultimatum was written early the next morning, the twenty-ninth. Every hour of continued delay, he wrote, was proof of the inability of the Mexican government to act effectively to obtain peace. "And now the limit of these delays has been reached." Although it would be "the most painful act of his life," he would be forced to bring the negotiations to a close unless there was immediate action by the Mexican government.[34] Doyle met later that morning with the commissioners and probably delivered Trist's note. Doyle told them that some of Scott's officers were now pressing for a forward movement. The commissioners urged Doyle to write directly to Rosa in Queretaro.

Doyle wrote Rosa that afternoon that Scott had hitherto "been able to delay sending troops into the interior of the country, but as fresh reinforcements had now arrived ... he should be compelled to do so; unless, he hinted to me, he might be able to come to another determination from the fact of a Treaty of Peace having been signed. The General added that, much as he should regret being obliged to take such a step, his orders were most peremptory to march upon Queretaro and not allow the General Government an opportunity of establishing itself in any other point of the Republic."[35]

The origins of Doyle's threat have remained a mystery. Justin Smith wrote that "Scott was placed by his orders under a military obligation to drive the government from Queretaro."[36] But indications of such an obligation are nowhere to be found in the secretary of war's meager instructions to Scott. Charles W. Elliott, a biographer of Scott, concluded that the threat of a march on Queretaro was Scott's own.[37] Scott had adopted Polk's tactic; after standing aside for weeks while Trist waved the olive branch, Scott now threatened to take up the sword again. This time the tactic worked.

The agitated commissioners wrote to Rosa by the same courier that carried Doyle's letter: "We are impressed by the difficulties the supreme government has had in giving us definite orders. If we do not receive them by Tuesday or if by some misfortune ... letters come from Washington, negotiations will be broken off, according to the statements of Mr. Trist and the English chargé d'affaires." They added that they had received proposals from a "banker," probably Ewen Macintosh, for a loan of up to $300,000 to help the government through the transition period until it received some of the funds to be paid by the United States under the treaty.[38]

The government in Queretaro was impressed by Scott's threat and by the promise of money. It was probably also influenced by evidence of the growing support in Mexico for the annexation of Mexico by the United States. On January 29, General Scott was among the 50 persons attending a festive lunch at a resort outside the capital organized by a Puro leader, Suarez Iriate, and other prominent figures of the capital. Toasts were drunk in seven kinds of wine to the victory of the Americans in the war and to the annexation of Mexico by the United States.[39]

During the previous week, Scott had received an astonishing offer from the annexationists. He would be paid $1,250,000 by five of the wealthiest men in Mexico if he would resign his commission in the U.S. Army and accept the interim presidency of Mexico as a "stepping stone" to the annexation of Mexico by the United States. Scott admitted in a letter in 1852 that the offer had been "highly seductive as to power and fortune."[40] At the time of the banquet on the twenty-ninth, the annexationists apparently thought Scott might accept. During this period a number of other American officers, including Lt. Ulysses S. Grant, were invited to conclaves by Mexican annexationists.[41] Scott stated in 1852 that the offer to him was secretly supported by more than half of the members of both the executive and legislative branches of the Mexican government. If so, Peña and Rosa must have known of the annexationists' offer, which formed a sinister backdrop for Doyle's threat that Scott would march to Queretaro and disperse the government that opposed annexation.

On January 31 the provisional president of Mexico, Peña y Peña, instructed the Mexican commissioners through Foreign Minister Rosa to sign the treaty

ELEVEN / *An Exceedingly Laborious Negotiation*   163

they had negotiated with Trist. Rosa's letter to the commissioners listed many reasons for the president's decision: "The extreme scantiness of resources, ... the probability that the United States may prove every day more exacting in their demands, the consideration that the treaty ... does not contain a single condition dishonorable to Mexico, the duty imposed on the government to put an end to the calamities from which the country is suffering and of checking the projects of annexation to North America, ... and many others."[42]

The messenger from Queretaro arrived in the capital in the evening of February 1. It may have been Trist who suggested that the treaty be signed at the shrine of Mexico's patron, Our Lady of Guadelupe Hidalgo. It was a spot considered by Mexicans as "the most sacred on earth, as being the scene of the miraculous appearance of the Virgin for the purpose of declaring that Mexico was taken under Her protection."[43] The next morning Trist and the commissioners traveled to the shrine a few miles north of the capital. The treaty was signed at midday in the sacristy of the cathedral. Commissioners Couto, Atristain, and Cuevas signed for Mexico. The sole signature for the United States was that of Nicholas P. Trist.

TWELVE

A Solemn Duty

In the Thirtieth Congress, elected in the fall of 1846 but convened only in December 1847 in accordance with the leisurely timetable of that era, the opposition Whigs had a majority in the House of Representatives. They believed they had a mandate from the voters to oppose "Mr. Polk's War," and they missed no opportunity for criticism of the president regarding the origin, conduct, or aims of the war.

The Whigs were especially critical of Polk's arrangements for Santa Anna's return to Mexico in August 1846. Just as Congress convened, Polk was appalled to learn that there had been another unsuccessful effort to strike a bargain with Santa Anna while the army was in Puebla in July 1847. On December 6, the day before the president's annual message to Congress, the Baltimore *Sun* reprinted a letter to the St. Louis *Republican* from its correspondent in Mexico, who signed himself "Gomez." It contained a detailed account of Scott's July 17 meeting with his generals on the plan to "purchase a peace."[1] The letter had been written in Puebla on August 6 but could not be sent to St. Louis at that point because of the suspended communication with the coast, the August and September battles, and the fall rains that closed the road to the coast. The letter did not reach St. Louis until November.

About the same time as Polk read the "Gomez" letter, he received a letter from his friend General Pillow with an account of the July 17 meeting. The president understood the letter to mean that the money was intended as a personal bribe to Santa Anna. Polk told the cabinet on December 11 that he had "received information that General Scott and Mr. Trist had ... entered into an agreement to pay Santa Anna a million dollars as secret money if he would agree to make a treaty of peace."[2] Buchanan also recorded his understanding that the money was to be paid to Santa Anna "on his private account."[3] (Pillow apparently indicated in a later letter on January 18 that payments were to be made to members of the Mexican Congress; at that time

Polk noted that Pillow had written about a plan "to bribe the authorities of Mexico to procure a peace."⁴)

Polk, who had not had anything to do with this effort to make a deal with Santa Anna, made sure his strong disapproval was on record. He "expressed in the strongest terms my condemnation of such conduct" and directed Buchanan and Marcy to demand a full explanation from Trist and Scott.⁵ "The President anxiously hopes," Buchanan wrote Trist, "that you have not been engaged in a transaction which would cover with merited disgrace all those who may have participated in it, and fix an indelible stain upon the character of our country."⁶

On December 30, Polk received Trist's initial reaction to the October 6 order recalling him. Although the November 27 dispatch reflected Trist's disappointment and frustration, there was no hint that he might ignore the order. It arrived the same day as Scott's charges against Generals Pillow and Worth. Polk thought the charges arose primarily from "the vanity and tyrannical temper of General Scott and his want of prudence and common sense" and that Scott was abetted by Trist, who was "ministering to his malignant passions, in persecuting General Pillow and others who are supposed to be friendly to me."⁷ This viewpoint was derived mainly from a letter from Pillow, although Trist mentioned in his dispatch that he expected to give important testimony in the case against Pillow. Polk's very negative comments about Trist on December 30, a week before he received the first indication that Trist had ignored the recall order, indicate that Polk's subsequent very negative reactions to Trist's decision were highly influenced by Trist's involvement in the charges against Polk's friend.

For a few days around the year's end, Polk considered sending a new commissioner to Mexico. On December 30 he received Peña's October 31 note regarding the appointment of new commissioners, along with Trist's comment, just before learning of his recall, that "the prospect for a treaty is ... very good." The next day Senator Jefferson Davis of Mississippi showed Polk a letter from Brigadier General David Twiggs, now commander in Vera Cruz, stating that a treaty might be signed if the United States had a commissioner in Mexico who was authorized to negotiate. Davis, agreeing with Twiggs, pointed out that a treaty could only be negotiated by an American commissioner in Mexico; Mexican commissioners sent to Washington would fear reprisals if their government were overthrown in their absence.⁸ Polk told the cabinet on January 3 that dispatches from Scott and Trist indicated that the government at Queretaro had appointed commissioners to treat for peace and that "we should have a commissioner in Mexico to meet them." Walker thought the ranking Democratic general with Scott, Major General William O. Butler, should be vested with diplomatic powers, but Buchanan thought another civilian envoy should be appointed.⁹

The next day Polk learned that the British courier had arrived in Vera Cruz in mid–December without letters for Washington but with a story that Trist had renewed negotiations with Mexican commissioners. Polk wrote in his diary that Trist was "acting, no doubt, upon General Scott's advice.... He is defying the authority of his Government ... and lending himself to all Scott's evil purposes. He may, I fear, greatly embarrass the Government."[10]

On January 5, Buchanan told Polk of the coded postscript to Trist's December 4 letter to his wife, which he had asked her to read to Buchanan. Polk recorded his understanding that "on the day he wrote (4th December) at twelve o'clock, he would open negotiations with the Mexican commissioners."[11] The confusion of the approximate date of Trist's decision to stay in Mexico with the actual opening of peace talks was probably based on the British courier's inaccurate report that negotiations had begun in early December. Polk, who did not see why the Mexicans should need much time to agree to his peace terms, thought that talks begun a month earlier might already be completed or at least would be completed by the time his reactions reached Trist. His erroneous assumption regarding the beginning of the negotiations was one reason why Polk took no action to interfere with them while they were in progress.

Another reason was probably Polk's secret hope, despite his angry reaction to Trist's decision, that his insubordinate envoy might sign an acceptable peace treaty. On January 3 the Whig majority in the House of Representatives approved a resolution introduced by ex-president John Quincy Adams which proclaimed that the war was "unnecessarily and unconstitutionally begun by the President of the United States." It called for the immediate withdrawal of the U.S. Army from Mexico, a U.S.-Mexican boundary between the Nueces and the Rio Grande, and a peace settlement without the acquisition of any territory from Mexico.[12] The House resolution gave Polk a stronger reason to hope that Trist might sign a peace treaty based on his original peace terms, before the "no territory" movement grew strong enough to prevent the ratification of such a treaty by the Senate.

While he waited for further news on Trist's unauthorized negotiations, Polk was preoccupied with a decision to remove Winfield Scott from the command of the army in Mexico. The only reason for the decision given in Polk's diary was the collision between the generals in Mexico, which Polk thought arose entirely from "the vanity and tyranny of General Scott." The decision was undoubtedly also influenced by Scott's role in the plan to "purchase a peace," by Polk's inaccurate assumption that Scott had encouraged Trist to ignore the recall order, and, especially, by the possibility that Scott might become a Whig candidate for the presidential election later that year. On January 7, Polk received private letters from Mexico with additional information on the "feuds and strifes" in the army, undoubtedly including one from Pillow and possibly one from the president's brother William, a major in the Third Dragoons.[13]

Orders were sent to Scott on January 13. He was directed to turn over his command to Major General William O. Butler. After attending sessions in Mexico of a Court of Inquiry established to investigate the plan to "purchase a peace" and the charges against Pillow and Worth, Scott was to return to Washington.[14] The timing was neatly calculated to bring Scott home under a cloud not long before the Whig convention.

The decision to relieve Scott was made only a month after Polk told Congress that "the war should be prosecuted with increased energy and power until a just and satisfactory peace can be obtained." Although Polk thought Trist's negotiations had begun a month earlier and might already be completed, he had no idea of the result. The dispatches he had received from Trist provided little basis for optimism that the Mexicans would now accept his original peace terms, and Polk had been thinking of tougher terms, including a lower border and a reduced payment. Polk had told Congress that the war should be carried on with increased vigor until the Mexicans acceded to his peace terms. Yet there is no indication in his diary or elsewhere that Polk considered the possibility that he might need an experienced commander to carry out further military operations in Mexico.

General Butler, a former Democratic congressman from Kentucky, had been in the war of 1812 and was one of Zachary Taylor's division commanders in northern Mexico, but he was an unknown quantity as an army commander. Despite the strong dissatisfaction with Zachary Taylor's performance in northern Mexico, four members of the cabinet, including Buchanan and Marcy, initially favored sending Taylor to replace Scott. They withdrew their objections to the Butler appointment only when the president said he would accept the whole responsibility for the decision.[15] The decision to replace Scott with Butler made sense from a military standpoint only under the assumption that the active phase of the war was already over. The timing of the decision suggests that when Polk heard that the Mexicans had agreed to new negotiations, he assumed that they would now finally accept his peace terms and that he would no longer need a competent combat commander in Mexico.

Two days after the order relieving Scott, Polk received Trist's long December 6 dispatch defending his decision to remain in Mexico. Polk completely failed to understand or appreciate Trist's motives. His indignation was fully recorded in his diary:

> His dispatch is arrogant, impudent, and very insulting to his Government, and even personally offensive to the President. He admits he is acting

> without authority and in violation of the positive order recalling him.... He has become the tool of General Scott.... I have never in my life felt so indignant.... He has acted worse than any man in the public employ whom I have ever known. His dispatch proves that he is destitute of honor or principle, and he has proved himself a very base man.[16]

Polk's first reaction was to tell Marcy to write to General Butler "directing him, if Trist was still with the headquarters of the army, to order him off, and to inform the authorities of Mexico that he had no authority to treat."[17] Although Scott had been ordered by Marcy in October to inform the Mexicans that Trist had been recalled,[18] Polk assumed that neither Trist nor Scott had told the Mexicans of the recall order. But over the next several days, Polk's resolution was diluted by advice from several quarters. The main reason for withholding punitive action against the insubordinate envoy was the possibility that he might already have signed an acceptable treaty.

The chairman of the Senate Foreign Relations Committee, Senator Sevier of Arkansas, told Polk on January 23 that he should submit to the Senate for its consideration any treaty that Trist had negotiated. Buchanan told Polk the next day that he should send military orders forcing Trist to return only if he was sure that he would not want to submit for ratification any treaty Trist might have signed.[19] On the twenty-fifth, Polk outlined his April peace terms to Senator Hannegan of Indiana, a leading western expansionist; the senator thought it would be very embarrassing for the president to reject a treaty made on the basis of those terms even if it had been negotiated without authorization.[20]

In the cabinet on January 26, Buchanan and Walker opposed an order forcing Trist to return, but the other four cabinet members favored such an order. Polk's record of the discussion in his diary contains only arguments related to the domestic political ramifications of the proposed action, but nothing on its impact on the chances for peace.[21] Although Polk recorded that he had decided to send a letter to Butler the following day, there is no other evidence of orders to Butler in January concerning Trist. Since Polk thought negotiations had begun six weeks earlier and were probably already completed, he apparently decided that he should wait to hear the result of the talks before taking action against Trist.

Letters from the Mexican capital arrived in Washington on February 7, but there were none from Trist and Scott. "Neither General Scott nor Trist has written a line to the government by the train that left Mexico [City] on the 13th of January," Polk wrote in his diary. "There is a conspiracy between Scott and himself to put the government at defiance and make a treaty of some sort."[22]

TWELVE / A Solemn Duty

By then the treaty that would rescue James K. Polk and the nation from a quagmire in Mexico was on its way to Washington. Preparations for its rapid delivery had been made in January. Trist enlisted as a special courier his friend James Freaner, a former express rider who had organized the rapid delivery of his dispatches to the *Delta*. With a fresh horse and a fresh escort at the pass at Rio Frio, Freaner hoped to make the trip to the coast in only three days.[23] Trist drafted a message for Scott to send to General Twiggs at Vera Cruz "desiring that the swiftest vessel which offers a safe conveyance to the mouth of the Mississippi or to Mobile may be detained at Vera Cruz ready to start at a moment's warning."[24]

The USS *Iris* was waiting for Freaner when he arrived, having left his escort behind in his hard-riding passage down from Jalapa. Not far behind was a courier sent by Kendall of the *Picayune* with the momentous news story of the treaty of peace. On orders from Scott, the port commander held the steamer *New Orleans* for two days to give the official courier a chance to reach Washington before press accounts of the treaty. But the *New Orleans* made better time than the *Iris* and arrived at her home port about the same time as Freaner reached Mobile.

The *Picayune* printed a special edition and set into motion the courier system which had carried war news to the press in the north. A *Picayune* courier caught up with Freaner at Charleston. When this courier reached Petersburg, Virginia, the southern end of the telegraph line, the news of the treaty was flashed to newspapers in Washington and other northern cities. The *Union* was setting type on the story when Freaner reached Washington on Saturday afternoon, February 19, just 17 days after Trist signed the treaty at Guadalupe. He arrived at Buchanan's house unshaven, in tattered clothing, and exhausted. At first he was told the secretary of state was taking a nap and couldn't be disturbed. Freaner replied that he would be glad to join him, as he had not slept a wink in six days.[25]

When he read the treaty, President James K. Polk realized that he faced a very difficult decision. The treaty had been negotiated and signed in total disregard of very clear presidential instructions that had been issued in October and proclaimed to the Congress in December. And yet the treaty was remarkably similar to the draft treaty Polk had sent to Mexico with Trist in April. Moreover, it provided the president with a priceless opportunity to escape from the corner into which he had painted himself.

Polk convened the cabinet on Sunday evening, February 20, to discuss the question "whether the Treaty should be rejected by me or sent to the Senate." The secretary of state advised the president to reject the treaty because it did not give the United States enough territory. Polk thought Buchanan really wanted him to send it the Senate but advised against it to protect his political support by those who favoring the annexation of more Mexican territory.[26] Secretary of the Treasury Robert Walker totally opposed the treaty. He said he would not be satisfied with anything less than the annexation of all of Mexico and threatened to resign to lobby for the treaty's defeat in the Senate.[27] The other four cabinet members, including the secretaries of war and the navy, were for acceptance of the treaty.

The next day Polk told the cabinet that he had decided to submit the treaty to the Senate with the recommendation that it be ratified except for Article 10 concerning Mexican grants of land in Texas and in the territories to be ceded to the United States. His account of the decision in his diary indicates that he was primarily concerned with the politics of the decision:

> The treaty conformed on the main questions of limits and boundary to the instructions given to Mr. Trist.... A majority of one branch of the Congress is opposed to my administration.... If I were now to reject a treaty made upon my own terms ... the probability is that Congress would not grant either men or money to prosecute the war.... If I were now to reject my own terms ... I did not see how it was possible for my administration to be sustained.[28]

Polk sent the treaty to the Senate on February 22:

> It was not expected that Mr. Trist would remain in Mexico or continue in the exercise of the functions of the office of commissioner after he received his letter of recall. He has, however, done so, and the plenipotentiaries of the Government of Mexico, with a knowledge of the fact, have concluded with him this treaty.... Conforming as it does substantially on the main questions of boundary and indemnity to the terms which our commissioner ... was authorized to offer ... I have felt it to be my duty to submit it to the Senate for their consideration with a view to its ratification.[29]

Polk recommended, however, that the Senate reject the tenth article of the treaty regarding Mexican land grants.

Several days later, on February 24, Polk received dispatches from Trist written on December 29 and January 12. Freaner claimed they had been in his baggage but had been overlooked until that day; he may have been aware of Trist's tactless comments in the dispatches and deliberately delayed their delivery to avoid influencing the president's initial reaction to the treaty. The December 29 dispatch commented on the paragraph in Polk's message to Congress on the need to establish a Mexican government that desired peace: "There is no room for doing anything towards *establishing* a government. Nothing is necessary but to *maintain* what is already established, to protect it against military violence and usurpation." In the January 12 dispatch, Trist

TWELVE / *A Solemn Duty* 171

criticized the orders from Washington that prevented an immediate suspension of hostilities upon the signing of a treaty.[30]

Polk found these dispatches "arrogant, highly exceptionable, and even of an insulting character." Now that Trist's treaty had been received, there was no longer any reason to delay the punishment of the insubordinate envoy. Polk directed that orders be sent to General Butler to prevent Trist from taking any further official act and to require him to leave the Mexican capital as soon as safe escort could be furnished to Vera Cruz.[31] This action ranks with the most flagrant examples of presidential ingratitude in American history. Orders requiring Trist to leave the Mexican capital were carried to Mexico by his friend Freaner while Trist's treaty was debated in the United States Senate.

For several weeks it was doubtful that the Senate would give its "advice and consent" for the ratification of the treaty as required by the Constitution. Some senators opposed the treaty because it gave the United States no more territory than had been demanded a year earlier before Scott's campaign in central Mexico. Senator Sam Houston of Texas thought the United States should keep all territory north of a line drawn from Tampico to the head of the Gulf of California.[32] Senator Jefferson Davis of Mississippi proposed a boundary starting north of Tampico and proceeding northwestward in a manner that would have given the United States all of the state of Coahuila and large parts of Tamaulipas, Nuevo Leon, and Chihuahua.[33]

Other senators thought the treaty gave the United States too much new territory. Eighteen Whigs supported a proposal by Senator John Crittenden of Kentucky that the territorial provisions of the treaty be confined to a settlement of the boundary of Texas and the U.S. acquisition of San Francisco.[34] Senator Daniel Webster of Massachusetts, who opposed the acquisition of any new territory, proposed the rejection of Trist's treaty and the dispatch to Mexico of a three-man commission to negotiate a new treaty.[35] Senator Thomas Hart Benton of Missouri, chairman on the Military Affairs Committee, supported Webster's proposal. The chairman of the Foreign Relations Committee, Senator Ambrose Sevier of Arkansas, told the president that his committee could not support any treaty that had been negotiated after the commissioner had been recalled and that the committee also proposed a commission of three to five persons to negotiate a new treaty. Polk responded that if the Senate advised him to send out such a commission, he hoped they would also advise him what treaty terms they would accept.[36]

Polk now realized that his initial lukewarm recommendation of the treaty was not sufficient to prod the Senate into action. He sent another message on February 29 which was designed to blame the Senate for any further delay in ending the war:

> Believing that, if the present treaty be rejected, the war will be continued at a great expense of life and treasure for an indefinite period, and considering that the terms ... conformed substantially to those authorized by me in April last, I considered it to be my solemn duty, uninfluenced by the exceptional conduct of Mr. Trist, to submit this treaty to the Senate with a recommendation that it be ratified with the modifications suggested.[37]

While the Senate debated the treaty in secret sessions, the public expressed a strong desire for peace. The treaty provisions had not been made public, but there was strong support for a peace treaty in principle in the editorials of most newspapers. "The news of peace is generally credited, and it had a most cheering effect," the New York *Express* commented on February 22; "money is more abundant than it has been, and confidence is hourly increasing." Ratification was opposed only by the New York *Herald* and a few other papers that had supported the annexation of all of Mexico. In New Orleans the *Picayune* printed Kendall's comment that "Trist's treaty is very distasteful to the men who go for the whole of Mexico, but very good for the future of both countries."[38]

The Senate debate on the treaty continued for ten more days after Polk's second message. On March 10, 1848, ratification of a slightly amended treaty was approved by 38 senators, including 26 Democrats, 11 Whigs, and 1 independent. It was opposed by 14 senators, including 7 Democrats, 6 Whigs, and 1 independent. While the treaty was supported by 3 more senators than the 35 needed for the necessary two-thirds majority of those present and voting, 6 senators were absent. The vote for the treaty was 1 vote less than a two-thirds majority of the 58 members of the Senate.

The "all Mexico" movement was dead, and peace seemed at hand. The country generally rejoiced, and even the *Herald* in New York conceded that "the Senate has done right, the President has done right, and Mr. Trist has done right."

Many books on the Mexican war end with the approval of Trist's treaty by the United States Senate. But there would be no peace until the treaty was also ratified by the Mexican Congress. It was not in session, and members were not eager to participate in a session that would be asked to sanction the loss of half of Mexico's territory. A quorum was not achieved until the first week in May.

The treaty was bitterly opposed by many conservatives in the Mexican

TWELVE / *A Solemn Duty* 173

Congress. Manuel Rejon, Santa Anna's foreign minister in 1844 and 1846, condemned the treaty in a position paper dated April 17:

> This fatal treaty amounts to a sentence of death.... As almost all of us are descended from Indians, the North American people abominate us.... In their future conquests they will strip us of our land and thrust us aside. Has their conduct ... been any other in their treatment of the Indian tribes? ... Our race ... will have to become nomadic, searching for hospitality in foreign lands.[39]

General Paredes, who began the war, also opposed the treaty that would end it. A few weeks later Paredes would use the treaty as an excuse for an unsuccessful revolution against the moderate government headed by the man he had overthrown in 1845, General Herrera.

President Peña, addressing the Congress on May 7, appealed for ratification of the treaty as the only means of restoring order and avoiding chaos and anarchy:

> The territories ceded by the treaty have not been given up for the sum of fifteen million dollars, but to recover our ports and invaded cities, to put a definite stop to all types of evils and horrors, ... to bring regularity and order.... Already we have seen too much social disorganization, insecurity among our people, danger along the highways, paralyzation of all branches of public welfare, and general misery.... Contemplate what would be the confusion and anarchy into which we would see our country sink ... with the continuing of this foreign war.[40]

After a stormy debate, the treaty was approved by the Chamber of Deputies on May 19. Anticipating Senate approval, Peña invited the two commissioners appointed by Polk to receive Mexican ratification of the treaty—Senator Sevier and Attorney General Clifford—to proceed from Mexico City to the temporary capital at Queretaro. The Senate approved the treaty, 33 to 5, on May 25, the day the American commissioners arrived in Queretaro with a escort of dragoons commanded by the president's brother, Major William Polk. News of the approval of the treaty by the Mexican Congress reached President Polk on June 15, exactly two years after the U.S. Congress declared that the United States was at war with Mexico. Ratifications were exchanged in Queretaro on May 30, and the ratified treaty reached President Polk in Washington on July 4, 1848.

THIRTEEN

A Firm and Universal Peace

The Treaty of Guadalupe Hidalgo contained a few articles of lasting significance and others which were important only in the transition from war to peace.[1] The first article proclaimed that "there shall be a firm and universal peace" between the United States and Mexico. For nearly a century and a half, the peaceful relations between the two countries have occasionally been disturbed but never broken. The next three articles provided for the suspension of hostilities, the withdrawal of American troops, and the transfer to the Mexican authorities of customs duties, military facilities and equipment, and other public property.

The most important article in the treaty was Article V, which delineated the new U.S.-Mexican boundary described in Chapter Eleven. It gave the United States a clear title to an area more than one-third the size of the United States prior to the annexation of Texas. The total area gained from Mexico, including Texas, was 851,598 square miles, or 545,012,720 acres.[2] Polk stressed the immense importance of these acquisitions in a message to Congress after Mexican ratification of the treaty:

> Embracing nearly ten degrees of latitude, laying adjacent to the Oregon Territory, and extending from the Pacific Ocean to the Rio Grande, a mean distance of nearly 1,000 miles, it would be difficult to estimate the value of these possessions to the United States.... Their acquisition is second only in importance to that of Louisiana in 1803. Rich in mineral and agricultural resources, with a climate of great salubrity, they embrace the most important ports on the whole Pacific coast of the continent of North America. The possession of the ports of San Diego and Monterey and the Bay of San Francisco will enable the United States to command the already valuable and rapidly increasing commerce of the Pacific. The number of our whale ships alone now employed in that sea exceeds 700.... The excellent harbors of Upper California will under our flag afford security and repose to our commercial marine.... By the acquisition of these possessions we are brought into immediate proximity with the west coast of America [and]

THIRTEEN / *A Firm and Universal Peace* 175

with the islands of the Pacific Ocean, and by a direct voyage in steamers we will be in less than thirty days of ... ports of China. ... In this vast region ... great must be the augmentation of our commerce, and with it new and profitable demands for mechanic labor in all its branches and new and valuable markets for our manufactures and agricultural products.³

A few historians have suggested that by signing a treaty based on Polk's original terms, Trist precluded the possibility that the United States might have obtained an even better deal from Mexico in a later treaty. But except for an additional strip of land in New Mexico and Arizona needed by the United States for a transcontinental railway, the boundary in Trist's treaty was the best boundary obtainable from both Mexican and U.S. standpoints. It was the best possible boundary from the Mexican standpoint because it involved the loss of only underdeveloped lands with small Mexican populations and avoided the loss of more populous areas. It was the best possible boundary for the United States because it eliminated the danger that the United States would be mired in a quagmire below the Rio Grande. The enormous problems and massive negative effects that would have resulted from an effort by the United States to annex substantial additional territory below the Rio Grande are examined in the Epilogue.

The problems encountered in establishing the boundary on the ground that resulted from the errors in the Disturnell map have been reviewed in Chapter Eleven. Aside from these problems, the only defect in the boundary was its failure to include a feasible route for a railroad connecting Texas and California. This resulted in part from the inaccuracy of the Disturnell map and in part from Trist's effort to achieve a treaty which could be ratified by the Mexican Congress. Trist did not realize that the southern boundary of New Mexico shown on the map did not include a vital part of the railroad route in the present state of New Mexico. He probably did not know that the terrain in northern New Mexico was too rugged for a railroad and that the Mesilla valley was the only feasible route. In any case, because of the inaccuracy of the Disturnell map, he thought the Mesilla valley was north of his border.

Trist's only instruction from Buchanan with regard to a railroad route had dealt with the route in the Gila valley in present Arizona. As required by Buchanan's revised instructions in July, Trist tried to obtain a border on the 32nd parallel which would give the United States the entire Gila valley. But the Mexicans refused to accept the lower border. By accepting the Gila River as the border in Arizona, Trist only reverted to his position in the summer negotiations, which was based on his original instructions.

Trist tried to compensate for his failure to obtain a lower border in Arizona by including Article VI. It provided for U.S.-Mexican cooperation on the construction of a railway in the Gila valley. If there had been no other problem with the railroad route, this article might have been the basis for a U.S.-Mexican agreement on an internationalized rail route in the Gila valley, with some track on the Mexican side of the river. The Gadsden Purchase of additional territory in the southwest in 1853 was motivated primarily by the need for the Mesilla valley in present New Mexico, of which Trist was totally unaware, and only secondarily by the desirability of a railroad route in Arizona that was entirely within U.S. territory.

Article VI also gave Americans transit rights through the lower Colorado River and the Gulf of California. Since the mouth of the Colorado is no longer navigable because of reduced flow and silting, this article is no longer of importance. Article VII provided equal transit rights on the boundary segments of the Rio Grande and Gila for citizens of both countries and prohibited obstructions of navigation on these rivers without mutual consent. Application of this article to the Gila was erased by the Gadsden treaty in 1854, but Article VII laid the foundation for later U.S.-Mexican agreements on flood control, irrigation, and navigation in the Rio Grande valley.

In Articles VIII and IX, Trist tried to protect the rights of Mexicans living in the territories ceded to the United States. Those Mexicans could remain in the United States or move with their property to Mexico. If they didn't wish to remain Mexican citizens, they would "be admitted as soon as possible ... to the enjoyment of all the rights of citizens of the United States." Trist's Article IX also specifically protected Catholic churches and schools, but the Senate replaced it with a provision stating that until they became U.S. citizens, the former Mexicans would "be maintained and protected in the free enjoyment of their liberty and property and secured in the free exercise of their religion without restriction." As with other legal protections of minority rights, these treaty provisions were not adequately implemented in the very racist America of the nineteenth and early twentieth centuries.

Article X was the only article of Trist's treaty that was totally rejected by the president and Senate. It provided that all grants of land in the ceded areas that had been made by competent Mexican authorities would be respected as valid in the United States. Trist agreed to it under great pressure from the Mexicans; he knew it would cause no end of trouble in Texas and perhaps expected that it would be rejected by the Senate.

In transmitting the treaty to the Senate, Polk noted that Article X was not authorized by Trist's instructions and that the federal government had no power to change the conditions of land grants made by the state of Texas. He recommended that Article X be rejected. There was not a single vote in the Senate in favor of accepting this article. Buchanan wrote the Mexican foreign minister after the Senate action that "to revive dead titles and suffer

THIRTEEN / *A Firm and Universal Peace*

the inhabitants to be ejected under them from their possessions, would be an act of flagrant injustice if not wanton cruelty. Fortunately, this Government possess no power to adopt such a proceeding."[4]

In Articles XI through XV, the United States agreed to various obligations and payments in return for the territory ceded by Mexico.

Under Article XI the United States accepted obligations to restrain with force incursions into Mexico by Indian tribes residing in U.S. territory, to prohibit purchase of property stolen by Indians from Mexicans, to assist in the return of Mexicans captured by Indians, and to prohibit the sale of firearms and ammunition to the Indians. Although there was no reference to such an obligation in the hastily prepared treaty draft Trist took to Mexico, there had been a similar provision in the U.S.-Mexican treaty of 1831, and Buchanan's instructions to Slidell in 1845 authorized an obligation to restrain the Indians. A proclamation drafted in Washington in June 1846 told the Mexicans that "it is our wish to ... drive back the savage Comanches, to prevent their renewal of their assaults, and to compel them to restore to you from captivity your long lost wives and children." A proclamation issued by General Kearny in New Mexico in August 1846 stated that he had instructions from his government to "protect the persons and property of all quiet and peaceable inhabitants ... against their enemies, the Eutaws, the Navahoes, and others."[5]

Polk's annual message in December 1847, which Trist received before the January negotiations, cited the U.S. ability and willingness to restrain the Indians in the Southwest as a reason why the Mexican government might be glad to cede New Mexico to the United States. "It would be a blessing to all these northern [Mexican] states to have their citizens protected ... by the power of the United States.... If New Mexico were held and governed by the United States, we could effectively prevent these tribes from committing such outrages, and compel them to release these captives."[6]

The Mexicans insisted that these pledges be included in the treaty. Trist wrote that "the stipulations respecting the Indians ... were indispensable to make the treaty acceptable to the northern [Mexican] states."[7] In appealing to the Mexican Congress for ratification of the treaty, Peña cited "the suppression of barbarous tribes that could make incursions across our boundaries" as one of the major advantages to be derived from the treaty."[8] Neither Polk nor the Senate raised any general objection to Article XI, although the Senate struck out the prohibition of arms sale to the Indians on the ground that they were hunters and could not survive without firearms.

Before 1848, Americans had little experience with the Indians of the Southwest and greatly underestimated the strength and ferocity of the Southwestern tribes. The United States government discovered that it lacked the capacity to meet fully the obligations it had accepted under Article XI. The American forces sent to prevent Indian raids into Mexico were woefully inadequate to the task, and the Mexican government filed numerous claims against the United States in the early 1850s for losses resulting from the failure of the United States to comply with Article XI. The United States government was very glad to see the obligation to restrain the Indians erased in the Gadsden treaty with Mexico in 1854.[9]

Article XII provided that the United States would pay Mexico $15 million for the territory it acquired. Trist had been authorized by his original instructions to pay up to $20 million if the Mexicans ceded Texas, New Mexico, and upper California. He assumed, however, that the president would want the payment reduced because of the loss of life and property suffered by the United States in the battles which followed Mexican rejection of the original U.S. peace terms.[10] His coded message to his wife on December 4, which was passed on to Buchanan and Polk, said he would offer the Mexicans "fifteen millions beside the three million cash" already authorized by Congress, but he decided later to limit the total payment to $15 million. This was exactly the reduced payment discussed by the president and cabinet in early September, although this figure was never firmly set or communicated to Trist.

Articles XIII through XV provided for the payment by the U.S. government of claims by Americans against Mexican authorities. These claims arose from unpaid bills, the seizure of American ships and other property, imprisonment of Americans without proper cause, and other Mexican actions. Unsatisfactory Mexican responses to U.S. demands for payment of the accumulated claims had been a major barrier to improved Mexican-American relations for over a decade. The unpaid claims were cited by Polk in several messages to Congress as a major cause of the war. "To let them go unpaid," Justin Smith wrote early in this century, "in addition to being internationally immoral, would have wronged our aggrieved citizens; and to pay them from our own revenues, besides being immoral, pusillanimous, and ridiculous, would have been unfair to all our taxpayers."[11] Yet, if they had been given the choice, the taxpayers might have preferred to pay several millions in claims in advance in order to avoid a war that raised the national debt by over $27 million and cost about 11,000 American lives. In the end, the United States paid the claims as one form of payment to Mexico for the ceded territories. Senator Thomas Hart Benton thought "the treaty was a singular conclusion of the war. Undertaken to get indemnity for claims, the United States paid those claims herself."[12]

The articles in Trist's treaty regarding claims were essentially based on an article in the draft treaty he brought to Mexico. The United States agreed to pay all claims that had previously been decided against Mexico under procedures established by the U.S.-Mexican treaties of 1839 and 1843. Mexico was also relieved of responsibility for all other claims by Americans up to the time of exchange of ratifications of the treaty. The United States undertook to pay claims by Americans against Mexico up to an amount not exceeding $3,250,000 and to establish a U.S. Board of Commissioners to make the final decisions on these claims using principles set forth in the 1839 and 1843 treaties. The board was established by Congress in 1849 and was given two years to finish its work; it approved 198 awards totaling $3,208,314.[13]

Two treaty articles dealt with supplies for the American troops prior to their evacuation. Each party reserved the right to fortify any part of its territory. The U.S.-Mexican treaty of amity, commerce, and navigation of 1831 was revived for a period of at least eight years. The aggrieved party in any dispute between the two nations promised to give full consideration to the possibility of referring the dispute to international arbitration. The final substantive article provided rules that would govern the status and treatment of foreign merchants and prisoners of war in the unhappy event of a future war between the two nations.

The only provision in the draft treaty Trist took to Mexico which was totally absent in the final treaty was an article providing transit rights for U.S. citizens across the Isthmus of Tehuantepec, the 125-mile strip of land in southern Mexico separating the Atlantic Ocean and Gulf of Mexico from the Pacific Ocean. The need for a transit route between the oceans had grown in the 1840s because of increased U.S. trade with China and expanding Yankee whaling voyages in the South Pacific. The Isthmus was considerably closer to both New York and San Francisco than the other possible interoceanic routes through Nicaragua and Panama.

The inclusion of an article on Tehuantepec in the draft treaty had been urged by Secretary of the Treasury Walker, the most ardent expansionist in the cabinet. Polk would have been glad to obtain the transit rights, but was not willing to make them a sine qua non for a treaty. If Trist could obtain the transit rights plus the other cessions demanded by Polk, he was authorized to pay a total of $30 million.

Polk's interest in the Isthmus was sustained by the activities of Commodore Matthew Perry, the U.S. naval commander in the Gulf of Mexico. Perry ordered an exploration of the Isthmus area in the spring of 1847, apparently without authorization from Washington. Despite discouraging data on the suitability of the area for a canal or other transit route, Perry submitted a detailed proposal in October 1847 for a joint Army-Navy expedition to seize control of the Isthmus. Such an expedition was being seriously contemplated in Washington that winter. Secretary of the Navy Mason sent additional marines to the Gulf to be available for such an expedition, if authorized, and ordered the Pacific squadron to cooperate.[14] As Trist began his second round of negotiations with the Mexicans, a transit route across the Isthmus was still on Polk's minimum list of concessions from Mexico.[15]

The U.S. bid for transit rights across Tehuantepec was thwarted by conflicting British interests, however. In 1843, Santa Anna had given a concession for the construction of a transit route across the Isthmus to a prominent Mexican, Antonio Garay. In 1847, Garay sold these rights to a group of British investors that included the firm of the British consul general, Manning & Macintosh. During the August-September negotiations, the Mexican commissioners informed Trist that the Mexican government could not agree to his proposal on transit rights for Americans since exclusive rights had been granted to a Mexican and subsequently transferred to British subjects with the approval of the Mexican government.[16]

The British group discovered that the British government's Board of Admiralty was cool to the Tehuantepec project because it would provide a route from New York to China and the East Indies which was several days quicker than the route from London. Anticipating the Board's veto of British participation in the project several months later, Macintosh became interested in selling the rights to American investors. Trist's papers contain a draft article stating that the Mexican government consented to the transfer of the rights on the Isthmus to "any company which may be incorporated in the United States for this purpose."[17] But the British chargé, Percy Doyle, insisted that Macintosh give the British government a chance to sponsor the Tehuantepec project, and he supported the Mexican refusal to include any article on Tehuantepec in the U.S.-Mexican treaty.

In February 1849, Manning & Macintosh transferred the Tehuantepec rights to an American, D. A. Hargous.[18] The Isthmus question complicated U.S.-Mexican relations over the next several years. President Fillmore wrote the Mexican president in 1852 that U.S. citizens had "surveyed a route for a railroad and demonstrated the practicality of such a route" across the Isthmus.[19] Transit rights across the Isthmus were given to Americans under the Gadsden treaty with Mexico in 1853, but these rights were never used and were canceled by treaty in 1937.[20]

Although Trist's treaty did not include Lower California or the transit rights on Tehuantepec, it gave the United States all the other territory demanded by the president. Trist made every reasonable effort to obtain a treaty that would be as consistent as possible with his original instructions and would be acceptable to the president and Senate of the United States. He was successful in his efforts to obtain the Rio Grande as the border from

THIRTEEN / *A Firm and Universal Peace* 181

the Gulf to El Paso, a border between Upper and Lower California that gave the United States the port of San Diego, and a reduced payment to Mexico.

The provisions of the treaty that proved unsatisfactory — the segment of the boundary along the Gila, the provisions concerning land grants in Texas, and the commitment to restrain the Indians — resulted from Trist's efforts to make the treaty also acceptable to the president and Congress of Mexico. He probably knew that the provision regarding Mexican land grants in Texas would prove unacceptable to the American president and Senate but was unable to convince the Mexicans to relinquish their demand for it. The commitment on restraining the Indians resulted from American ignorance of the fierce Southwestern tribes and was accepted by the president and Senate without question. These objectional features of the treaty were eliminated by the Senate rejection of the article on land grants in Texas and by the subsequent Gadsden treaty with Mexico, which adjusted the border in the Southwest and canceled the obligations regarding Indians.

These relatively minor drawbacks were overshadowed by the enormous value of a treaty which ended America's first foreign war and increased the size of the country by more than one third. Yet the most important feature of the treaty was not found in any specific article but in its date. By persisting in his determination to negotiate a peace treaty as quickly as possible, Trist eliminated the chance of further bloodshed, removed the danger of a disastrous attempt to annex additional Mexican territories, canceled the threat that the United States would become trapped for some years in a Mexican quagmire, and avoided the severe internal problems in both Mexico and the United States that would have resulted from a prolongation of the war.

These major effects of the Treaty of Guadelupe Hidalgo will be explored in the Epilogue, following an analysis in Chapter Fourteen of James K. Polk's "bold and firm course" in dealing with Mexico during the first three years of his single presidential term.

FOURTEEN

A Bold and Firm Course

During his single presidential term, James K. Polk conducted the foreign policy of the United States on his own with very few constructive inputs from others.

Although Polk discussed all his major moves with his cabinet, its members also lacked diplomatic experience and rarely challenged the president's reactions to developments in the Mexican situation. The cabinet's effectiveness as an advisory body on Mexican affairs was limited by the extreme views of Polk's secretary of the treasury, who seems to have been conducting a vendetta against the nation he held responsible for his brother's death, and by the vacillating views of his secretary of state, who tended to advocate positions that might appeal to voters in the next presidential election. Polk tolerated Buchanan's ineffective performance because he wished to retain for himself all the important diplomatic decisions.

The secretary of state and the president received no policy advice from the State Department; it had no foreign policy analysts, only clerks. Effective policy making was greatly inhibited by the extremely slow and very uncertain communications between Washington and Mexico. The president was too dependent on the inadequate political reporting and analysis of the diplomatic agents he sent to Mexico, including Trist. His view of events in Mexico was skewed by his partisan distrust of the two senior American generals in Mexico, both Whigs, and by the self-serving opinions in the letters from Mexico of his friend General Pillow.

Several factors limited congressional influence on Polk's foreign policies. More than half of the time during the three-year Mexican crisis the Congress was not in session. There were nine-month adjournments in both 1845 and 1847 and a shorter recess in 1846. Even when Congress was in session, it was neither well informed nor effectively consulted by the president. Secretive by nature, Polk kept secret several of his most important decisions regarding Mexico in part to avoid congressional interference. Congress did not

FOURTEEN / *A Bold and Firm Course*

learn about the Slidell mission, Taylor's march to the Rio Grande, and the Trist mission until in each case it was much too late for useful congressional input.

There were few constructive ideas in the Congress for avoiding the war and, once it began, no agreement on how it should be ended. Before and during the war, there was little support in the Congress or public for a more moderate policy toward Mexico. Although the actions which led to "Mr. Polk's war" were severely criticized by the Whigs, the badly divided opposition could not agree on constructive proposals for ending the war. The inability of Congress to participate effectively in the making of U.S. policy toward Mexico resulted to a considerable degree from the divergent views within both parties on any issue related to slavery, especially the admission of slavery into new territories to be gained from Mexico. Although the question of the extent of the territory to be acquired from Mexico was vigorously debated in the Congress and the country beginning in the summer of 1846, there was no consensus on the issue. This congressional stalemate allowed Polk to conceal his peace terms from the Congress—even after they had been revealed to the Mexicans—until the arrival of Trist's treaty.

No other significant sources of policy advice and analysis were available to the president. The press of the 1840s typically appealed to the readers' nationalistic and partisan feelings and was unaccustomed to the careful analysis of foreign policy options. As a result of Polk's highly secretive manner of conducting foreign relations, most of the press coverage of foreign issues consisted of rumors, speculation, and uninformed commentary that was not seriously considered by the president. The era in which the academic community would participate actively in the nonpartisan evaluation of foreign policy options had not yet begun.

Lacking both previous diplomatic experience and useful advice on diplomatic issues from others, President James K. Polk relied on his basic instincts and perceptions. Initial miscalculations were inevitable. But Polk, a slow learner in diplomacy, made similar errors of judgment during five distinct but similar cycles of his policy toward Mexico. Each cycle consisted of aggressive military moves followed by peace initiatives. In each cycle he first brandished the sword, then waved the olive branch.

In the first cycle (spring 1845 to January 1846), Polk sent an army to Texas and then sent Slidell to Mexico to attempt to negotiate a treaty. This cycle ended when Polk heard that the Herrera government was reluctant to receive Slidell.

The second cycle (January to September 1846) began with the orders to General Taylor to march to the Rio Grande which, along with Taylor's blockade of the river, led to a Mexican attack and the U.S. declaration of war. Only a few weeks after the war began, Polk attempted to negotiate with both the Paredes government and the exiled former dictator, Santa Anna. This cycle ended when the Mexican government, again headed by Santa Anna, rejected these peace feelers.

In the third cycle (September 1846 to March 1847) Polk ordered an invasion of central Mexico and then sent Beach and Atocha to Mexico to explore possibilities for peace. This cycle ended when Beach was forced to leave Mexico and Atocha returned with another Mexican rejection of negotiations.

The fourth cycle (March to October 1847) began with Polk's exclusive preoccupation with the invasion of central Mexico. After Polk learned of victories by Scott at Vera Cruz and Taylor at Buena Vista, he send Trist to Mexico to deliver his peace terms. The cycle ended when Polk learned that the Mexicans had rejected his terms.

The fifth and final cycle (October 1847 to February 1848) began with Polk's recall of Trist and his orders for an expanded military occupation of Mexico. He was planning to send a new envoy with a new olive branch when he heard that Trist had ignored the recall and begun negotiations with a new civilian government. The cycle ended when Polk received Trist's treaty.

In each of these cycles, Polk's premature peace initiative was based on misjudgments of the reactions of the Mexican leaders and the Mexican people to the preceding American military movements. He saw Mexico as a weak, disorganized, unstable, and chaotic country. He could not believe that such a country could sustain a war with the powerful United States for very long. Polk viewed Mexico as a country dominated by dictators in which politics and public opinion were of little importance. He consistently underrated the political and psychological factors that were mainly responsible for the behavior of Mexican leaders.

In several of the cycles from sword to olive branch, Polk thought the Mexican president could make a deal with the American president without worrying very much about the reactions of political opponents or the general public in Mexico. Slidell was sent to Mexico in 1845 because of Polk's naive assumption that Herrera would be willing to resume full diplomatic relations with the United States before receiving any indication of the American terms for a settlement of the dispute with Mexico. For a while in the spring of 1846, Polk thought he could make a deal with Paredes by supplying money to support the Mexican army. A few months later he believed that if Santa Anna returned to Mexico, he would resume dictatorial powers and would be able and willing to make a deal with Polk without consulting the Mexican Congress. Polk never fully understood that after his return, the

FOURTEEN / *A Bold and Firm Course*

former dictator's power was severely limited by political opposition from both monarchists and federalists. When Santa Anna rejected Polk's peace terms brought by Trist, Polk saw only bad faith and treachery, and ignored the possibility that the Mexican leader simply found the U.S. peace terms politically unacceptable as well as subversive of Mexican honor. In each of these cases Polk, always preoccupied with American politics, failed to understand that the imperatives of Mexican politics prevented Mexican leaders from accepting his olive branch.

While misjudging three Mexican presidents, Polk also misjudged the Mexican people. Although a Jacksonian Democrat, he was no populist. His political career had been based on connections and maneuvers within political elites. He was not very interested in the reactions or feelings of ordinary people — Americans or Mexicans. As Charles Sellers wrote, "Polk was not remotely equipped to understand the emotions men brought to the emerging slavery controversy."[1]

A nationalist who often appealed to the pride of Americans in their country, Polk consistently ignored Mexican national pride and the important Hispanic ideas of personal and national honor as major forces preventing the peace settlement he sought. David Pletcher wrote that Polk "epitomized the self-centered, aggressive nationalism prevalent in the Mississippi Valley during much of the 19th century.... He lacked ... the ability to appreciate a foreign people's hopes, fears, and driving impulses."[2]

In each of the cycles described above, Polk shifted back to the sword at the first indication that the Mexicans had rejected his olive branch. In each case he thought that further brandishing of the sword would eventually convince the Mexican leaders that they had no choice but to accept the olive branch on his terms. Although Polk had spent his life in law and politics, he was not a negotiator or a compromiser. He thought that in diplomacy and war, as in law and politics, his goals could be obtained by maintaining unrelenting pressure on his opponents. Polk never envisioned a true negotiation with the Mexicans that would lead to a compromise between the U.S. and Mexican positions. As Pletcher wrote, "he felt contemptuous impatience toward a weak, corrupt, disorganized government, much given to delay and evasion.... Such a government would respond only to strong words and a show of force."[3]

Until the arrival of Trist's treaty, Polk never wavered from his determination to "conquer a peace." The peace terms Trist took to Mexico in the spring of 1847 were essentially the same as those Slidell would have presented if he had been received by the Mexicans in the fall of 1845. Because of Scott's capture of Vera Cruz and Taylor's victory at Buena Vista, Polk thought the Mexicans would have no choice but to accept his "ultimatum."

Although Polk was planning in the first days of 1848 to send another envoy to Mexico, he was no more ready then for real negotiations than before. Indeed, he was thinking of tougher terms, including a lower border and a reduced payment to Mexico. The only new ideas about Mexico in his message to Congress that winter were the formation of a more tractable and compliant Mexican government under the protecting wing of the American army or, if peace on his terms continued to be elusive, a long-term military occupation of Mexico. Either policy, if implemented, would have involved the United States in extraordinarily difficult long-term roles and commitments.

James K. Polk had set the United States on the road to disaster in Mexico. It was saved from entrapment in a Mexican quagmire by Trist's decision to ignore Polk's recall order and complete his peace mission.

Epilogue:
A Friend of Peace

The period from his decision to ignore the recall order to the signature of the treaty was Nicholas Trist's finest hour. In these weeks he used all his knowledge, skill, and judgment to the fullest. After that, his emotions supplanted his judgment and his life slid downhill rapidly.

Even before his decision to ignore Polk's recall order, Trist had concluded that he could no longer remain a government employee. He was profoundly shocked and outraged at the evidence of a political plot by the president and associates against his friend, General Scott, and he refused to continue to work for politicians with such base political motives. He wrote his wife on November 28 that "I have bid adieu forever to official life. This decision is irrevocable."[1] His subsequent decision to remain in Mexico and negotiate a treaty was based in part on his conviction that after receiving the recall order, he was again a private citizen free to do whatever he believed necessary in the national interest.

After the treaty was signed, Trist spent ten more weeks in Mexico waiting for reactions to the treaty in Washington and Queretaro. A few days after Freaner departed with the treaty, Trist was shattered by the news that Polk had recalled General Scott. He thought it was "the height of human audacity and effrontery." Trist became convinced that the "Leonidas" letter, Pillow's claim to have masterminded the August and September victories, and the recall of Scott and himself were all part of a plan by Polk to undermine the peace process and pave the way for the annexation of all of Mexico to the United States. He began a long memorial to Congress which was intended to expose this plot. It was mainly written in a period in February and early March when Trist had too much time for indignation and speculation but too little solid information on the president's motives and actions. His belief that there had been a plot against the treaty persisted even after he learned that Polk had submitted it to the Senate for ratification.[2]

When Freaner returned in mid–March, the dispatches he brought for General Butler included the February 24 order that Trist be required to leave Mexico immediately. This was the military order of expulsion from Mexico that Trist had feared during the negotiation. Just as the United States Senate was about to ratify the peace treaty he had negotiated, the peacemaker was required to leave Mexico before the ratification process was completed. At first Trist told General Butler he was now a private citizen over whom the president had no authority, but he acquiesced when Butler said it would be his unpleasant duty to "enforce" the president's order.[3] Before leaving Mexico, Trist received notification from Buchanan that the ungrateful president would not allow him to return to the State Department and refused to pay his salary and expenses for the period following his receipt of the recall order in mid–November. This meant that he would receive no pay or expenses for the period in which the treaty was negotiated.

Many in the army were shocked by Polk's treatment of Scott and Trist. Ulysses S. Grant recalled in his memoirs that "there were many who regarded the treatment of General Scott as harsh and unjust."[4] Grant evidently believed that Trist had also been badly treated; twenty-two years later he would be the only president of the United States to act affirmatively in recognition of Trist's unique contribution to the nation. "I presume it is perfectly fair," Robert E. Lee commented with irony, "after having made use of [Trist's] labors, that he should be kicked off as General Scott has been [and] turned out as an old horse to die."[5]

After testifying before the court of inquiry on Scott's charges against Pillow, Trist began the trip home. On the road down to Vera Cruz, he passed Senator Sevier and Attorney General Clifford, the commissioners Polk had sent to Mexico to receive Mexican ratification of the treaty.[6] Senator Benton noted later that Sevier and Clifford received the full pay and expenses of plenipotentiaries "for bringing home a treaty on which their names do not appear," while Trist was recalled, dismissed, and denied salary and expenses for the period in which he negotiated the treaty.[7]

Trist reached New Orleans on April 30, just over a year after he left there for Mexico. While he was on his way back to Washington, the Mexican Congress ratified the treaty. Two days after he reached home on June 10, the American army marched out of the Mexican capital. Trist was only a few blocks from the White House on July 4, 1848, when Polk received the Mexican ratification of the treaty, but he was not among those invited to witness the signature of the president's proclamation that hostilities with Mexico had been terminated. The last American troops left Mexico by the end of July. Thanks to Nicholas P. Trist, America's first foreign war was over.

Trist's contribution to peace was recognized by the Mexican commissioners in their report to the Mexican Congress: "Happy has it been for both countries that the choice of the American government should have been fixed upon a person of such worth, upon a friend of peace so loyal and sincere. Of him there remains in Mexico none but gratified and honoring recollections."[8]

Nicholas Trist did not receive such recognition in the United States. The Congress and public knew very little about the circumstances under which the treaty had been negotiated. In that era the public was accustomed to treaties negotiated in secret and debated by the Senate in closed sessions. There is no indication that anyone from the press attempted to obtain the full story from Trist.

A few weeks after his return to Washington, Trist sent the Speaker of the House of Representatives a large package of documents, including the 111-page memorial he had written in Mexico, 116 pages of notes and appendices, and 67 pages of supporting documents. His covering letter stated his belief "that the Congress and the country has been deceived by the ... President of the U.S. and that the object for which that deception has been practiced was the indefinite protraction of the war ... having for its end the conquest of Mexico and her absorption into our Union."[9]

Although the memorial and attachments contained important facts about Trist's activities in Mexico, they were not intended to provide a general account of his peace mission. Moreover, the mass of papers contained few facts or arguments that effectively supported Trist's charge that Polk had wanted to prevent or suppress the peace treaty as a prelude to the annexation of all of Mexico.

Congress was about to adjourn, and few members had an opportunity to examine Trist's memorial. Democrats in the House naturally opposed dissemination of any criticism of their president, and some Whigs wanted to limit controversy about the war now that they had chosen its hero, Zachary Taylor, as their candidate for president. Although 83 members of the House voted for printing Trist's memorial, 96 voted against it. Trist's documents were quietly filed in the National Archives and remained there virtually untouched for 135 years.[10] After this abortive effort, Trist made no other effort to tell the story of the ending of the war with Mexico.

Trist's education, his unique associations with many of the leading figures of the first half of the nineteenth century, and his diplomatic experience had prepared him well for a useful career in public affairs in the remaining decades of his life. But, except for a very minor post at the very end of his life, his mission in Mexico was his last public service.

When Trist returned from Mexico, he was 48 years old. He lived for 26 more years, until 1874. Most of these years were spent in poverty and obscurity. "I will live on bread and water before I will again hold office of any kind," he wrote his wife the day before the treaty was signed.[11] It was not a bad prediction of his later life.

Although well qualified for a career in public service, Trist lacked the ability to make a decent living in private employment. For a year or two, he held a minor position with a Wall Street law firm, handling the complicated but unprofitable affairs of Spanish-speaking clients. In 1853 the Trists opened a school for young ladies in Philadelphia, hoping their connection with Jefferson would attract young ladies from the Southern states. But Southern leaders were now discouraging Southern families from patronizing schools in the North. The closing of the school left Trist with a debt of $750 for school supplies.

In 1856, Trist became an agent for the inventor of a grate bar used in furnaces and in the fireboxes of railroad locomotives. His contacts with railroaders led to a job as paymaster for the railroad that ran between Philadelphia and Baltimore. The position paid only $1,200 per year, but Trist was glad to accept it. He remained in the railroad job for eleven years, a period which included the Civil War.

During the war Trist remained a steadfast supporter of the Union, despite his family ties in the South. His son, Dr. Hore Browse Trist, was a medical officer in the Confederate army. His daughter and all of Virginia Trist's family remained in Virginia. Virginia's brother, Thomas Jefferson Randolph, was a Confederate colonel. The railroad Trist worked for ran through Maryland countryside which was full of Confederate sympathizers. The president of the railroad knew that Trist retained the friendship of General Scott, who still commanded the Federal army in the first months of the war. Trist was sent to Washington in December 1860 and in April 1861 to see Scott and discuss security measures to protect the railroad.

In 1869, four years after the Civil War, poor health forced Trist to give up his railroad job, and he moved with his wife to Alexandria, Virginia, near his married daughter. For twenty years an appeal for his salary and expenses for his period in Mexico after receipt of the recall order had seemed futile because the White House was occupied by either a president of the opposite party (Taylor, Filmore, Lincoln, Johnson) or an unsympathetic Democratic president (Pierce, Buchanan). In 1869 the chance of getting his back pay and expenses plus twenty years' interest seemed somewhat better because of the election of President Ulysses S. Grant, who knew from his service in Mexico how much Trist had contributed to the nation. Trist decided to petition Congress for his back pay and expenses plus interest on the debt. A bill to pay Trist $14,569 was passed in 1870 by the Senate and in 1871 by the House, but payment was delayed until 1872 by an unsubstantiated charge that a lobbyist had been paid a fee to get it through Congress.[12]

Meanwhile, in July 1870, President Grant appointed Trist postmaster of Alexandria, Virginia. Trist held the post until his death at 73 on February 11, 1874. He was buried in the Ivy Hill cemetery which overlooks Alexandria and, in the distance across the Potomac, the nation's capital.

The full story of Trist's role in ending the nation's first foreign war remained untold in his lifetime and thereafter. Seven books on the military history of the Mexican war were published in the decade after the war, but they contained little information on the origins of the war or the process by which it was ended. These books set a pattern followed by most subsequent histories of the war. About the only positive statement in the 1850s about Trist's contribution appeared in the memoirs of Senator Thomas Hart Benton of Missouri, published in 1856:

> The treaty was a fortunate event for the United States, and for the administration which made it. The war had disappointed the calculation on which it began. Instead of being cheap and bloodless, it had become long, costly, and sanguinary.... Peace was the only respite from so many dangers, and it was gladly seized upon.... Trist, who made the treaty which secured the objects of the war and released the administration from dangers, was recalled and dismissed.[13]

A decade after his mission, the continuing mystery about Trist's role in Mexico was summed up by J.F.H. Claiborne:

> His operations are to this date, to some extent, a matter of conjecture.... He never disclosed enough of his secret instructions and proceedings to rebuke his employer or to vindicate himself.... What was the extent of his powers, what his secret instructions, and how far he was sustained by the President ... will be a problem until Mr. Trist himself gives the solution.[14]

Trist was not able to provide the solution to the mystery. Although he thought he should write a history of his mission, he lacked both the necessary leisure and the ability to write about his service in Mexico without being overwhelmed by a flood of memories. But he saved almost every scrap of paper related to his mission and the 11,000 items of his accumulated papers were contributed to the Library of Congress after his death.

Thirteen years after Trist's mission, the Mexican war story was totally overshadowed by the larger drama of the Civil War. During the remainder of the nineteenth century, material on the Mexican war appeared mainly in the early chapters of books by or about men who had been in Mexico and then served prominently in the Civil War.

There was no scholarly study of the origins of the Mexican war until the publication in the first decades of the twentieth century of several articles and books which reflected the expansionist perspectives of that era.[12] In 1913, George Lockhart Rives's *The United States and Mexico, 1821-48* provided a rather detailed but negative account of Trist's mission in Mexico. In 1919, Justin Smith's two-volume history of *The War with Mexico* defended Polk against charges in several journals that he had "wished for war" with Mexico, but it contained only a minimal account of the Trist mission.[15] During subsequent decades, military and diplomatic historians were preoccupied with World War I and then with World War II.

In the 1960s and 1970s, the Mexican war was rediscovered by military historians. Seven histories of the Mexican war were published between 1960 and 1974, but none contained much detail on the origins or termination of the war and none provided an extensive account of Trist's mission. Many of the brief comments on Trist in these histories of the war and in general histories of the United States contain important factual errors or distortions of the Trist story. David Pletcher's *The Diplomacy of Annexation*, published in 1973, includes about fifty pages on the period of Trist's mission but does not provide a comprehensive account of the mission itself.

Trist's persistent obscurity is the result in part of the traditional American attitude toward the expansion of the country to the Pacific. The idea that it was the "manifest destiny" of citizens of the United States to inhabit the middle latitudes of the North American continent from the Atlantic to the Pacific appeared in a magazine article in the summer of 1845. It quickly became an important part of America's self-image. The concept of Manifest Destiny was a convenient rationalization for pushing aside the Indians and Mexicans who stood in the way of the "destined" march of Americans to the Pacific.

In this century, most of those enrolled in a high school or college course in American history have read about the Mexican war in a section of their textbook entitled "Manifest Destiny" or "Westward Expansion." The typical textbook leaves the impression that the treaty which gave the United States about one third of its contiguous territory was only another step in this inevitable process of fulfilling our manifest national destiny. But the signing of an acceptable peace treaty between the United States and Mexico in 1848 or soon thereafter was not inevitable. It happened in spite of orders from the president of the United States recalling the negotiator and directing further military operations in Mexico. It happened only because of the determination and persistence of one man — Nicholas Trist.

EPILOGUE / *A Friend of Peace*

In his later years, Trist remained convinced that he had saved his country from the many perils associated with an attempt to annex all of Mexico. Several American historians have written that if the "all Mexico" movement had not been nipped in the bud by Trist's treaty, Mexico would probably have been absorbed by the United States. "The agitation for 'all of Mexico' was well started and needed only time to become really formidable," Edward G. Bourne concluded in 1900. "It was deprived of that requisite element of time by the astonishing course of Mr. Trist."[16] John Fuller, author of the only comprehensive study of the "all Mexico" movement, wrote in 1936 that "it seems probable that had Polk's policy as regards further negotiations been carried out, Mexico would now be a part of the United States."[17]

Thomas A. Bailey commented in 1940 that "Trist, by violating his instructions, probably saved the United States from the staggering problems that would have come from trying to absorb the more densely settled portions of Mexico — problems that the U.S. was to learn more about when it later took over the Philippines and Puerto Rico."[18] "It is possible, even probable," Glyndon Van Deusen wrote in 1959, "that Trist's refusal to obey his final instructions prevented the absorption of Mexico by the United States."[19] Nevertheless, an examination of the military, social, and political ramifications of the "all Mexico" idea leads to the conclusion that it would have faded away as soon as Americans had time to consider those ramifications.

First, they would soon have realized that an attempt to annex all of Mexico was totally impractical from a military standpoint. It would have required an army of occupation far larger than the 24,000 American troops in central Mexico in early 1848. General Quitman, the first U.S. military governor of the Mexican capital, thought that controlling just the state capitals and a few other important cities would require at least 50,000 men.[20] A much larger force would have been required to maintain effective control over the entire country.

There are many reasons for doubting that a large army of occupation could have been raised in the United States and maintained for an extended period in Mexico. The administration had no authority to draft men, and the war had been fought by regular army units and volunteer regiments. Even at the height of wartime patriotism, most of the volunteers had enlisted for only a year or less and very few had been willing to extend their enlistments to the duration of the war. Enlistments would have declined in 1848 because of growing opposition to the war and virtually ceased in 1849 when all of the footloose part of the American population rushed to California in search of gold.

Moreover, the Whig majority in the House of Representatives, where money bills must originate, would have been very reluctant to authorize expenditures for this new phase of "Mr. Polk's War." Even if appropriations had been authorized by Congress, the money could have been obtained only by borrowing. From Polk's inauguration to July 1848, the national debt increased from $18 to $66 million,[21] and the government's credit had already been stretched to near the limit.[22]

Second, if they had been given a chance to consider the idea, most Americans would have doubted the desirability of attempting to assimilate such a large and racially diverse population. Support for "all Mexico" came mostly from areas on or near the frontier where expansionist sentiment was always strong and from northeastern cities with ethnically mixed and heavily Catholic populations that believed the American "melting pot" could absorb an unlimited number of immigrants. But these frontier and urban communities were not strongly represented in the state legislatures, which elected United States senators. Mainstream America was still very conservative and very racist.

Although the United States had assimilated many individuals from other countries, it had never tried to absorb a whole population with a different culture, language, and racial pattern. The Mexican population of eight million was a mixture of persons of Spanish birth or descent, *mestizos* of mixed Spanish and Indian blood, Indians, and others. Even during the short period in which additional annexations below the Rio Grande were being discussed in late 1847 and early 1848, several prominent leaders rejected such annexations on racial grounds.[23]

When the idea of annexing Mexican territory east of the Sierra Madre was suggested to Secretary of State James Buchanan early in 1847, he replied that the United States could not govern the "mongrel race" that inhabited the area or admit representatives of that race to the House or Senate.[24] The term *mongrel* was rather frequently used in the United States in the 1840s to describe the Mexican population. General Scott told a campaign audience in 1852 that he had opposed annexation of Mexico in 1847 because its population contained seven million Indians and mixed races and "as a lover of my own country, I was opposed to mixing up that race with our own."[25]

Senator John C. Calhoun of South Carolina, the leading defender of slavery in the Congress, told Senate colleagues early in 1848 that "ours is the government of the white man" and that in enacting annexation legislation, Congress should not make "the fatal mistake of placing the colored race on an equality with the white."[26] This attitude was shared by many Northern leaders. "If all Mexico were taken," Frederich Merk wrote in 1963, "citizenship would have to be conferred on colored people — on Indians, on Negroes, on mixed races.... The idea of a wholesale raising to citizenship of the mixed races in Mexico ... was horrifying. A cheerful optimism was felt by Americans concerning the power of man over physical nature. This was part of the theory of Manifest Destiny.... But of human nature little was expected."[27]

Third, any move to annex all of Mexico would have been strongly opposed for different reasons related to the slavery issue by most House and Senate members from the old South and the Northeast and many members from other regions. After the admission of Texas, Calhoun and other leaders of the old South opposed additional annexations because they thought these areas would become free states.[28] Ironically, many Northern leaders — notably Daniel Webster and Martin Van Buren — wanted to limit annexations because they feared the new territories might become slave states. Others, including Henry Clay, opposed additional annexations because they realized that the issue of slavery in the new territories threatened to lead to civil war.

Another thesis is that although Trist did not prevent an attempt to annex all of Mexico, he saved the nation from a disastrous attempt to annex more territory below the Rio Grande.

The acquisition of a wide band of territory below the Rio Grande was discussed by various leaders at various times between mid-1846 and the Senate ratification of Trist's treaty in March 1848. All these proposals were rather vague, and there was no consensus among the advocates on the extent of the desirable acquisitions. In the early months of the war, expansionist Secretary of the Treasury Robert J. Walker talked of a southern border along the 26th parallel.[29] Such a border would have given the United States most or all of the Mexican states of Coahuila, Chihuahua, and Sonora and the upper half of Baja California. New York editor Moses Beach discussed a border on the 26th parallel with Mexican leaders during his mission to Mexico for Polk early in 1847, but he had no authorization from the president or secretary of state to propose such a boundary.

Others proposed a less southern boundary that was vaguely defined but was based at least in part on the Sierra Madre mountains. The Sierra Madre Oriental runs south from Monterrey to near Jalapa. Some advocates of the "Sierra Madre line" were thinking of the annexation of some of the area east of these mountains which includes most or all of the states of Tamaulipas, Nuevo Leon, and Vera Cruz and the torrid and unhealthy coastal zone that had been quickly evacuated by Winfield Scott to minimize the ravages of the vómito (yellow fever). In October 1846, Zachary Taylor thought the northern part of this region could be held with a strong garrison at Saltillo and a small corps at Monclova, Linares, Victoria, and Tampico.[30] Buchanan, who had earlier opposed acquisitions below the Rio Grande, told Polk in

January 1848 that the United States should take "Tamaulipas and all of the country east of the Sierra mountains." Polk thought Buchanan had switched positions to increase support among expansionists for his presidential aspirations.[31]

The "Sierra Madre line" was most frequently proposed by those who thought that if the Mexicans refused to sign an acceptable treaty, the United States should withdraw to a defensive line of its own choosing. Most Americans knew the Sierra Madres only as the mountains beyond Monterrey that had been the southern limit of Taylor's campaign, and many thought of the chain as a barrier running east and west. James Gadsden of South Carolina wrote Calhoun in January 1848 that "the Sierra Madre is intended by nature to separate the people of Texas and New Mexico from what is old Mexico.... It is the great natural barrier which should be placed between the Anglo Saxon and the Spanish race."[32] The future negotiator of the Gadsden Purchase from Mexico of additional territory in Arizona and New Mexico had apparently not yet discovered that the Sierra Madre Oriental is over a thousand miles from New Mexico.

Polk realized that taking additional territory below the Rio Grande would involve very serious problems. One was the inevitable controversy over the introduction of slavery into such territory. Polk told Senator Crittenden in January 1847 that he did not want to acquire territory farther south than New Mexico and California "because I did not desire by so doing to give occasion for agitation on a question [slavery] which might endanger the Union itself."[33] In January 1848 he was also doubtful about the feasibility of annexing northeastern Tamaulipas and adjacent areas because of the problems of assimilating the region's large population.[34]

When Trist's treaty arrived in February, Polk noted in his diary that "if the treaty was now to be made, I should demand more territory, perhaps to make the Sierra Madre the line."[35] But he made this entry after he had decided to accept Trist's treaty, and there is no evidence that he ever seriously considered an attempt to obtain a boundary along the Sierra Madre or any other acquisitions below the Rio Grande.

During the debate on Trist's treaty in March 1848, eleven senators supported Senator Jefferson Davis' motion for a boundary starting north of Tampico and giving the United States a wide band below the Rio Grande, including large parts of Tamaulipas, Nuevo Leon, and Chihuahua and all of Coahuila.[36] This gesture to the expansionists was not accompanied by any serious effort to build support for further acquisitions.

An attempt by the United States to occupy and annex any large area below the Rio Grande would have been fraught with enormous practical difficulties and would almost certainly have proved to be a disastrous failure.

Epilogue / *A Friend of Peace*

Despite early hopes in the United States that some of the northern Mexican provinces would welcome independence from the rest of Mexico, the Mexicans in the Rio Grande valley considered the Yankees to be invaders, not liberators. It is hardly conceivable that any Mexican government would have been willing to sign a treaty ceding a large area below the Rio Grande. Such an area could have been acquired and held only with a large army.

The manpower problem would have proved insurmountable. Occupation duty in Mexico would have attracted few volunteers after the great gold rush to California began early in 1849, and the occupation force would have depended mainly on regular army units. Neither Taylor nor Scott had been able to maintain control over very much of the Mexican countryside even at the apogee of the strength of their forces, and no occupation commander would have been able to do much better after 1848. The vómito would have taken a large toll among any troops stationed in the unhealthy coastal zone.

Moreover, annexation of large territories below the Rio Grande would have involved the same major problems as annexing all of Mexico, especially the difficulties of assimilating a large and racially mixed population with a different language and culture and the intensification of sectional conflict in the United States over the extension of slavery to the new territories.

If Trist had left Mexico as ordered in December 1847, Americans would have had plenty of time to contemplate all these pitfalls. The appointment of one or more new American commissioners, which was being considered by Polk just before he heard that Trist had ignored his recall, would have proved more difficult in 1848 than in 1847. Trist was sent to Mexico secretly just after the 29th Congress expired. In early 1848 the 30th Congress was in its long first session, which would last till summer. Polk could not have appointed peace commissioners that winter or spring without obtaining Senate confirmation of the appointments.

The idea of sending commissioners bearing instructions similar to Trist's would not have been greeted with enthusiasm by senators who wanted to limit the territory acquired from Mexico (including Southern senators who opposed any territory which might become free soil states) or by senators who supported the annexation of more Mexican territory. At the least, opposition to the peace mission in the Senate would have delayed the departure of commissioners and intensified the debate over the extent of the territory to be acquired from Mexico. As the presidential election approached, Whig leaders might have decided that their political interests were better served by the continuation of "Mr. Polk's War"—without further battles—until after the election.

A substantial delay in the peace process would probably not have greatly affected the eventual territorial settlement. Even before the discovery of gold in California, there was never any doubt that the United States would hold the Pacific province that contained the valuable bays of San Francisco and San Diego. Despite the brash talk in 1847 about taking "all Mexico" or Mexican territory to the "Sierra Madre line," acquisitions below the Rio Grande had been never been carefully considered or widely supported in the United States. Delay in the negotiation of a peace treaty would have permitted the American public to become fully aware of the many problems and pitfalls associated with the acquisition of additional Mexican territory.

But delay in the peace process would have had very serious internal consequences — in Mexico and in the United States.

In Mexico, delay might have been fatal to the pro-peace government in Queretaro. Trist thought the odds were against the political survival of the government in Queretaro for more than a few months. By the time new American commissioners arrived, the government might have been voted out of office by the Mexican Congress or been overthrown in a new revolution. The procrastinating tactics of the Herrera, Paredes, and Santa Anna governments between 1845 and 1847 offer models for predicting the behavior of another shaky government that was as unwilling as its predecessors to take responsibility for a treaty involving a large territorial loss by Mexico.

If Trist had left Mexico as ordered in December 1847, the government in Queretaro would have also faced a threat from the American army. With no prospect for early negotiations, General Scott could not have continued to ignore the specific orders from the secretary of war to expand the occupation to include at least the mining districts of Zacatecas and San Luis Potosí. Such an operation might have been carried out in December or January before Scott heard of Polk's interest in appointing new commissioners. The route to these cities ran through Queretaro, the temporary capital of Mexico. At best, the occupation of Queretaro would have forced the Mexican government to flee to some other city and would have further delayed the beginning of new negotiations. At worst, it would have dispersed the government, eliminated any chance of negotiations that year, and produced a prolonged period of anarchy and utter confusion in Mexico.

If the pro-peace government had fallen because of action by the Mexican Congress, a revolution, or the American occupation of Queretaro, the negotiation of a peace treaty might have appeared to be impossible for the foreseeable future. The United States would then have faced the very difficult choices that were already being debated in the winter of 1847–48 between a prolonged occupation of central Mexico or a withdrawal without a treaty.

In his message to Congress in December 1847, Polk had rejected withdrawal

EPILOGUE / *A Friend of Peace* 199

without a treaty and indicated that a military occupation for a considerable period would be necessary. Such an occupation would have involved most of the manpower, morale, health, security, and financial problems discussed above in connection with an occupation for the purposes of annexation. Moreover, Polk had told the Congress that if the current Mexican government proved unable to make peace, a new government should be installed with the encouragement and protection of the American army. The creation of such a "puppet" government under the protecting wing of the American army would have been unacceptable to most Mexicans and would have led to guerrilla warfare while the American army was still in Mexico and the overthrow of the puppet regime as soon as the American army was withdrawn. In short, Polk's idea was a recipe for disaster in Mexico.

Delay in the signing of a peace treaty would also have had grave consequences in the United States. The ratification of Trist's treaty in March 1848 permitted a breathing spell during the presidential election of 1848. Both the Democrats and the Whigs were able to paper over their internal divisions on the slavery issue and to conduct campaigns in which discussion of the Wilmot Proviso was minimized on both sides. The treaty also limited the geographic scope of the controversy over slavery in the territories gained from Mexico. Even so, the acrimonious debate was resumed after the election and developed over the next two years into the most serious internal crisis in the nation's history up to that time.

Without Trist's treaty, the United States would still have been at war with Mexico during most or all of the presidential election campaign in 1848. The continuation of the war would clearly have changed the nature of the election campaign and might have affected its outcome. The war and its outcome would have been the most important election issue in 1848. The question of the extent of the territory to be acquired from Mexico would have been inseparable from the question of the admission of slavery into the newly acquired territories. The two political parties, each badly divided on slavery issues, would scarcely have been able to develop coherent positions on these very complicated and controversial issues. The inevitable result would have been to accelerate the polarization of sectional positions on the extension and continuation of slavery, a process already well advanced prior to the election.

The bitter public debate and hardening of positions during the election of 1848 could have prevented the great compromise masterminded in 1850 by Henry Clay and might have led to secession and civil war in the early 1850s. Most historians believe that the increases in population, industry, agriculture, and railroads in the Northern states in the 1850s provided an essential margin of strength for a Union victory in the Civil War. If the war had begun a decade earlier, the North and South would have been more evenly matched and an eventual Union victory much less certain.

Nicholas P. Trist's act of courage and determination in Mexico provided an early and relatively easy termination of America's first foreign war and its only war with an independent neighboring country. He eliminated the danger that the United States would be drawn into disastrous policies in Mexico, including a prolonged occupation of central Mexico, the establishment of a puppet government under the wing of the American army, and an attempt to annex additional Mexican territories. He snuffed out the movement for the annexation of all of Mexico and eliminated the talk of acquisitions below the Rio Grande before they could further poison the future relations between the two countries. By cutting off the debate in the United States on the acquisition of additional territories, he limited the scope of the raging controversy over slavery in the territories acquired from Mexico and made possible a sectional compromise which kept the peace in the United States during the 1850s.

He was indeed, as the Mexican commissioners said, a friend of peace.

Notes

ABBREVIATIONS

JB	James Buchanan
LC	Library of Congress
NA	National Archives
NPT	Nicholas P. Trist
UNC	University of North Carolina
UVA	University of Virginia

Prologue: Talents, Integrity, and Honor

1. Thomas Jefferson to John Turnbull, December 18, 1786, *Papers of Thomas Jefferson,* vol. 10 (Princeton: 1950–73), 611.
2. Virginia Moore, *The Madisons* (New York: 1979), 125.
3. NPT to Henry S. Randall, undated, Jefferson Papers, LC.
4. James Madison to Henry Clay, October 14, 1828, Nicholas P. Trist Papers, LC.
5. W. C. Rives to Martin Van Buren, March 18, 1829, Trist Papers, LC.
6. NPT to Ellen Randolph Coolidge, July 4, 1826, Coolidge Papers, UVA.
7. [NPT], "Nullification Theory," *Enquirer,* Richmond, September 22, 1831.
8. Henry Clay to NPT, October 10, 1828, Trist Papers, LC.
9. Andrew Jackson to NPT, September 16, 1835, Trist Papers, LC.
10. Joseph Coolidge to NPT, September 30, 1831, Trist Papers, LC.
11. Madison to NPT, December 17, 1828, Trist Papers, LC.
12. [NPT], "A Virginian," *Globe,* Washington, August 23, September 1, 1831.
    [NPT], "One of the '98 School," *Enquirer,* Richmond, September 20, 1831.
    [NPT], "One of the '98 School," *Globe,* Washington, D.C., September 22, 1831.
    [NPT], "Nullification Theory," *Enquirer,* Richmond, September 22, 1831.
    [NPT], "Mr. Jefferson and Nullification," *Globe,* Washington, D.C., August 27, 1832.
    [NPT], "Vindex," *Enquirer,* Richmond, March 26, 1833.
    [NPT], "One of the '98 School," *Virginia Advocate,* Charlottesville, December 13, 1833.

13. Jackson to John Coffee, April 19, 1833, in Burke Davis, *Old Hickory* (New York: 1977), 323.

14. NPT to British commissioners, July 2–August 29, 1839, House Executive Document 115, 26th Cong., 2d sess., 461.

15. Lord Palmerston to Andrew Stevenson, December 17, 1836, House Executive Document 115, 26th Cong., 2d sess., 4.

16. British commissioners to NPT, January 8, 1838, House Executive Document 34, 27th Cong., 1st. sess., 26.

17. NPT to British commissioners, July 2 to August 29, 1839, House Executive Document, 26th Cong., 2d sess., 386.

18. Henry Fox to Forsyth, October 30, 1839, House Executive Document 115, 26th Cong., 2d sess., 112.

19. NPT to Forsyth, February 13, 1841, House Executive Document 115, 26th Cong., 2d sess., 497.

20. David Turnbull, *Travels in the West: Cuba* (London: 1840), 435.

21. NPT to Forsyth, December 17, 1838, House Executive Document 115, 26th Cong., 2d sess., 309–22.

22. NPT to Forsyth, December 10, 1839, in "Reply of N. P. Trist to the Preamble and Resolutions Adopted by the Meeting of Shipowners on August 4, 1839 (pamphlet), Havana, 1839, New York Public Library.

23. House Report 707, 26th Cong., 2d sess., July 21, 1840.

24. Alexander Everett to Forsyth, July 21, 1840, House Executive Document 115, 26th Cong., 2d sess., 481.

25. NPT, "Examination of Mr. Everett's Report," February 18, 1841, House Executive Document 115, 26th Cong., 2d sess., 541–42.

26. House Executive Document 115, 26th Cong., 2d sess., 766 pages.

27. Daniel Webster to NPT, September 4, 1841, Trist Papers, LC.

28. Thomas Fleming, *The Man from Monticello* (New York: 1969), 384.

29. NPT to Speaker of the House of Representatives, August 7, 1848, *Congressional Globe*, 30th Cong., 1st sess., 1058.

30. NPT to Andrew Jackson Donelson, February 10, 1830, Trist Papers, LC.

31. NPT Memorandum, May 4, 1833, Trist Papers, LC; James Parton, *Life of Andrew Jackson* (New York: 1861), 437; Robert V. Remini, *Andrew Jackson and the Course of American Democracy, 1833–1845* (New York: 1984), 196.

Chapter One: Our Flag Is Insulted

1. John Quincy Adams, Diary, January 10 and 12, 1823; April 19, 1824; and May 27, 1824; Alan Nevins, ed., *The Diary of John Quincy Adams* (New York: 1929), 294–95, 321, 325; Andrew Jackson to James Monroe, February 19, 1823, in Marquis James *Life of Andrew Jackson* (New York: 1938), 356–60; Robert V. Remini, *Andrew Jackson and the Course of American Freedom, 1822–1832* (New York: 1981), 50, 234.

2. Herbert E. Putnam, *Joel Roberts Poinsett: A Political Biography* (Washington: 1935), 20–43; James M. Callahan, *American Foreign Policy in Mexican Relations* (New York: 1932), 189.

3. Henry Clay to Joel Poinsett, August 25, 1829, in William R. Manning, ed., *Diplomatic Correspondence of the United States*, vol. 8 (Washington, D.C.: 1937), 3–8.

4. Martin Van Buren to Joel Poinsett, August 25, 1829, in Manning, *Diplomatic Correspondence of the United States*, vol. 8, 3–8.

5. William R. Manning, "Poinsett's Mission to Mexico," *American Journal of International Law* (October 1913): 817–19.
6. Anthony Butler to Andrew Jackson, June 23, 1831, Jackson Papers, LC.
7. Jackson to Butler, August 17, 1831, Jackson Papers, LC.
8. Butler to Jackson, February 10, 1833, *Diplomatic Correspondence of the United States*, vol. 8, 260.
9. Butler to Jackson, October 28, 1833; Jackson to Butler, November 27, 1833, Jackson Papers, LC; Remini, *Jackson, 1822–1832*, 354.
10. Butler to Jackson, February 6, 1834, Jackson Papers, LC; Remini, *Jackson*, vol. 2, 354.
11. Brantz Mayer, *Mexico — Aztec, Spanish, and Republican* (Hartford: 1852), 318.
12. Butler to John Forsyth, June 17, 1835, *Diplomatic Correspondence of the United States*, vol. 8, 289.
13. Jackson, note on above letter, June 22, 1835, *Diplomatic Correspondence of the United States*, vol. 8, 293.
14. John M. Belohlavek, *Let the Eagle Soar: The Foreign Policy of Andrew Jackson* (Lincoln, Neb.: 1985), 226.
15. Forsyth to Butler, July 2, 1835, *Diplomatic Correspondence of the United States*, vol. 8, 293.
16. James Schouler, *Atlantic Monthly* (February 1905): 200; Jesse S. Reeves, *American Diplomacy Under Tyler and Polk* (Baltimore: 1907): 75.
17. Robert V. Remini, *Andrew Jackson and the Course of American Democracy, 1833–1845* (New York: 1984), 536.
18. Herbert I. Priestly, *The Mexican Nation* (New York: 1926), 282.
19. Paul Horgan, *Great River: The Rio Grande in North American History*, vol. 2 (New York: 1954), 526.
20. Richard Coxe, *Review of the Relations Between the U.S. and Mexico* (New York: 1846), 21.
21. Remini, *Jackson, 1833–1845*, 366–67.
22. *Ibid.*
23. *Ibid*, 368.
24. Forsyth to Powhatan Ellis, July 20, *Diplomatic Correspondence of the United States*, vol. 8, 52–54.
25. Ellis to Jose Monasterio, December 7, 1836, *Diplomatic Correspondence of the United States*, vol. B, 391–400.
26. Ellis to Jackson, August 26, 1836, *Diplomatic Correspondence of the United States*, vol. 8, 343–45.
27. Forsyth to minister of foreign affairs, May 27, 1837, *Diplomatic Correspondence of the United States*, vol. 8, 79.
28. Hubert H. Bancroft, *History of Mexico*, vol. 5 (San Francisco: 1885), 315.
29. Forsyth to Ellis, May 3, 1839, *Diplomatic Correspondence of the United States*, vol. 8, 95.
30. Frederick Merk, *History of the Western Movement* (New York, 1978), 360.
31. Forsyth to Memucan Hunt, August 25, 1837, in *Globe*, Washington, D.C., October 18, 1837.
32. Henry P. Thompson. *Waddy Thompson*, privately printed, 1929, 18–21.
33. Horgan, *Great River*, vol. 2, 585.
34. *Ibid*, 585–600.
35. Thompson to Webster, April 11, 1843, *Diplomatic Correspondence of the United States*, vol. 8, 544.

36. Ellis to Forsyth, June 7, 1840, *Diplomatic Correspondence of the United States*, vol. 8, 463.
37. Forsyth to Ellis, August 21, 1840, *Diplomatic Correspondence of the United States*, vol. 8, 100.
38. Ellis to Forsyth, October 1 and 17, 1840, *Diplomatic Correspondence of the United States*, vol. 8, 473–75.
39. Jose Maria de Bocanegra to Thompson, May 12 and 31, 1842, *Diplomatic Correspondence of the United States*, vol. 8, 487–90.
40. Bocanegra to Thompson, December 19, 1842, *Diplomatic Correspondence of the United States*, vol. 8, 527.
41. Webster to Thompson, January 31, 1843, *Diplomatic Correspondence of the United States*, vol. 8, 128
42. Thompson to Webster, April 11, 1843, *Diplomatic Correspondence of the United States*, vol. 8, 544.
43. Thompson to John Tyler, May 9, 1842, *Diplomatic Correspondence of the United States*, vol. 8, 485.
44. George Lockhart Rives, "Mexican Diplomacy on the Eve of the War with the U.S.," *American Historical Review* (January 1913): 275–95.
45. Lord Aberdeen to Richard Pakeham, December 26, 1843, *The Record of American Diplomacy* (New York: 1954), 193–94.
46. Bocanegra to Thompson, August 23, 1843, *Diplomatic Correspondence of the United States*, vol. 8, 557.
47. Thompson to Abel P. Upshur, August 25, 1843, *Diplomatic Correspondence of the United States*, vol. 8, 558.
48. Thompson to Upshur, October 29, 1843, *Diplomatic Correspondence of the United States*, vol. 8, 565.
49. Juan Almonte to Upshur, October 29, 1843, *Diplomatic Correspondence of the United States*, vol. 8, 567.
50. Upshur to Almonte, November 8, 1843, *Diplomatic Correspondence of the United States*, vol. 8, 1414.
51. Jesse S. Reeves, *American Diplomacy Under Tyler and Polk*, vol. 2 (Baltimore: 1907), 138–61.
52. Edward Channing, *A History of the United States*, vol. 5 (New York: 1927), 342–49.

Chapter Two: A Common Destiny

1. Charles G. Sellers, *James K. Polk: Jacksonian, 1795–1843* (Princeton: 1957), 336.
2. Andrew Jackson to A. V. Hoin, February 12, 1844; Polk to S. P. Chase and Thomas Heaton, April 23, 1844, unidentified newspapers, Nicholas P. Trist Papers, LC.
3. Samuel F. Bemis, *A Diplomatic History of the United States* (New York: 1942), 22; Glyndon G. Van Deusen, *The Jackson Era, 1828–1848* (New York: 1959), 186.
4. Benjamin Green to Jose Maria de Bocanegra, May 23, 1844, in William R. Manning, ed., *Diplomatic Correspondence of the United States*, vol. 8 (Washington, D.C.: 1937), 586.
5. Wilson Shannon to John C. Calhoun, May 23, 1844, "Correspondence Addressed to Calhoun," *Annual Report of the American Historical Association for 1929* (Washington, D.C.: 1930), 235.
6. Henry B. Parkes, *A History of Mexico* (Boston: 1970), 208
7. Brantz Mayer, *Mexico—Aztec, Spanish, and Republican* (Hartford: 1852), 367, 405.

8. T. R. Fehrenbach, *Fire and Blood: A Bold and Definitive Modern Chronicle of Mexico* (New York: 1985), 391.

9. *National Intelligencer*, Washington, February 15, 1846.

10. Joint Resolution of Annexation, U.S. Congress, February 27, 1845, in Ruhl J. Bartlett, ed., *The Record of American Diplomacy* (New York: 1954), 200.

11. J. D. Richardson, ed., *Messages and Papers of the Presidents, 1789-1897*, vol. 4 (Washington D.C.: 1908), 373-82.,

12. Juan Almonte to Calhoun, March 6, 1845, *Diplomatic Correspondence of the United States*, vol. 8, 600.

13. Waddy Thompson to Daniel Webster, November 30, 1842, *Diplomatic Correspondence of the United States*, vol. 8, 524; John Black to John Slidell, December 15, 1845, *Diplomatic Correspondence of the United States*, vol. 8, 778.

14. Luis Gonzago Cuevas to Mexican Congress, March 11, 1845, in Thomas Cotner, *The Military and Political Career of Jose Joaquin de Herrera* (Austin: 1949), 124.

15. Herbert Gambrell, *Anson Jones: The Last President of Texas* (Austin: 1964), 391-400.

16. Cotner, *Herrera*, 122.

17. Cuevas to Shannon, March 28, 1845, *Diplomatic Correspondence of the United States*, vol. 8, 705-6.

18. William Parrott to JB, April 26, 1845, *Diplomatic Correspondence of the United States*, vol. 8, 712.

19. Parrott to JB, April 26, 1845, *Diplomatic Correspondence of the United States*, vol. 8, 712.

20. April 24, 1845, entry in Milo Milton Quaife, ed., *The Diary of James K. Polk*, vol. 1 (Chicago: 1910), 350; Donelson to JB, May 6, 1845, House Executive Document 2, 29th Cong., 1st sess., 44.

21. Donelson to JB, May 11 and 22, 1845, House Executive Document 2, 29th cong., 1st sess., 45.

22. JB to Donelson, May 23, 1845, House Executive Document 2, 29th Cong., 1st sess., 46.

23. William Marcy to Zachary Taylor, May 28, 1845, House Executive Document 60, 29th Cong., 1st sess., 80.

24. George Bancroft to Taylor, June 15, 1845, House Executive Document 60, 29th Cong., 1st sess., 81-82.

25. Andrew Jackson Donelson to JB, May 24, 1845, House Executive Document 2, 29th Cong., 1st sess., 47.

26. Donelson to JB, June 2 and 4, House Executive Document 2, 29th Cong., 1st sess., 53-54.

27. Justin H. Smith, *The Annexation of Texas* (New York: 1911), 447

28. Glenn W. Price, *Origins of the War with Mexico: The Polk-Stockton Intrigue* (Austin: 1967), 111-12; Anson Jones, *Memorandum and Official Correspondence Relating to the Republic of Texas and Its History and Annexation* (New York: 1859), 46.

29. Jones, *Memorandum*, 46-51.

30. Smith, *Annexation of Texas*, 447.

31. Donelson to JB, July 11, 1845, in Richard B. Stenberg, "The Failure of Polk's War Intrigue of 1845," *Pacific History Review* 55 (March 1935), 36-39.

32. Polk to Sam Houston, June 6, 1845, in Charles Sellers, *James K. Polk: Continentalist* (Princeton: 1966), 224-25.

33. Polk to Donelson, June 15, 1848, in Paul H. Bergeron, *The Presidency of James K. Polk* (Lawrence, Kans.: 1987), 62.

34. John Bach MacMaster, *A History of the People of the United States*, vol. 5 (New York: 1900), 12.

35. Glyndon Van Deusen, *The Jackson Era, 1828–1848* (New York: 1959), 215; Frederick Merk, *The Monroe Doctrine and American Expansionism, 1843–49* (New York: 1966), 147–48; Price, *Origins of the War*, 156.

36. Sellers, *Polk: Continentalist*, 224–25.

37. Taylor to Adjutant General, July 8, 1845, House Executive Document 60, 29th Cong., 1st sess., 81–82.

38. Donelson to Taylor, June 28, 1845, House Executive Document 60, 29th Cong., 1st sess., 804–6.

39. Taylor to Adjutant General, July 8, 1845, House Executive Document 60, 29th Cong., 1st sess., 802–3.

40. Marcy to Taylor, July 30, 1845, House Executive Document 60, 29th Cong., 1st sess., 807.

41. Eugene Irving MacCormac, *James K. Polk: A Political Biography* (Berkeley: 1922), 379; Polk Diary, vol. 4, November 4, 1848, 179–80.

42. *El Siglo XIX*, Mexico, quoted in *Niles' National Register*, Washington, D.C., July 19 and 26, 1845, 306, 324, cited in David M. Pletcher, *The Diplomacy of Annexation: Texas, Oregon, and the Mexican War* (Columbia, Mo.: 1973), 256.

43. Polk to JB, August 7, 1845, in George Ticknor Curtis, *Life of James Buchanan*, vol. 1 (New York: 1883), 589.

44. Marcy to Taylor, August 23, 1845, House Executive Document 60, 29th Cong., 1st sess., 85.

45. Taylor to Adjutant General, August 15, 1845, House Executive Document 60, 29th Cong., 1st sess., 99.

46. Taylor to Adjutant General, September 6, 1845, House Executive Document 60, 29th Cong., 1st sess., 105.

47. Gene M. Brack, "Mexican Opinion, American Racism, and the War of 1846," *Western Historical Quarterly* 1 (April 1970), 164.

48. Ramon E. Ruiz, *Triumph and Tragedy: A History of the Mexican People* (New York: 1992), 212.

49. Andrew Jackson to Polk, December 10, 1844, *Correspondence of James K. Polk*, vol. 8 (Knoxville: 1994), 418–19.

50. Philip S. Klein, *President James Buchanan: A Biography* (Philadelphia: 1962), 165.

51. NPT recollections, 1853, Trist Papers, LC.

52. NPT undated draft, Trist Papers, LC.

53. Leonard D. White, *The Jeffersonians: A Study in Administrative History, 1801–1829* (New York: 1951), 11.

54. Justin H. Smith, *The War with Mexico*, vol. 1 (Austin: 1920), 128.

55. Sellers, *Polk: Continentalist*, 109, 309.

56. Bergeron, *Presidency of Polk*, 49.

57. James P. Shenton, *Robert John Walker: A Politician from Jackson to Lincoln* (New York: 1961), 24.

Chapter Three: The Cup of Forbearance

1. William Parrott to JB, August 5, 1845, in William R. Manning, *Diplomatic Correspondence of the United States*, vol. 8 (Washington, D.C.: 1937), 745; John Black to JB, August 23, 1845, *Diplomatic Correspondence of the United States*, vol. 8, 745.

2. Parrott to JB, August 26, 1845, *Diplomatic Correspondence of the United States*, vol. 8, 746.

3. Thomas Cotner, *The Military and Political Career of Jose Joaquin de Herrera, 1792–1854* (Austin: 1949), 129–30.

4. September 16, 1845, entry in Milo Milton Quaife, ed., *The Diary of James K. Polk*, vol. 1 (Chicago: 1910), 33.

5. Polk Diary, September 17, 1845, vol. 1, 35.

6. JB to John Black, September 17, 1845, *Diplomatic Correspondence of the United States*, vol. 8, 168.

7. Manuel de la Peña y Peña to Black, October 15, 1845, *Diplomatic Correspondence of the United States*, vol. 8 (Washington, D.C.: 1937), 763.

8. Charles Sellers, *James K. Polk: Continentalist, 1843–46* (Princeton: 1966), 265, citing statement by Benjamin E. Green, August 8, 1889, in L. G. Tyler, *The Letters and Times of the Tylers*, vol. 3, (Richmond, 1896) 174–77, and Joel Poinsett to Martin Van Buren, May 26, 1846, Van Buren Papers.

9. Eugene I. McCormac, *James K. Polk: A Political Biography* (New York: 1922), 393.

10. Sellers, *Polk: Continentalist*, 265.

11. Frederick Merk, *Manifest Destiny and Mission in American History* (New York: 1963), 85–86.

12. Polk Diary, January 16 and 20, 1846, vol. 3, 170, 185.

13. David M. Pletcher, *The Diplomacy of Annexation: Texas, Oregon, and the Mexican War* (Columbia, Mo.: 1973), 422.

14. Powhattan Ellis to John Forsyth, September 24, 1836, *Diplomatic Correspondence of the United States*, vol. 8, 358.

15. Robert V. Remini, *Andrew Jackson and the Course of American Freedom* (New York: 1981), 355, 367.

16. George Bancroft to James Schouler, 1887, in James Schouler, *History of the United States*, vol. 4 (New York: 1880–99), 498.

17. Bancroft to John D. Sloat, June 24, 1845, *Diplomatic Correspondence of the United States*, vol. 8, 231.

18. *Union*, Washington, June 6, 1845, in Sellers *Polk: Continentalist*, 231.

19. Thomas O. Larkin to JB, July 10, 1845, *Diplomatic Correspondence of the United States*, vol. 8, 735.

20. JB to Larkin, October 17, 1845, *Diplomatic Correspondence of the United States*, vol. 8, 169.

21. Polk to Congress, December 2, 1845, in James D. Richardson, ed., *Messages and Papers of the Presidents, 1789–1897*, vol. 5 (Washington, D.C.: 1908), 2248.

22. Polk Diary, October 24, 1846, vol. 1, 71.

23. Pletcher, *Diplomacy*, 96.

24. Edward Channing, *A History of the United States*, vol. 5 (New York: 1927), 567.

25. Pletcher, *Diplomacy*, 424, citing Arthur Stanmore, *The Earl of Aberdeen* (London: 1905), 183–88.

26. Polk to John Slidell, November 10, 1843, letterbook, Polk Papers, in Sellers, *Polk: Continentalist*, 338.

27. JB to Slidell, November 10, 1845, *Diplomatic Correspondence of the United States*, vol. 8, 180.

28. Black to JB, December 18, 1845, *Diplomatic Correspondence of the United States*, vol. 8, 783.

29. Slidell to JB, December 17, 1845, *Diplomatic Correspondence of the United States*, vol. 8, 777.

30. JB to Slidell, November 19, 1845, *Diplomatic Correspondence of the United States*, vol. 8, 183–84.
31. Peña to Slidell, December 20, 1845, House Executive Document 60, 29th Cong., 1st sess., 38–39; Slidell to Polk, December 29, 1845, Polk Papers, in Sellers, *Polk: Continentalist*, 400.
32. Pletcher, *Diplomacy*, 230, 262–63.
33. Polk Diary, September 6, 1845, vol. 1, 35.
34. John H. Schroeder, *Mr. Polk's War: American Opposition and Dissent, 1846–48* (Madison, Wisc.: 1973), 12.
35. NPT to Slidell, December 7, 1845, Nicholas P. Trist Papers, LC.
36. Merk, *Manifest Destiny*, 75.
37. Pletcher, *Diplomacy*, 610.
38. Zachary Taylor to Adjutant General, November 7, 1845, House Executive Document 60, 29th Cong., 1st sess., 112.
39. David Conner to Taylor, November 7, 1845, House Executive Document 60, 29th Cong., 1st sess., 112.
40. Marcy to Taylor, January 13, 1846, House Executive Document 60, 29th Cong., 1st sess., 91.
41. JB to Slidell, January 20, 1846, *Diplomatic Correspondence of the United States*, vol. 8, 186.
42. Black to JB, December 20, 1845, *Diplomatic Correspondence of the United States*, vol. 8, 785; Taylor to Adjutant General, January 7, 1846, House Executive Document 60, 29th Cong., 1st sess., 115.
43. JB to Slidell, January 28, 1846, *Diplomatic Correspondence of the United States*, vol. 8, 187.
44. Polk Diary, February 17, vol. 1, 1846, 234; April 7, 1846, 319; April 21, 1846, 343; April 25, 1846, 354; April 28, 1846, 363.
45. Polk to Congress, December 8, 1846, in Richardson, *Messages and Papers*, vol. 5, 2324.
46. Andrew Jackson to Congress, February 6, 1837, *Addresses and Messages of the Presidents of the United States*, vol. 2 (New York: 1846), 945.
47. Black to JB, December 30, 1845, *Diplomatic Correspondence of the United States*, vol. 8, 806.
48. Slidell to JB, January 14, 1846, and February 6, 1846, *Diplomatic Correspondence of the United States*, vol. 8, 808, 812.
49. Polk Diary, February 13 and 16, 1846, vol. 1, 225.
50. Sellers, *Polk: Continentalist*, 402–45.
51. Bernard DeVoto, *Year of Decision—1846* (Boston: 1943), 362.
52. Frederick Merk, *History of the Westward Movement* (New York: 1978), 325.
53. Taylor to Betty Taylor, January 9, 1846, *The Autograph* 1 (April 1917), 34.
54. JB to Slidell, March 12, 1846, *Diplomatic Correspondence of the United States*, vol. 8, 189.
55. Polk Diary, Marcy 28, 1846, vol. 1, 189.
56. Slidell to JB, February 6 and 17, *Diplomatic Correspondence of the United States*, vol. 8, 811, 813.
57. Polk Diary, March 28, 1846, vol. 1, 305.
58. Polk Diary, April 3, 1846, vol. 1, 317.
59. Bancroft to Louis McLane, March 29, 1846, *Life and Letters of George Bancroft*, vol. 1 (New York: 1908), 282.
60. Polk to Senate, March 24, 1846, in Richardson *Messages and Papers*, vol. 5, 2260.
61. Polk Diary, March 31, 1846, vol. 1, 314.

62. George Bancroft, "Biographical Sketch of James K. Polk," Bancroft Collection, New York Public Library.
63. Slidell to Joaquin M. de Castillo y Lanzas, March 1, 1846, *Diplomatic Correspondence of the United States*, vol. 8, 814.
64. Castillo y Lanzas to Slidell, March 12, 1846, *Diplomatic Correspondence of the United States*, vol. 8, 818.
65. Slidell to JB, April 9, 1846,m in George Tichnor Curtis, *Life of James Buchanan*, vol. 1 (New York: 1883), 599.
66. JB to Slidell, March 12, 1846, *Diplomatic Correspondence of the United States*, vol. 8, 192.
67. Polk to Slidell, April 17, 1846, Polk Papers, LC, cited by Pletcher, *Diplomacy*, 379–80.

Chapter Four: Hostilities May Be Considered as Commenced

1. Zachary Taylor to Adjutant General, March 21, 1846, House Executive Document 60, 29th Cong., 1st sess., 124.
2. Minutes of interview between General Worth and General Vega, March 28, 1846, House Executive Document 60, 29th Cong., 1st sess., 134–38.
3. Taylor to Adjutant General, March 29, 1846, House Executive Document 60, 29th Cong., 1st sess., 132.
4. Taylor to Betty Taylor, April 7, 1846, *The Autograph*, vol. 1 (1917), 74.
5. George G. Meade to wife, April 7, 1846, in George C. Meade, *Life and Letters of George Gordon Meade*, vol. 1 (New York: 1913), 54.
6. J. Jack Bauer, *Zachary Taylor: Soldier, Planter, Statesman of the Old Southwest* (Baton Rouge: 1985), 148.
7. Pedro Ampudia to Taylor, April 12, 1846, House Executive Document 60, 29th Cong., 1st sess., 140.
8. Taylor to Ampudia, April 12, 1846, House Executive Document 60, 29th Cong., 1st sess., 139.
9. Ramon Alcarez, *The Other Side* (New York: 1849), 40–41.
10. Cadmus M. Wilcox, *History of the Mexican War* (Washington, D.C.: 1892), 42; Alcarez, *Other Side*, 39; *News*, Galveston, in *Niles's Register* (Washington: May 9), 1846.
11. Buchanan Papers, Historical Society of Pennsylvania, cited in David M. Pletcher, *The Diplomacy of Annexation: Texas, Oregon, and the Mexican War* (Columbia, MO.: 1973), 287.
12. February 16, 1846, entry in Milo Milton Quaife, ed., *The Diary of James K. Polk*, vol. 1 (Chicago: 1910), 230.
13. April 2, 1846, entry in W. A. Croffut, ed., *Fifty Years in Camp and Field: Diary of Major General Ethan Allen Hitchcock, USA* (New York: 1909), 220; Polk to Senate, July 5, 1848, in James D. Richardson, ed., *Messages and Papers of the Presidents, 1789–1897*, vol. 5 (Washington, D. C.: 1908), 2437.
14. David Connor to Taylor, March 2, 1846, House Executive Document 60, 29th Cong., 1st sess., 122; Diary of W. S. Henry, April 9, 1946, *Campaign Sketches of the War with Mexico* (New York: 1847), 73.
15. George G. Meade to wife, April 15, 1845, in Meade, *Life and Letters*, vol. 1, 57–59.
16. April 15, 1846, entry in Rhoda Doubleday, ed., *Journal of the Late Brevet Major Philip Norbourne Barbour* (New York: 1936), 38.
17. Ulysses S. Grant to Julia Dent, April 20, 1846, *Papers of U. S. Grant*, vol. 1 (Carbondale, Ill.: 1967), 81.

18. April 19, 1846, entry in Doubleday, *Journal of Philip Barbour*, 40; George C. Meade to wife, April 19, 1846, in Meade, *Life and Letters*, vol. 1, 61.

19. Polk to Congress, May 11, 1846, House Executive Document 60, 29th Cong., 1st sess., 7.

20. Marcy to Taylor, January 13, 1846, House Executive Document 60, 29th Cong., 1st sess., 91.

21. Taylor to Adjutant General, February 26, 1846 House Executive Document 60, 29th Cong., 1st sess., 118.

22. Worth-Vega interview, March 28, 1846, House Executive Document 60, 29th Cong., 1st sess., 134.

23. Polk to House of Representatives, July 24, 1848, in Richardson, *Messages and Papers*, vol. 5, 2445.

24. Glenn W. Price, *Origins of the War with Mexico* (Austin: 1967), 153; Thomas A. Bailey, *A Diplomatic History of the American People* (New York: 1946), 271; Ivor D. Spencer, *The Victor and the Spoils: A Life of William L. Marcy* (Providence: 1959), 151; Eugene McCormac, *James K. Polk* (New York: 1967), 412.

25. Taylor to R. C. Wood, July 14, August 4, August 23, 1845, *Taylor Letters*, 28, 37, 49, cited in McCormac, *Polk*, 432.

26. Taylor to Adjutant General, November 7, 1845, House Executive Document 60, 29th Cong., 1st sess., 112.

27. Taylor to Adjutant General, April 6, 1846 and May 3, 1846, House Executive Document 60, 29th Cong., 1st sess., 133, 303; Diary of W. S. Henry, April 11, 1846, in Henry, *Campaign Sketches*, 74.

28. Taylor to Adjutant General, April 23, 1846, House Executive Document 60, 29th Cong., 1st sess., 143.

29. Taylor to Adjutant General, February 16, 1846, House Executive Document 60, 29th Cong., 1st sess., 117.

30. Report of Captain W. T. Hardee, April 26, 1846, House Executive Document 60, 29th Cong., 1st sess., 291.

31. Taylor to Adjutant General, May 3, 1846, House Executive Document 60, 29th Cong., 1st sess., 289.

32. Bauer, *Zachary Taylor*, 129.

33. Taylor to Ampudia, April 22, 1846, House Executive Document 60, 29th Cong., 1st sess., 146.

34. Justin H. Smith, "Mexico Wanted War," excerpt from *The War with Mexico* (New York: 1919), in R. E. Ruiz, ed., *The Mexican War: Was It Manifest Destiny?* (New York: 1963), 95-96.

35. *Ibid.*, 97-99.

36. Juan Almonte to Ministry of Foreign Affairs, March 15, 1844, in George Lockhart Rives, *The United States and Mexico, 1821-48*, vol. 2 (New York: 1913), 243-44.

37. Miguel Soto, "The Monarchist Conspiracy," *Essays on the Mexican War* (Arlington, Texas: 1986). 74.

38. Black to JB, May 23, 1846, in William R. Manning, ed., *Diplomatic Correspondence of the United States*, vol. 8 (Washington, D.C.: 1937), 853-54.

39. Soto, "Monarchist Conspiracy," 78.

40. Eugene I. McCormac, *James K. Polk: A Political Biography*, vol. 2 (Berkeley: 1922, 413; Rives, *U.S. and Mexico*, vol. 2, 141-42.

41. McCormac, *Polk*, 413.

42. Mariano Arista to Taylor, April 24, 1846, House Executive Document 60, 29th Cong., 1st sess., 1205.

43. Taylor to Arista, April 24, 1846, House Executive Document 60, 29th Cong., 1st sess., 1206.
44. Pletcher, *Diplomacy*, 292; Frederick Merk, *History of the Westward Movement* (New York: 1978), 325.
45. Polk Diary, vol. 1, April 7, 1846, 319.
46. Black to JB, December 30, 1846, *Diplomatic Correspondence of the United States*, vol. 8, 806.
47. JB to Slidell, March 12, 1846, *Diplomatic Correspondence of the United States*, vol. 8, 191.
48. Slidell to JB, February 6, 1846, *Diplomatic Correspondence of the United States*, vol. 8, 811.
49. Slidell to JB, February 17, 1846, *Diplomatic Correspondence of the United States*, vol. 8, 813.
50. Slidell to JB, March 18, 1846, *Diplomatic Correspondence of the United States*, vol. 8, 831.
51. Black to JB, March 19, 1845, *Diplomatic Correspondence of the United States*, vol. 8, 833.
52. Polk Diary, April 28, 1846, vol. 1, 363.
53. Polk Diary, May 2, 1846, vol. 1, 374.
54. Polk Diary, May 3, 1846, vol. 1, 376.
55. Polk Diary, May 6, 1846, vol. 1, 381.
56. Louis McLane to JB, April 17–18, 1846, in Pletcher, *Diplomacy*, 383.
57. Polk Diary, May 8, 1846, vol. 1, 382.
58. Polk Diary, May 9, 1846, vol. 1, 384.
59. Polk to Congress, December 8, 1846, in Richardson, *Messages and Papers*, vol. 5, 2323–28.
60. Taylor to Adjutant General, April 26, 1846, House Executive Document 60, 29th Cong., 1st sess., 141.
61. Polk Diary, May 9, 1846, vol. 1, 386.
62. Polk to Congress, May 11, 1846, House Executive Document 60, 29th Cong., 1st sess., 410.
63. Charles Sellers, *James K. Polk: Continentalist, 1843–46* (Princeton: 1966), 418, 427.
64. Merk, *Westward Movement*, 363.

Chapter Five: A Peace Must Be Conquered

1. May 13, 1846, entry in Milo Milton Quaife, ed., *The Diary of James K. Polk*, vol. 1 (Chicago: 1910), 397.
2. JB to Louis McLane, May 14, 1846, in Carlos B. Garcia, *Material para la Histsorica de Mexico* (Mexico: 1956), 570.
3. Polk Diary, May 30, 1846, vol. 1, 438.
4. Ivor D. Spencer, *The Victor and the Spoils: A Life of William L. Marcy* (Providence: 1959), 153.
5. George Bancroft to John D. Sloat, June 24, 1845, House Executive Document 60, 29th Cong., 1st sess., 231.
6. Bancroft to Sloat, May 15, 1846, House Executive Document 60, 29th Cong., 1st sess., 235.
7. Bancroft to Louis McLane, June 23, 1846, in Mark A. Howe, *Life and Letters of George Bancroft*, vol. 1 (New York: 1908), 286.

8. Dwight L. Clarke, *Stephen Watts Kearny: Soldier of the West* (Norman, Okla.: 1961), 92.
9. William Goetzman, *Exploration and Empire* (New York: 1966), 250.
10. John Bigelow, *Memoir of the Life and Public Service of John Charles Fremont* (New York: 1856); J. Jack Bauer, *The Mexican War: 1846-48* (New York: 1974), 164-96; Frederick Merk, *History of the Westward Movement* (New York: 1978), 347-58.
11. Bauer, *Mexican War*, 145-59.
12. James K. Polk to William Polk, July 14, 1846, Polk Papers, LC, cited in Thomas R. Hietala, *Manifest Design: Anxious Aggrandizement in Late Jacksonian America* (Ithaca, N.Y.: 1985), 157.
13. William Marcy to Zachary Taylor, May 28, 1846, House Executive Document 60, 29th Cong., 1st sess., 281.
14. Marcy to Taylor, June 8, 1846, House Executive Document 60, 29th Cong., 1st sess., 325.
15. Taylor to Marcy, July 2, 1846, House Executive Document 60, 29th Cong., 1st sess., 329.
16. Polk Diary, July 8, 1846, vol. 2, 17.
17. George Lockhart Rives, *The United States and Mexico, 1821-48*, vol. 2 (New York: 1913), 233-35.
18. John Black to JB, June 9, 1846, in William R. Manning, ed., *Diplomatic Correspondence of the United States*, vol. 8 (Washington, D.C.: 1937), 193.
19. JB to Minister of Foreign Affairs of Mexico, July 27, 1846, *Diplomatic Correspondence of the United States*, vol. 8, 193.
20. Polk Diary, March 28, 1846, vol. 1, 307.
21. Polk Diary, March 31, 1846, vol. 1, 315.
22. Polk Diary, August 1, 1846, vol. 2, 70.
23. George Lockhart Rives, *The United States and Mexico, 1821-48*, vol. 2 (New York: 1913), 235.
24. Polk Diary, August 10, 1846, vol. 2, 77.
25. Bancroft to David Conner, May 13, 1846, House Executive Document 60, 29th Cong., 1st sess., 774.
26. Brantz Mayer, *Mexico—Aztec, Spanish, and Republican*, vol. 1 (Hartford: 1852), 356.
27. Antonio Lopez de Santa Anna, address, August 16, 1846, House Executive Document 60, 29th Cong., 1st sess., 777.
28. Mayer, *Mexico*, vol. 1, 360.
29. Manuel Rejon to JB, August 31, 1846, *Diplomatic Correspondence of the United States*, vol. 8, 885.
30. Polk Diary, September 10 and 11, 1846, vol. 2, 129, 132.
31. Polk Diary, September 19, 1846, vol. 2, 145.
32. NPT draft, Nicholas P. Trist Papers, LC.
33. Howe, *George Bancroft*, vol. 1, 289.
34. Polk Diary, August 29, 1846, vol. 2, 103; Marcy to Taylor, July 9, 1846, House Executive Document 60, 29th Cong., 1st sess., 355.
35. Polk Diary, October 17, 1846, vol. 2, 197.
36. Polk Diary, October 12, 1846, vol. 2, 183.
37. Marcy to Taylor, October 13, 1846, House Executive Document 60, 29th Cong., 1st sess., 355.
38. Scott to Marcy, November 12, 1846, House Executive Document 60, 29th Cong., 1st sess., 1271.
39. Polk Diary, November 19, 1846, vol. 2, 246.

40. Marcy to Scott, November 23, 1846, House Executive Document 60, 29th Cong., 1st sess., 836.
41. Polk to Congress, December 8, 1846, in James D. Richardson, ed., *Messages and Papers of the Presidents, 1789–1897*, vol. 5 (Washington, D.C.: 1908), 2324.
42. David M. Pletcher, *The Diplomacy of Annexation: Texas, Oregon, and the Mexican War* (Columbia, Mo.: 1973), 477, 495; M. S. Beach, " A Secret Mission to Mexico," *Scribner's Monthly*, 18 (May 1879).
43. Polk Diary, January 14, 1847, vol. 2, 325.
44. JB to Foreign Minister of Mexico, January 18, 1847, *Diplomatic Correspondence of the United States*, vol. 8, 197.
45. Pletcher, *Diplomacy*, 475.
46. *Ibid.*, 479.
47. Jose Monasterio to JB, February 22, 1847, *Diplomatic Correspondence of the United States*, vol. 8, 896.
48. Polk Diary, March 20, 1847, vol. 2, 433.
49. Polk Diary, December 6, 1846, vol. 2, 262.
50. Polk Diary, January 18, 1847, vol. 2, 338.
51. Polk Diary, April 10, 1847, vol. 2, 456–57.
52. *Ibid.*
53. NPT, undated draft letter to *Post*, New York, Trist Papers, LC.
54. JB to NPT, April 15, 1847, *Diplomatic Correspondence of the United States*, vol. 8, 205.
55. Jesse S. Reeves, "The Treaty of Guadelupe Hidalgo," *American Historical Review* vol. 10, (January 1905); 309, 324.
56. Polk Diary, October 21, 1847, vol. 3, 196.

Chapter Six: Bread Upon the Waters

1. William Marcy to Winfield Scott, April 14, 1847, House Executive Document 60, 29th Cong., 1st sess., 941.
2. NPT, draft letter to newspaper, 854, Nicholas P. Trist Papers, LC.
3. Scott to NPT, May 7, 1847, House Executive Document 60, 29th Cong., 1st sess., 960.
4. Marcy to Scott, November 23, 1847, House Executive Document 60, 29th Cong., 1st sess., 836.
5. Winfield Scott, *Memoirs of Lt. General Scott* (New York: 1864), 576.
6. June 12, 1847, entry in Milo Milton Quaife, ed., *The Diary of James K. Polk*, vol. 3 (Chicago: 1910), 57.
7. Scott, *Memoirs*, 576.
8. Nicholas P. Trist, Memorial to Congress, August 7, 1848, NA, Record Group 58, Original Miscellaneous Documents, No. 23–101, 30th Cong., 1st sess., House of Representatives, 7.
9. NPT to Scott, May 9, 1847, House Executive Document 60, 29th Cong., 1st sess., 822.
10. NPT memo, 1868, Trist Papers, LC; NPT to Samuel Felton, June 4, 1870, Trist Papers, LC.
11. NPT to Scott, May 20, 1847, in William R. Manning, ed., *Diplomatic Correspondence of the United States*, vol. 8 (Washington, D.C.: 1937), 903.
12. Scott to NPT, May 29, 1847, *Diplomatic Correspondence of the United States*, vol. 8, 904.

13. Scott to Marcy, May 28, 1847, House Executive Document 60, 29th Cong., 1st sess., 993.

14. Carlos Bosch Garcia, *La Historia de Las Relaciones Entre Mexico y Los Estados Unidos, 1819–1848* (Mexico D.F.: 1961), in Cecil Robinson, ed., *The View from Chapultepec: Mexican Writers on the Mexican-American War* (Tucson: 1989), 172.

15. Jose F. Ramirez, *Mexico During the War with the U.S.* (Columbia, Mo.: 1950), 131.

16. Lord Palmerston to Charles Bankhead, August 15, 1846, in Jasper Ridley *Lord Palmerston* (London: 1970), 305.

17. Virginia Randolph Trist to Ellen Randolph Coolidge, February 7, 1832, Coolidge Papers, UVA.

18. Nicholas P. Trist, Memorial to Congress, 1848, UVA, 19.

19. NPT to Bankhead, June 6, 1847, Trist Papers, LC.

20. Mexican Law of April 21, 1847, House Executive Document 60, 29th Cong., 1st sess., 951–52.

21. Ramirez, *Mexico*, 122–26, 129.

22. *Ibid.*, 131.

23. Edward Thornton to Bankhead, June 14, 1847, Foreign Office Archives, in Alice Katherine Shuster, "Nicholas Philip Trist: Peace Mission to Mexico," (Ph.D. diss., University of Pittsburgh, 1947), 70.

24. NPT to JB, draft, July 21, 1847, Nicholas P. Trist Papers, UVA.

25. NPT to JB, June 13, 1847, *Diplomatic Correspondence of the United States*, vol. 8, 912; NPT to JB, draft, July 21, 1847, Trist Papers, UVA.

26. NPT to JB, June 13, 1847, *Diplomatic Correspondence of the United States*, vol. 8, 908.

27. NPT to JB, draft, July 21, 1847, Trist Papers, UVA.

28. Domingo Ibarra to JB, June 22, 1847, *Diplomatic Correspondence of the United States*, vol. 8, 94.

29. NPT to JB, draft, July 21, 1847, Trist Papers, UVA.

30. NPT to Scott, June 25, 1847, Trist Papers, LC.

31. NPT to Scott, January 12, 1861, Trist Papers, LC.

32. Scott to Marcy, July 25, 1847, House Executive Document 60, 29th Cong., 1st sess., 1013.

33. Eba A. Lawton, ed., *An Artillery Officer in the Mexican War: Letters of Robert Anderson, Captain, 3rd Artillery, USA* (New York: 1911), 229.

34. NPT to JB, draft, July 21, 1847, Trist Papers, UVA.

35. NPT to Virginia Randolph Trist, October 18, 1847, Trist Papers, LC.

36. NPT to Thornton, July 3, 1847, Trist Papers, LC.

37. Scott to Persifor Smith, July 6, 1847, Trist Papers, LC; James Madison to NPT, June 6, 1829, Madison Papers, LC.

38. Lawton, *Robert Anderson*, 240.

39. NPT to JB, July 7, 1847, Trist Papers, LC; NPT to Virginia Randolph Trist, July 29, 1847, Trist Papers, LC.

40. NPT to JB, July 23, 1847, *Diplomatic Correspondence of the United States*, vol. 8 (Washington, D.C.: 1937), 916; Scott to Marcy, July 25, 1847, House Executive Document 60, 29th Cong., 1st sess., 1012.

41. NPT to Edward Thornton, July 15, 1847, Trist Papers, LC.

42. Thornton to NPT, July 8, 1847, Trist Papers, LC.

43. Chapter One, 20.

44. Polk to Congress, April 20, 1846, *Messages and Papers of the Presidents, 1789–1897*, vol. 5 (Washington, D.C.: 1908), 2285; Polk Diary, April 15, 1847, vol. 1, 331; George Ticknor Curtis *Life of Daniel Webster*, vol. 2 (New York: 1872), 266.

45. JB to John Slidell, March 12, 1847, *Diplomatic Correspondence of the United States*, vol. 8, 190.
46. N. C. Hughes, and R. P. Stonesifer, Jr., *The Life and Wars of Gideon J. Pillow* (Chapel Hill: 1993),48-50.
47. Gideon Pillow to Marcy, January 18, 1848, Court of Inquiry Records, 1848, NA.
48. *Ibid.*
49. Gideon Pillow, "Letters to the People of Tennessee" (pamphlet), Nashville, 1857.
50. Pillow to Marcy, January 18, 1848, Court of Inquiry Records, NA.
51. John A. Quitman to Marcy, March 9, 1848, in J.F.H. Claiborne, *Life and Correspondence of John A. Quitman*, vol. 1 (New York: 1860), 327.
52. NPT to Scott, July 16, 1847, Trist Papers, LC.
53. July 18, 1847, entry in W. A. Croffut, ed., *Fifty Years in Camp and Field: Diary of Major General Ethan Allen Hitchcock, USA* (New York: 1909), 267-68.
54. Quitman to Marcy, March 9, 1848, in Claiborne, *Quitman*, 327.
55. James Shields to Marcy, March 11, 1848, Court of Inquiry Records, NA.
56. Polk Diary, December 28, 1848, vol. 3, 262.
57. Hitchcock Diary, July 18, 1847, 267-68.
58. Scott to NPT, July 17, 1848, Trist Papers, LC.
59. NPT to JB, July 21, 1847 draft, Trist Papers, UVA; NPT to VRT, August 6, 1847, Trist Papers, LC.
60. Scott to Marcy, February 6, 1848, House Executive Document 60, 29th Cong., 1st sess., 1085.
61. Scott to Court of Inquiry, April 17, 1848, Trist Papers, LC.
62. Finding and Opinion of Court of Inquiry, Senate Executive Document 65, 30th Cong., 1st sess., 328-35.
63. Polk Diary, November 14, 1848, vol. 4, 196.
64. *North American*, Mexico City, October 5, 1847, and March 3, 1848.
65. Ministry of Relations of Mexico, *Memorial*, 1852; Pletcher, *Diplomacy* 524.
66. NPT to JB, October 26, 1847, *Diplomatic Correspondence of the United States*, vol. 8, 960.
67. NPT to JB, draft, July 21, 1847, Trist Papers, UVA.
68. Thornton to NPT, July 21, 1847, Trist Papers, LC; NPT to JB, July 23, 1847, *Diplomatic Correspondence of the United States*, vol. 8, 917.
69. NPT to JB, August 22, 1847, *Diplomatic Correspondence of the United States*, vol. 8, 928.
70. Pillow testimony, Court of Inquiry, April 1848, Court of Inquiry Records, NA.
71. George W. Kendall to *Picayune*, August 27, 1847, in *Picayune*, New Orleans, September 9, 1847; Kendall to *Picayune*, September 4, 1847, in *Picayune*, October 17, 1847.
72. Scott to Marcy, November 14, 1848, Senate Executive Document 34, 34th Cong., 3d sess., 25.
73. J. R. Pacheco to Mexican Congress, July 16, 1847, Senate Executive Document 52, 30th Cong., 1st sess., 303-5.
74. Hitchcock Diary, September 10, 1847, 299.
75. Ministry of Relations of Mexico, *Memorial*, 1852, U.S. Department of State Library.
76. *North American*, March 17, 1848.
77. Thornton to NPT, July 21, 1847, Trist Papers, LC (decoding completed by author).
78. NPT note, July 25, 1847, on copy of NPT to JB, July 23, 1847, Trist Papers, LC.
79. Hitchcock Diary, July 25, 1847, 269.
80. J. Jack Bauer, *The Mexican War, 1846-48* (New York: 1974), 286.

81. Hitchcock Diary, July 29, 1847, 269.
82. Thornton to NPT, July 29, 1847, Trist Papers, LC.
83. NPT to JB, July 31, 1847, *Diplomatic Correspondence of the United States*, vol. 8, 918.
84. Pillow to March, January 14, 1848, Court of Inquiry Records, NA.
85. *Ibid.*
86. Undated draft on envelope, Trist Papers, LC; Ethan Allen Hitchcock to *Sun*, New York, January 23, 1848, in Senate Executive Document 65, 39th Cong., 1st sess., 524.
87. Edward Mansfield, *Life and Military Services of Lt. General Winfield Scott* (New York: 1862), 223.

Chapter Seven: Too Much Blood Has Been Shed

1. NPT to JB, August 14, 1847, in William R. Manning, ed., *Diplomatic Correspondence of the United States*, vol. 8 (Washington, D.C.: 1937), 920.
2. Cadmus M. Wilcox, *History of the Mexican War* (Washington, D.C.: 1892), 341.
3. NPT to JB, August 14, 1847, *Diplomatic Correspondence of the United States*, vol. 8, 921.
4. NPT to JB, August 22, 1847, *Diplomatic Correspondence of the United States*, vol. 8, 924.
5. Matthew F. Steel, *American Campaigns*, vol. 1 (Washington D.C.: 1909), 113–15; J. Jack Bauer, *The Mexican War: 1846–48* (New York: 1974), 291–301.
6. NPT recollection, Trist Papers, LC.
7. Douglas S. Freeman, *R. E. Lee*, vol. 1 (New York: 1936), 249–72.
8. Bauer, *Mexican War*, 295.
9. Winfield Scott to Court of Inquiry, April 17, 1848, Court of Inquiry Records, NA.
10. *Ibid.*
11. NPT to JB, August 22, 1847, *Diplomatic Correspondence of the United States*, vol. 8, 925.
12. Ethan Allen Hitchcock to wife, August 24, 1847, Hitchcock Papers, LC.
13. Scott to William Marcy, September 18, 1847, Trist Papers, LC.
14. Ulysses S. Grant to Julia Dent, August 22, 1847, *Papers of U. S. Grant*, vol. 1 (Carbondale, Ill.: 1967), 144.
15. Scott to Court of Inquiry, April 17, 1848, Court of Inquiry Records, NA; Winfield Scott, *Memoirs of Lt. General Scott* (New York: 1864), 498.
16. William D. Wilkins to Ross Wilkins, October 22, 1847, in G. W. Smith, and C. Judah, eds., *Chronicles of the Gringos* (Albuquerque: 1968), 270.
17. Ramon Alcaraz, *The Other Side* (New York: 1849), 301.
18. NPT to JB, December 6, 1847, *Diplomatic Correspondence of the United States*, vol. 8, 1020.
19. Scott, *Memoirs*, 498.
20. Hitchcock Diary, August 22, 1847, 284.
21. J. R. Pacheco to JB, August 20, 1847, *Diplomatic Correspondence of the United States*, vol. 8, 921.
22. Edward Mansfield, *Life and Military Services of Lt. General Winfield Scott* (New York: 1862), 433.
23. Scott, *Memoirs*, 499.
24. Scott to Santa Anna, August 21, 1847, *Diplomatic Correspondence of the United States*, vol. 8, 922.

25. Manuel Alcorta to Scott, August 21, 1847, *Diplomatic Correspondence of the United States*, vol. 8, 923.
26. NPT to JB, August 22, 1847, *Diplomatic Correspondence of the United States*, vol. 8, 924.
27. Scott to Marcy, August 28, 1847, Senate Executive Document 1, 30th Cong., 1st sess., 303–15.
28. Scott to Marcy, August 28, 1847, Senate Executive Document 1, 30th Cong., 1st sess., 303–15; Bauer, *Mexican War*, 301.
29. Ehrain Kirby Smith, *To Mexico with Scott* (Cambridge, Mass.: 1917), 208.
30. Senate Executive Document 52, 30th Cong., 1st sess., 310–12.
31. Roswell Ripley, *War with Mexico*, vol. 2 (New York: 1849), 344.
32. Wilcox, *Mexican War*, 426; Francis Collins, August 21, 1848, "Journal of Francis Collins, an Artillery Officer in the Mexican War," *Quarterly Publication of the Historical and Philosophical Society of Ohio*, vol. 10 (1915), 83; John Sedgwick to sister, August 28, 1847, *Correspondence of John Sedgwick, Major General*, vol. 1 (New York: 1902), 113.

Chapter Eight: The Painful Necessity

1. NPT statement, Senate Report 261, 41st Cong., 2d sess.
2. Cadmus M. Wilcox, *History of the Mexican War* (Washington, D.C.: 1892), 415; George Lockhart Rives, *The United States and Mexico, 1821–48*, vol. 2 (New York: 1913), 510.
3. NPT to JB, August 29, 1847, in William R. Manning, ed., *Diplomatic Correspondence of the United States*, vol. 8 (Washington, D.C.: 1937), 932.
4. Ramon Alcaraz, *The Other Side* (New York: 1849), 320.
5. P. G. Beauregard Diary, August 21, 1847, in G. W. Smith, and C. Judah, eds., *Chronicles of the Gringos* (Albuquerque: 1968), 250.
6. Roswell Ripley, *War with Mexico*, vol. 2 (New York: 1949), 649.
7. NPT to JB, September 4, 1847, *Diplomatic Correspondence of the United States*, vol. 8, 936.
8. NPT to JB, December 6, 1847, *Diplomatic Correspondence of the United States*, vol. 8, 1007; August 29, 1846, entry in W. A. Croffut, ed., *Fifty Years in Camp and Field: Diary of Major General Ethan Allen Hitchcock, USA* (New York: 1909), 289; Justin H. Smith, *The War with Mexico*, vol. 2 (New York: 1919), 135.
9. NPT to JB, September 4, 1847, *Diplomatic Correspondence of the United States*, vol. 8, 933–35.
10. NPT to Mexican commissioners, September 7, 1847, *Diplomatic Correspondence of the United States*, vol. 8, 948.
11. NPT to JB, December 6, 1847, *Diplomatic Correspondence of the United States*, vol. 8, 1012–15.
12. *Ibid.*
13. NPT to JB, August 22, 1847, *Diplomatic Correspondence of the United States*, vol. 8, 926.
14. NPT to JB, August 24, 1847 *Diplomatic Correspondence of the United States*, vol. 8, 927.
15. Smith, *War with Mexico*, vol. 2, 135.
16. NPT note, September 1847, Trist Papers, LC.
17. Santa Anna to Manuel Rejon, August 31, 1847, in Raphael Semmes, *The Campaign of General Scott in the Valley of Mexico* (Cincinnati: 1852), 303–4.
18. NPT to JB, September 4, 1847, *Diplomatic Correspondence of the United States*, vol. 8, 940.

19. John Black to JB, May 26, 1846, *Diplomatic Correspondence of the United States*, vol. 8, 855; George Lockhart Rives, *The United States and Mexico, 1821–48*, vol. 2 (New York: 1913), 518.

20. NPT to JB, November 27, 1847, *Diplomatic Correspondence of the United States*, vol. 8, 982.

21. Charles Bankhead to Lord Palmerston, September 28, 1847, in Rives, *U.S. and Mexico*, vol. 2, 510.

22. NPT to JB, October 25, 1847, *Diplomatic Correspondence of the United States*, vol. 8, 963.

23. Mexican commissioners to NPT, September 6, 1847, *Diplomatic Correspondence of the United States*, vol. 8, 940–45.

24. *Ibid.*

25. "Contestaciones," Senate Executive Document 52, 30th Cong., 1st sess., 350–82.

26. J. Jack Bauer, *The Mexican War: 1846–48* (New York: 1974), 307.

27. NPT to Mexican commissioners, September 7, 1847, *Diplomatic Correspondence of the United States*, vol. 8, 945.

28. NPT to Virginia Randolph Trist, September 28, 1847, Trist Papers, LC.

29. Mexican commissioners to Minister of Foreign Relations to Mexico, September 7, 1847, in Wilcox, *Mexican War*, 548.

30. Brantz Mayer, *Mexico—Aztec, Spanish, and Republican*, vol. 1 (Hartford: 1852), 406.

31. Bauer, *Mexican War*, 308–11.

32. Fayette Copeland, *Kendall of the Picayune* (Norman, Okla.: 1943), 318.

33. J.F.H. Claiborne, *Life and Correspondence of John A. Quitman*, vol. 1 (New York: 1860), 353; Bauer, *Mexican War*, 312.

34. Kendall to *Picayune*, September 13, 1847, in *Picayune*, New Orleans, October 15, 1847.

35. Nicholas P. Trist, Memorial to Congress, 1848, Trist Papers, UVA, 73.

36. Mayer, *Mexico*, vol. 1, 431–33.

Chapter Nine: Mr. Trist Is Recalled

1. JB to John C. Fremont, June 11, 1847, Buchanan Papers, LC.

2. June 12, 1847, entry in Milo Milton Quaife, ed., *The Diary of James K. Polk*, vol. 3 (Chicago: 1910), 57.

3. William Marcy to Winfield Scott, June 14, 1847, House Executive Document 60, 29th Cong., 1st sess., 975.

4. JB to NPT, June 14, 1847, in William R. Manning, ed., *Diplomatic Correspondence of the United States*, vol. 8 (Washington, D.C.: 1937), 208.

5. JB to NPT, July 13, 1847, *Diplomatic Correspondence of the United States*, vol. 8, 210; Polk Diary, July 17, 1847, vol. 3, 91.

6. JB to NPT, personal, July 13, 1847, Nicholas P. Trist Papers, LC.

7. Polk Diary, September 7, 1847, vol. 3, 163.

8. *Ibid.*

9. NPT to JB, August 29, 1847, *Diplomatic Correspondence of the United States*, vol. 8, 931; Polk Diary, September 14, 1847, vol. 3, 171.

10. Polk Diary, September 15, 1847, vol. 3, 173.

11. *Ibid.*

12. Marcy to P. M. Wetmore, September 26, 1847, in Norman Graebner, "Party Politics and the Trist Mission," *Journal of Southern History*, vol. 10 (May 1953), 142.

NOTES / *Chapter Ten* 219

13. Senate Executive Document 52, 30th Cong., 1st sess., 350–82; *Union*, Washington, October 4, 1847.
14. Polk Diary, September 27 to October 4, 1847, vol. 3, 183–85; JB to NPT, personal, October 7, 1847, Trist Papers, LC.
15. Polk Diary, October 5, 1847, vol. 3, 185.
16. JB to NPT, October 6, 1847, *Diplomatic Correspondence of the United States*, vol. 8, 216.
17. JB to NPT, personal, October 24, 1847, Trist Papers, LC.
18. *Weekly Union*, Washington, October 9, 1847.
19. NPT to JB, December 6, 18747, *Diplomatic Correspondence of the United States*, vol. 8, 999.
20. JB to NPT, personal, October 7, 1847, Trist Papers, LC.
21. Marcy to Scott, October 6, 1947, House Executive Document 60, 29th Cong., 1st sess., 1007.
22. *Ibid.*
23. NPT to JB, September 27, 1847, *Diplomatic Correspondence of the United States*, vol. 8, 953.
24. Polk Diary, October 21, 1847, vol. 3, 196.
25. JB to NPT, October 25, 1847, *Diplomatic Correspondence of the United States*, vol. 8, 217.
26. JB to NPT, personal, October 25, 1847, Trist Papers, LC.
27. Paul Lambert, "The Movement for the Acquisition of All Mexico," *Journal of the West*, vol. 1 (April 1972), 317–27.
28. John Schroeder, *Mr. Polk's War: American Opposition and Dissent, 1847–48* (Madison, Wisc.: 1973), 128.
29. *Sun*, Baltimore, October 5, 1847, in Frederick Merk, *Manifest Destiny and Mission in American History* (New York: 1966), 44.
30. *Sun*, New York, October 22, 1847, and *Public Ledger*, Philadelphia, October 25, 1847, in Merk, *Manifest Destiny*, 122–25; *National Whig*, Washington, November 10, 1847, in John D. P. Fuller, *The Movement for the Acquisition of All Mexico, 1847–48* (Baltimore: 1936), 84.
31. Polk Diary, November 9, 1847, vol. 3, 216.
32. Marcy to Scott, November 19, 1827, House Executive Document 60, 29th Cong., 1st sess., 1014.
33. NPT to JB, September 27 and October 1, 1847, *Diplomatic Correspondence of the United States*, vol. 8, 953, 957.
34. Polk Diary, November 18, 1847, vol. 3, 225.
35. Polk Diary, November 20, 1847, vol. 3, 226.
36. NPT to JB, October 25 and 31, 1847, *Diplomatic Correspondence of the United States*, vol. 8, 958, 969.
37. Polk to Congress, December 7, 1847, James D. Richardson, ed., *Messages and Papers of the Presidents, 1789–1897*, vol. 5 (Washington, D.C.: 1908), 2389.
38. Polk Diary, December 18, 1847, vol. 3, 250–51.

Chapter Ten: I Will Make a Treaty

1. NPT to JB, January 25, 1848, in William R. Manning, ed., *Diplomatic Correspondence of the United States*, vol. 8 (Washington, D.C.: 1937), 1035.
2. NPT to JB, September 27, 1847, *Diplomatic Correspondence of the United States*, vol. 8, 956.

3. George Lockhart Rives, *The United States and Mexico, 1821–48*, vol. 2 (New York: 1913), 586.

4. *North American*, Mexico City, October 15, 1847.

5. Winfield Scott to Gideon Pillow, October 2 and 3, 1847, House Executive Document 60, 29th Cong., 1st sess., 1016, 1018.

6. Charles W. Eliot, *Winfield Scott* (New York: 1937), 568.

7. Otis A. Singletary, *The Mexican War* (Chicago: 1960), 135–36.

8. J. Jack Bauer, *The Mexican War: 1846–48* (New York: 1974), 372.

9. William J. Worth to William Marcy, October 30, 1847, in John D. P. Fuller, *The Movement for the Acquisition of All Mexico, 1846–48* (Baltimore: 1936), 94.

10. John A. Quitman to A. S. Foote, October 15, 1847, in G. W. Smith and C. Judah, eds., *Chronicles of the Gringos* (Albuquerque: 1968), 395.

11. JB to James Shields, April 23, 1847, *Works of James Buchanan*, vol. 7 (Philadelphia: 1908–11), 286.

12. Enclosure with NPT to JB, September 28, 1847, Marcy Papers, LC, in David M. Pletcher, *The Diplomacy of Annexation: Texas, Oregon, and the Mexican War* (Columbia, Mo.: 1973), 536.

13. *Delta*, New Orleans, November 27, 1847.

14. *Delta*, September 23, 1847; *American Star*, Mexico City, October 28, 1847.

15. NPT to Edward Thornton, December 4, 1847, *Diplomatic Correspondence of the United States*, vol. 8, 984.

16. Nicholas P. Trist, Memorial to Congress, August 7, 1848, NA, Record Group 58, Original Misc. Documents No. 23–101, 30th Cong., 1st sess., House of Representatives, 26.

17. NPT to Luis de la Rosa, October 20, 1847, Nicholas P. Trist Papers, LC.

18. NPT to JB, November 27, 1847, *Diplomatic Correspondence of the United States*, vol. 8, 982.

19. Thornton to NPT, November 22, 1847, Trist Papers, LC.

20. Manuel de la Peña y Peña to NPT, November 22, 1847, *Diplomatic Correspondence of the United States*, vol. 8, 973.

21. NPT statement, Senate Report 261, 41st Cong., 2d sess., July 14, 1870.

22. Thornton to NPT, November 22, 1847, Trist Papers, LC.

23. NPT to Peña, November 24, 1847, *Diplomatic Correspondence of the United States*, vol. 8, 980.

24. NPT to Bernardo Couto, November 24, 1847, in Rives, *U.S. and Mexico*, vol. 2, 596.

25. James Freaner to *Delta*, September 17, 1847, in *Delta*, New Orleans, October 15, 1847.

26. Freaner to *Delta*, November 26, 1847, in *Delta*, December 20, 1847.

27. Scott to Marcy, December 25, 1847, House Executive Document 60, 29th Cong., 1st sess., 1046.

28. NPT to TJ, August 3, 1822, Jefferson Papers, LC.

29. NPT to JB, October 25, 1847, *Diplomatic Correspondence of the United States*, vol. 8, 963.

30. NPT to JB, December 6, 1847, *Diplomatic Correspondence of the United States*, vol. 8, 888.

31. NPT, draft, 1848, Nicholas P. Trist Papers, UNC.

32. NPT draft, "To My Country," undated, Trist-Burke papers, UVA.

33. NPT to JB, September 4, 1847, *Diplomatic Correspondence of the United States*, vol. 8, 938.

34. NPT to JB, November 27, 1847, *Diplomatic Correspondence of the United States*, vol. 8, 980; NPT to VRT, November 28, 1847, Trist Papers, LC.

35. NPT to Thornton, December 4, 1847, *Diplomatic Correspondence of the United States*, vol. 8, 985.
36. Nicholas P. Trist, Memorial to Congress, 1848, 10, UVA.
37. April 14, 1847, entry in Milo Milton Quaife, ed., *The Diary of James K. Polk*, vol. 3 (Chicago: 1910), 470.
38. Freaner to *Delta*, December 1, 1847, in *Delta*, New Orleans, December 24, 1847.
39. NPT undated draft, "Links of Proof," Trist Papers, LC.
40. NPT, Memorial to Congress, 1848, 26, UVA.
41. NPT to S. M. Felton, April 5, 1870, Trist Papers, LC.
42. Couto to Peña, December 3, 1847, in Rives, *U.S. and Mexico*, vol. 2, 597.
43. NPT to Thornton, December 4, 1847, *Diplomatic Correspondence of the United States*, vol. 8, 984.
44. NPT to VRT, December 4, 1847, Trist Papers, LC.
45. NPT to JB, December 4, 1847, *Diplomatic Correspondence of the United States*, vol. 8, 987.
46. *Ibid.*, 990.
47. *Ibid.*, 995.
48. *Ibid.*, 1000.
49. Thornton to NPT, December 11, 1847, Trist Papers, LC; Winfield Scott, *Memoirs of Lt. General Scott* (New York: 1864), 576.
50. Percy Doyle to Lord Palmerston, December 13, 1847, in Rives, *U.S. and Mexico*, vol. 2, 600.
51. Scott, General Order 370, December 15, 1847, House Executive Document 60, 29th Cong., 1st sess., 1050.
52. Scott to Marcy, December 14, 1847, House Executive Document 60, 29th Cong., 1st sess., 1039.
53. NPT to JB, December 29, 1847, *Diplomatic Correspondence of the United States*, vol. 8, 1028.
54. *Ibid.*

Chapter Eleven: An Exceedingly Laborious Negotiation

1. NPT notes, January 2, 1848, meeting with Mexican commissioners, Nicholas P. Trist Papers, LC.
2. NPT notes, January 3, 1848, meeting with Mexican commissioners, Trist Papers, LC.
3. NPT, draft letter to New York *Post*, 1851, Trist Papers, LC.
4. JB to NPT, July 13, 1847, in William R. Manning, ed., *Diplomatic Correspondence of the United States*, vol. 8 (Washington, D.C.: 1937), 213.
5. NPT to JB, January 25, 1848, *Diplomatic Correspondence of the United States*, vol. 8, 1049.
6. JB to NPT, July 13, 1847, *Diplomatic Correspondence of the United States*, vol. 8, 213.
7. Hubert Howe Bancroft, *Works of Hubert H. Bancroft*, vol. 17 (San Francisco: 1863–90), 470.
8. Odie B. Faulk, *Too Far North ... Too Far South* (Los Angeles: 1967), 58.
9. Bancroft, *Works*, vol. 17, 470.
10. David Hunter Miller, *Treaties and Other International Acts of the United States of America*, vol. 5 (Washington, D.C.: 1942), 420.

11. JB to NPT, April 15, 1847, *Diplomatic Correspondence of the United States*, vol. 8, 205.

12. Mexican commissioners to NPT, September 6, 1847, *Diplomatic Correspondence of the United States*, vol. 8, 941.

13. NPT, note on copy of JB to NPT, July 13, 1847, Trist Papers, LC.

14. NPT, memo on January 4, 1848, meeting with Mexican commissioners, Trist Papers, LC; Hunter Miller, *Treaties*, vol. 5, 318.

15. Hunter Miller, *Treaties*, vol. 5, 317.

16. JB to NPT, July 19, 1847, *Diplomatic Correspondence of the United States*, vol. 8, 214.

17. NPT memorandum, January 7, 1848, *Diplomatic Correspondence of the United States*, vol. 8, 1044.

18. *Ibid.*, 1047.

19. *Ibid.*, 1049.

20. Virginia Randolph Trist to Tuckerman, July 8, 1864, Nicholas P. Trist Papers, UNC, in Robert W. Drexler, *Guilty of Making Peace: A Biography of Nicholas P. Trist* (Lanham, MD.: 1991), 129–30.

21. NPT to JB, January 25, 1848, *Diplomatic Correspondence of the United States*, vol. 8, 1043.

22. *Ibid.*

23. Marcy to Scott, December 14, 1847, House Executive Document 60, 29th Cong., 1st sess., 1037.

24. Scott to Marcy, January 28, 1848, in J.F.H. Claiborne, *Life and Correspondence of John A. Quitman*, vol. 1 (New York: 1860), 320–21.

25. NPT to JB, January 12, 1848, *Diplomatic Correspondence of the United States*, vol. 8, 1034.

26. *Ibid.*

27. *North American*, Mexico City, January 22, 1848.

28. Mexican commissioners to Luis de la Rosa, January 23, 1848, in George Lockhart Rives, *The United States and Mexico, 1821–48*, vol. 2 (New York: 1913), 60–65; Percy Doyle to NPT, January 23, 1848, Trist Papers, LC.

29. NPT to JB, January 25, 1848, *Diplomatic Correspondence of the United States*, vol. 8, 1034.

30. Rosa to Mexican commissioners, January 26, 1847, in Rives, *U.S. and Mexico*, vol. 2, 604.

31. Rosa to Mexican commissioners, January 27, 1847, in Rives, *U.S. and Mexico*, vol. 2, 609.

32. NPT to Scott, January 28, 1848, Trist Papers, LC.

33. Doyle to Lord Palmerston, February 1, 1848, Foreign Office Archives, cited in Rives, *U.S. and Mexico*, vol. 2, 608.

34. NPT to Mexican commissioners, January 29, 1848, Trist Papers, LC.

35. Doyle to Rosa, January 29, 1848, Foreign Office Archives, cited in Rives, *U.S. and Mexico*, vol. 2, 609.

36. Justin Smith, *The War with Mexico*, vol. 2 (New York: 1919), 240.

37. Charles W. Elliott, *Winfield Scott* (New York: 1937), 561.

38. Mexican commissioners to Rosa, January 29, 1848, in Rives, *U.S. and Mexico*, vol. 2, 611.

39. James A. Magner, *Men of Mexico* (Milwaukee: 1942), 342; Elliott, *Winfield Scott*, 563–64.

40. Scott to J. M. Clayton, March 1852, New York Public Library.

41. Lloyd Lewis, *Captain Sam Grant* (Boston: 1950), 272.

42. Rosa to Mexican commissioners, January 31, 1848, in Rives, *U.S. and Mexico*, vol. 2, 612.
43. NPT to JB, February 2, 1848, *Diplomatic Correspondence of the United States*, vol. 8, 1059.

Chapter Twelve: A Solemn Duty

1. *Republican*, St. Louis, November 22, 1847; *Sun*, Baltimore, December 6, 1847.
2. December 11, 1847, entry in Milo Milton Quaife, ed., *The Diary of James K. Polk*, vol. 3 (Chicago: 1910), 246; Polk to Pillow, December 19, 1847, in J. Jack Bauer, *The Mexican War: 1846-48* (New York: 1974), 372.
3. JB to NPT, December 21, 1847, in William R. Manning, ed., *Diplomatic Correspondence of the United States*, vol. 8 (Washington, D.C.: 1937), 218.
4. Polk Diary, February 16, 1848, vol. 3, 341.
5. Polk Diary, December 11, 1847, vol. 3, 246.
6. JB to NPT, December 21, 1847, *Diplomatic Correspondence of the United States*, vol. 8, 218; Marcy to Scott, December 24, 1847, Court of Inquiry Records, NA.
7. Polk Diary, December 30, 1847, vol. 3, 267.
8. NPT to JB, November 7, 1847, *Diplomatic Correspondence of the United States*, vol. 8, 972; Polk Diary, December 31, 1847, vol. 3, 269.
9. Polk Diary, January 3, 1848, vol. 3, 290.
10. Polk Diary, January 4, 1848, vol. 3, 294.
11. Polk Diary, January 5, 1848, vol. 3, 296.
12. Bauer, *Mexican War*, 370.
13. Polk Diary, January 7, 1848, vol. 3, 288.
14. William Marcy to Winfield Scott, January 13, 1848, House Executive Document 60, 29th Cong., 1st sess., 1044.
15. Polk Diary, January 9, 1948, vol. 3, 294.
16. Polk Diary, January 15, 1848, vol. 3, 300.
17. *Ibid.*
18. Marcy to Scott, October 6, 1847, House Executive Document 60, 29th Cong., 1st sess., 1008.
19. Polk Diary, January 23, 1848, vol. 3, 310.
20. Polk Diary, January 25, 1848, vol. 3, 315.
21. Polk Diary, January 26, 1848, vol. 3, 315.
22. Polk Diary, February 7, 1848, vol. 3, 329.
23. James Freaner to NPT, January 18, 1848, Nicholas P. Trist Papers, LC.
24. NPT undated draft, Trist Papers, LC.
25. Fayette Copeland, *Kendall of the Picayune* (Norman, Okla.: 1943), 235-38.
26. Polk Diary, February 20 and 21, 1848, vol. 3, 347-50.
27. James P. Shenton, *Robert John Walker* (New York: 1961), 137.
28. Polk Diary, February 21, 1848, vol. 3, 347-48.
29. Polk to Senate, February 22, 1848, in James D. Richardson, ed., *Messages and Papers of the Presidents, 1789-1897*, vol. 5 (Washington, D.C.: 1897), 242.
30. NPT to JB, December 29, 1847, and January 12, 1848, *Diplomatic Correspondence of the United States*, vol. 8, 1028-34.
31. Polk Diary, February 24 and 25, 1848, vol. 3, 359-61.
32. Frederick Merk, *A History of the Westward Movement* (New York: 1978), 372.
33. Robert S. Henry, *The Story of the Mexican War* (Indianapolis: 1950), 387.
34. Polk Diary, February 28, 1848, vol. 3, 365.

35. Claude Moore Fuess, *Daniel Webster*, vol. 2 (Hamden: Conn.: 1963), 82.
36. Polk Diary, February 28, 1848, vol. 3, 365.
37. Polk to U.S. Senate, February 29, 1848, in Richardson, *Messages and Papers*, vol. 5, 2425.
38. Kendall to *Picayune*, February 4, 1848, in Robert A. Brent, "Reaction in the U.S. to Nicholas Trist's Mission to Mexico," *Revista de Historica de America*, vol. 35 (1953), 105–18.
39. Manuel Crescencio Rejon, translated from "Observaciones Sobre Los Tratados de Guadelupe," *Pansamiento Politicio* (Mexico D.F.: 1968), 116–22, in Cecil Robinson, ed., *The View from Chapultepec: Mexican Writers on the Mexican-American War* (Tucson: 1989), 100.
40. Manuel de la Peña y Peña, "An Address in Support of the Treaty of Guadalupe Hidalgo," translated from Alberto Maria Carreno, *Mexico y Los Estados Unidos de America* (Mexico D.F.: 1962), 192–94, in Robinson, *Mexican Writers*, 109–12.

Chapter Thirteen: A Firm and Universal Peace

1. David Hunter Miller, "Treaty of Guadelupe Hidalgo," *Treaties and Other International Acts of the United States of America*, vol. 5 (Washington: 1942), 236–438.
2. Polk to Congress, December 5, 1848, in James D. Richardson, *Messages and Papers of the Presidents, 1789–1895*, vol. 5 (Washington, D.C.: 1908), 2446.
3. Polk to Congress, July 6, 1848, Richardson, *Messages and Papers*, vol. 5, 2438–39.
4. JB to Minister of Foreign Affairs, March 18, 1848, *Diplomatic Correspondence of the United States*, vol. 8 (Washington, D.C.: 1937), 224–25.
5. Proclamation to the People of Mexico, enclosure with William Marcy to Zachary Taylor, June 4, 1846, House Executive Document 60, 29th Cong., 1st sess., 167; Proclamation of General S. V. Kearny, August 22, 1846, House Executive Document 60, 29th Cong., 1st sess., 170.
6. Polk to Congress, December 7, 1847, in Richardson, *Messages and Papers*, vol. 5, 2390.
7. NPT to JB, January 25, 1848, in William R. Manning, ed., *Diplomatic Correspondence of the United States*, vol. 8 (Washington, D.C.: 1937), 1058.
8. Manuel de la Peña y Peña, "An Address in Support of the Treaty of Guadelupe Hidalgo" (translated from A. M. Carreno, *Mexico y Los Estados Unidos de America* [Mexico: 1962], 192–94), in Cecil Robinson, ed., *The View from Chapultepec: Mexican Writers on the Mexican War* (Tucson: 1989), 107.
9. Frederick S. Dunn, *The Diplomatic Protection of Americans in Mexico* (New York: 1933), 66.
10. NPT to JB, January 25, 1848, *Diplomatic Correspondence of the United States*, vol. 8 (Washington, D.C.: 1937), 1051.
11. Justin H. Smith, *The War with Mexico*, vol. 1 (New York: 1919), 134.
12. Thomas Hart Benton, *Thirty Years View*, vol. 2 (New York: 1856), 710.
13. Dunn, *Diplomatic Protection*, 51–53.
14. Frederick Merk, *Manifest Destiny and Mission in American History* (New York: 1966), 140–43; J. Jack Bauer, *The Mexican War: 1847–48* (New York: 1974), 343.
15. January 2, 1848, entry in Milo Milton Quaife, ed., *The Diary of James K. Polk*, vol. 3 (Chicago: 1910), 291.
16. Mexican commissioners to NPT, September 6, 1847, *Diplomatic Correspondence of the United States*, vol. 8 (Washington, D.C.: 1937), 944.
17. NPT, draft "Additional Article," December 21, 1847, Nicholas P. Trist Papers,

LC; David M. Pletcher, *The Diplomacy of Annexation: Texas, Oregon, and the Mexican War* (Columbia, Mo.: 1973), 524.

18. Paul N. Garber, *The Gadsden Treaty* (Pittsburgh: 1924), 167; Senate Executive Document 97, 32d Cong., 1st sess.

19. Fred J. Rippy, *The U.S. and Mexico* (New York: 1926), 62.

20. Samuel F. Bemis, *Diplomatic History of the United States* (New York: 1942), 325–26.

Chapter Fourteen: A Bold and Firm Course

1. Charles Sellers, *James K. Polk: Continentalist, 1843–46* (Princeton: 1966), 467.
2. David M. Pletcher, *The Diplomacy of Annexation: Texas, Oregon, and the Mexican War* (Columbia, Mo.: 1973), 693.
3. *Ibid.*

Epilogue: A Friend of Peace

1. NPT to Virginia Randolph Trist, November 28, 1847, Nicholas P. Trist Papers, LC.
2. Nicholas P. Trist, Memorial to Congress, 1848, UVA.
3. William O. Butler to NPT, March 17, 1848; NPT to Butler, March 17, 1848; Butler to NPT, March 18, 1848; NPT to Butler, March 18, Trist Papers, LC.
4. Ulysses S. Grant, *Personal Memoirs of U. S. Grant*, vol. 1 (New York: 1888), 173.
5. Alfred Hoyt Bill, *Rehearsal for Conflict: The War with Mexico, 1846–48* (New York: 1969), 319.
6. NPT recollection, undated, Trist Papers, LC.
7. Thomas Hart Benton, *Thirty Years View*, vol. 2 (New York: 1856), 711.
8. Norman A. Graebner, *Empire on the Pacific* (New York: 1955), 207.
9. NPT to Speaker of the U.S. House of Representatives, August 7, 1848, *Congressional Glove*, 30th Cong., 1st sess., 1057–58.
10. Nicholas P. Trist Memorial to Congress, August 7, 1848, NA, Record Group 58, Original Miscellaneous Documents, #23-101, 30th Cong., 1st sess., House of Representatives.
11. NPT to Virginia Randolph Trist, February 1, 1848, Trist Papers, LC.
12. Senate Report 261, 41st Cong., 2d sess., Trist Papers, LC; *Evening Telegraph*, Philadelphia, February 11, 1874.
13. Thomas Hart Benton, *Thirty Years View*, vol. 2 (New ;York: 1856), 711.
14. J.F.H. Claiborne, *Life and Correspondence of John A. Quitman*, vol. 1 (New York: 1860), 312–13.
15. Jesse S. Reeves, *American Diplomacy Under Tyler and Polk* (Baltimore: 1907); George Lockhart Rives, *The United States and Mexico, 1821–48* (New York: 1913); Justin Smith, *The War with Mexico* (New York: 1919).
16. Edward G. Bourne, "A Proposed Absorption of Mexico in 1847–48," *Annual Report of the American Historical Association for 1899* (Washington, D.C.: 1900), 165–66.
17. John D. P. Fuller, *The Movement for the Acquisition of All Mexico* (Baltimore: 1936), 93.
18. Thomas A. Bailey, *A Diplomatic History of the American People* (New York: 1946), 278.
19. Glyndon Van Deusen, *The Jacksonian Era* (New York: 1959), 239.

20. Robert A. May, *John A. Quitman: Old South Crusader* (Baton Rouge: 1985), 196–97.

21. Polk to Congress, July 6, 1848, in James D. Richardson, ed., *Messages and Papers of the Presidents, 1789–1897*, vol. 5 (Washington, D.C.: 1908), 2441.

22. Marcy to P. M. Wetmore, January 28, 1848, in Ivor D. Spencer, *The Victor and the Spoils: A Life of William L. Marcy* (Providence: 1959), 172.

23. Thomas P. Hietala, *Manifest Design: Anxious Aggrandizement in Late Jacksonian America* (Ithaca, N.Y.: 1985), 152–66.

24. JB to James Shields, *The Works of James Buchanan*, vol. 6 (Philadelphia: 1908–11), 286.

25. *National Intelligencer*, Washington, D.C., October 15, 1852.

26. Hietala, *Manifest Design*, 162.

27. Frederick Merk, *Manifest Destiny and Mission in American History* (New York: 1963), 192–93.

28. Merk, *Manifest Destiny*, 171; Margaret L. Coit, *John C. Calhoun* (Boston: 1950), 443.

29. June 30, 1846, entry in Milo Milton Quaife, ed., *The Diary of James K. Polk*, vol. 1 (Chicago: 1910), 497.

30. Taylor to Adjutant General, October 15, 1846, House Executive Document 60, 29th Cong., 1st sess., 353.

31. Polk Diary, January 2, 1848, vol. 3, 291.

32. James Gadsden to John C. Calhoun, "Correspondence Addressed to Calhoun," *Annual Report of the American Historical Association for the Year 1929* (Washington, D.C.: 1930), 426.

33. Polk Diary, January 23, 1847, vol. 2, 350.

34. Polk Diary, January 2, 1848, vol. 3, 291.

35. Polk Diary, February 21, 1848, vol. 3, 347.

36. Robert S. Henry, *The Story of the Mexican War* (Indianapolis: 1950), 357.

Index

Aberdeen, Earl of (British foreign sec.) 28, 29
Adams, John Quincy (U.S. sec. of state, president) 8, 17, 18, 31
Alcorta, Lino Jose (Mexican brig. gen., minister of war) 114
"All Mexico" movement for annexation of 132, 139, 140, 142–144, 150, 158, 162, 169, 172, 187, 189, 193, 198, 200
Allen, William (U.S. senator, Ohio) 82
Almonte, Juan N. (Mexican min. to U.S.) 29, 33, 68, 69
American Star (American newspaper in Mexico City) 141, 142, 159
Ampudia, Maj. Gen. Pedro de (Mexico) 25, 63, 67, 71
Anaya, Pedro (Mexican gen., prov. president) 141, 157
Anderson, Capt. Robert (U.S.) 98
Arista, Gen. Mariano (Mexico) 39, 40, 56, 63, 64, 67, 69, 74, 75
Arizona 17, 175, 196
Arrangoiz (Mexican consul in New Orleans) 113
Atocha, Col. Alexander (Spanish) 57, 58, 64, 71, 84, 86, 87, 184
Atristain, Commissioner Miguel (Mexico) 116, 149, 151, 163
Austin, Stephen (Texas founder) 18, 37
Ayolta, Mexico 108, 109

Bailey, Thomas A. (historian) 192
Baja (Lower) California 89, 155, 156, 180, 195
Bancroft, George (U.S. sec. of the navy) 43, 50, 60, 71, 84

Bancroft, Hubert (historian) 154
Bankhead, Charles (British min. to Mexico) 95, 96, 104, 105, 114, 119, 141
Baranda, Manuel (Mexican for. min.) 95
Barbour, Major Philip (U.S.) 64
Bartlett, John Russell (U.S. boundary commissioner) 154
Bartlett-Conde Line 154, 155
Bauer, K. Jack (biographer, historian) 67, 120
Beach, Moses (editor, U.S. agent in Mexico) 86
Beauregard, Lt. P.G. (U.S.) 110
Behohlavek, John M. (historian) 20
Benton, Thomas Hart (U.S. senator, Missouri) 7, 50, 51, 71, 74, 82, 87, 88, 89, 171, 178, 188, 191\
Bergeron, Paul (historian) 42
Black, John (U.S. consul in Mexico) 47, 48, 56, 69, 71, 81
Black Hawk War 80
Bourne, Edward G. (historian) 192
Bravo, Nicholas (Mexican gen.) 83
Brazos Santiago (Texas) 62, 63
Buchanan, James (U.S. sec. of state) 1, 5, 31, 32, 35, 37, 39, 40, 41, 43, 47, 48, 56, 59, 70, 72, 73, 81, 83, 85, 87–89, 91, 92, 95, 96, 99, 105, 106, 113, 115, 118, 125, 126, 130, 131, 133, 143–145, 147, 150, 152, 153, 155, 156, 158, 164, 165, 167–169, 176, 182, 188, 190, 194, 195
Buena Vista, Battle of 87, 88, 89, 184, 185
Butler, Anthony (U.S. chargé d'affaires in Mexico) 18, 19, 29, 99

228 INDEX

Butler, Maj. Gen. William O. (U.S.) 84, 165, 167, 171, 188

Cadwalader, Brig. Gen. George (U.S.) 101, 102, 110, 111, 159
Calhoun, John C. (U.S. sen., U.S. sec. of state) 10, 28, 29, 31, 59, 74, 194, 195, 196
California 22, 26, 27, 29, 49, 50–53, 65, 70, 74–79, 82, 89, 94, 95, 117, 119, 120, 129, 132, 151, 152, 155, 156, 174, 181, 193, 197, 198
Carson, Kit 79
Cass, Lewis (U.S. senator) 82
Cerro Gordo, Battle of 91, 94, 98, 126, 139
Chapultepec, castle of 114, 115, 121, 139
Chihuahua (Mexican state) 80, 153, 171, 195, 196
Childs, Lt. Col. Thomas (U.S.) 91, 97
Christopher, Warren (U.S. sec. of state) 65
Churubusco, Battle of 111, 112, 127
Civil War 11, 191, 192, 200
Claiborne, J.F.H. (biographer of Quitman) 191
Claims by Americans against Mexico 23, 24, 73, 77, 85, 178, 179
Clay, Henry (U.S. sec. of state, U.S. senator, Kentucky) 8, 18, 30, 31, 195, 199
Clifford, Nathan (U.S. atty. gen., commissioner to Mexico) 44, 127, 130, 173, 188
Coahuila (Mexican state) 171, 195, 196
Colorado River 152, 153, 155, 156, 176
Congress, Mexican 20, 32, 83, 87, 94–97, 99, 103–105, 117–119, 137, 140, 141, 144, 145, 149, 157, 159, 162, 164, 172, 175, 184, 185, 188, 198
Congress, U.S. 20, 23, 49, 56–58, 61, 64, 65, 69, 70–74, 82, 83, 85–87, 96, 97, 131, 133, 134, 146, 149, 164, 166, 167, 168, 170, 182, 183, 185, 189, 190, 197, 198, 199
Conner, Commodore David (U.S.) 64, 83
Contreras, Battle of 110, 111, 127, 138
Corpus Christi, Texas 39, 62, 66
Couto, Jose Bernardo (Mexican commissioner) 47, 116, 141, 149, 151, 163

Crittenden, John (U.S. senator, Kentucky) 88, 171, 196
Cross, Col. Trueman (U.S.) 66
Cuba 11–16, 65, 96
Cuevas, Luis G. (Mexican for. min., commissioner) 34, 35, 141, 142, 151, 163

Dallas, George M. (U.S. vice president) 44
Davis, Jefferson (U.S. senator, Mississippi) 165, 196
Delta, New Orleans 127, 138, 140, 143, 145, 169
Democrats 8, 31, 32, 39, 55, 70, 74, 84, 85, 93, 98, 189
De Tocqueville, Alexis (French writer) 10
Dimond, F. M. (U.S. consul, Vera Cruz) 84
Disturnell Map 152–154, 156, 174
Donelson, Andrew Jackson (U.S. chargé d'affaires in Texas) 6, 8, 9, 15, 33, 35, 36
Doniphan, Col. Alexander W. (U.S.) 80, 153
Doyle, Percy (British chargé d'affaires in Mexico) 95, 149, 160–162, 180
Drexler, Robert W. (biographer of Trist) 157

Eaton Affair 9
Elections, U.S. Presidential: 1828 8; 1844 30, 31, 98; 1848 199
Eliot, Charles (British min. to Texas) 34, 35
Eliott, Charles W. (biographer of Scott) 162
Ellis, Powhattan (U.S. min. to Mexico) 23, 49
El Paso, Texas 80, 152, 153, 154, 155, 181
El Peñon, fortress of 109, 110
Emory, Major William H. (U.S.) 152, 155, 156
Everett, Alexander 14, 15
Express, New York 172

Federalists, Mexican 18, 71
Fillmore, Millard (U.S. president) 180

Index

Forbes, James (British vice consul in California) 51
Forsyth, John (U.S. sec. of state) 20, 23
France 9, 15, 42, 70
Freaner, James L. (*Delta* correspondent in Mexico) 127, 143, 145, 146, 169, 170, 171, 187, 188
Fremont, Lt. Col. John Charles (U.S.) 50, 78, 79, 125
Fort Leavenworth, Kansas 78, 79
Fuller, John (historian) 192

Gadsden, James (U.S. diplomat) 196
Gadsden Purchase 127, 155, 176, 178, 180, 181
Gaines, Brig. Gen. Edmund (U.S.) 22
Garay, Antonio (Mexican businessman) 180
Gerolt, Baron (Prussian min. to U.S.) 39
Gila River 152, 153, 155, 156, 175, 176, 181
Gillespie, Capt. Archibald H. (U.S.) 78
Goliad, Texas 21, 25
Gomez Farias (Mexican vice president) 87
Gorostiza, Manuel (Mex. min. to U.S.) 22
Grant, Lt. Ulysses S. (U.S.) 64, 109, 112, 162, 188, 190, 191
Great Britain 12–14, 16, 26, 27, 29, 30, 31, 34, 35, 49, 51, 52, 54, 58, 59, 61, 69, 70, 72, 83, 84, 94, 95, 149, 150
Green, Benjamin (U.S. chargé d'affaires ad interim in Mexico) 31, 48
Green, Duff (editor, U.S. agent in England) 28
Greenhow, Robert (U.S. bearer of despatches to Mexico) 23
Gulf of California 153, 155, 156, 171, 176

Hannegan, Edward (U.S. senator, Indiana) 168
Hargous, D.A. (American banker in Mexico) 180
Harlingen, Texas 62

Harrison, William Henry (U.S. president) 27
Havana, Cuba 11–16
Hayne, Robert (U.S. senator, South Carolina) 10
Herald, New York 143, 172
Herrera, Gen. Jose Joaquin de (Mexican president) 32, 35, 47, 52, 58, 59, 69, 82, 103, 116, 119, 141, 173, 184, 198
Hitchcock, Lt. Col. Ethan Allen (U.S.) 66, 101, 103, 104, 105, 106
Houston, Sam (Texas general, pres. of Texas, U.S. sen.) 21, 25, 35, 171
Huamantla, Mexico 113

Indians 152, 177, 181, 194

Jackson, Andrew (U.S. president) 5, 8, 11, 15, 16, 18, 19, 20, 21, 22, 30, 35, 40, 42, 49, 51, 57, 80, 82
Jalapa, Mexico 57, 58, 91, 93, 94, 107, 149, 169, 195
Jefferson, Thomas (U.S. president) 5–8, 15, 16, 143
Johnson, Cave (U.S. postmaster gen.) 44
Jones, Anson (president of Texas) 34, 35, 37, 38
Jones, Commodore Thomas ap Catesby (U.S.) 26

Kearny, Brig. Gen. Stephen W. (U.S.) 78, 79, 81, 152, 155, 177
Kendall, George W. (*Picayune* correspondent in Mexico) 104, 122, 127, 128, 169, 172

La Branch, Alicee (U.S. chargé d'affaires in Texas) 22
Lafayette, Marquis de 7
Lake Chalco 105
Lamar, Mirabeau B. (president of Texas) 24
Lane, Brig. Gen. Joseph (U.S.) 137
Laredo, Texas 25, 38
Larkin, Thomas O. (U.S. consul, Monterey, Calif.) 50, 51, 53, 78

230   INDEX

Lee, Capt. Robert E. (U.S.) 109, 110, 111, 122, 156, 188
"Leonidas" letter 138, 139, 187
Linaeres, Mexico 195
Livingston, Edward (U.S. sec. of state) 10, 11
Los Angeles, Calif. 79
Louisiana Purchase 6, 9, 31

McCormac, Eugene (biographer of Polk) 49
Macintosh, Ewen (British consul general in Mexico) 97, 103, 104, 105, 106, 110, 113, 116, 122, 162, 180
Mackenzie, Commander Alexander Slidell (U.S.) 81–84
Madison, Mrs. Dolley 41
Madison, James (U.S. president) 5, 6, 8, 10, 11, 15, 16
Maine boundary 9, 80, 99
Manifest Destiny 192, 195
Marcy, William L. (U.S. sec. of war) 44, 56, 60, 65, 72, 79, 80, 81, 84, 91, 92, 102, 103, 125, 128, 130, 132, 133, 139, 158, 165, 167, 168
Marshall, Brig. Gen. Thomas (U.S.) 160
Mason, John Y. (U.S. sec. of the navy) 44, 180
Matamoros, Mexico 62–69, 74, 75
Mayer, Brantz (U.S. diplomat in Mexico) 123
Meade, Lt. George C. (U.S.) 63, 64
Mejia, Brig. Gen. Francisco (Mexico) 44
Merk, Frederick (historian) 53, 194
Messila Valley, New Mexico 154, 175, 176
Mexican army 67, 68
Mexico City 81, 84, 85, 92, 94–96, 101, 105–109, 112, 113, 132, 133, 134, 138, 139, 189, 193
Mexican commisioners 34, 35, 47, 116, 119, 120, 121, 133, 141, 142, 144, 146, 149, 151, 159, 160, 162, 161, 163, 165
Mexican Constitution of 1824   17, 21, 83, 96, 104, 137, 141
Mier, Mexico 25, 63
Moderados 32, 141
Molino del Rey, Battle of 12, 122
Monarchists 57, 69, 70, 71, 83, 119, 140

Monclava, Mexico 195
Monroe, James (U.S. president) 17
Monroe Doctrine 70
Monterey, Calif. 26, 78, 79, 116, 155, 174
Monterrey, Mexico 81, 84, 113
Monticello 5–7
Mora y Villamil, Brig. Gen. Ignacio (Mexico) 113, 114, 116, 117, 141

Nacodoches, Texas 22
Natchez, Mississippi 5
National Era, Washington 132
National Whig, Washington 132
New Mexico 17, 29, 53, 65, 76, 77, 78, 89, 118, 119, 120, 129, 131, 148, 151–155, 175, 176, 196
New Orleans, Louisiana 6, 8, 64, 126, 127, 188
North American, Mexico City 105, 140, 142, 143, 158, 159
Nueces River 18, 37, 39, 62, 63, 69, 71, 74, 89, 117, 118, 120, 129, 131, 148, 151, 166
Nuevo Leon (Mexican state) 176, 195, 196
Nullification, crisis and proclamation 8, 10, 11, 16, 80, 144

Oregon 50, 58, 59, 61, 65, 70, 71, 72
Orizaba, Mexico 91

Pacheco, Jose M. (Mexican maj. gen., for. min.) 113, 114, 115, 116, 119
Padre Island, Texas 44, 65
Palo Alto, Battle of 75
Pakenham, Richard (British min. to Mexico, U.S.) 51, 58
Parades y Arrillaga, Mariano (Mexican gen., president of Mexico) 32, 39, 56, 57, 60, 64, 65, 67, 69, 70, 71, 75, 81, 82, 100, 119, 133, 173, 184, 198
Parrott, William S. (U.S. agent in Mexico) 34, 35, 47, 48, 56
Patterson, Maj. Gen. Robert (U.S.) 84
Payments to Mexican officials and legislators 19, 20, 96–102, 159, 164
Pedregal 110, 111

Index 231

Peña y Peña, Manuel (Mexican for. min., president of Mexico) 137, 141, 142, 146, 153, 157, 162, 165, 173
El Penon, fortress 105
Perote, fortress 94
Perry, Commodore Matthew (U.S.) 179
Philadelphia 5, 8, 190
Picayune, New Orleans 127, 128, 169, 172
Pierce, Brig. Gen. Franklin (U.S.) 97, 107, 115, 190
Pillow, Maj. Gen. Gideon J. (U.S.) 97–103, 106, 108, 128, 138, 139, 164, 165, 167, 182, 187
Pletcher, David (historian) 53, 87, 185, 192
Poinsett, Joel (U.S. min. to Mexico) 18, 34, 49
Polk, James K. (U.S. president) 1–3, 22, 30, 31, 33, 36, 38, 39, 41, 42, 44–46, 48, 52–61, 64, 65, 70–89, 92, 99, 100, 114, 120, 124–133, 138, 139, 145, 147, 149, 159, 165, 169, 170, 171, 180, 182–86, 198, 199
Polk, William (brother of James K. Polk) 80, 167, 173
Point Isabel, Texas 62, 67, 74
Public Ledger, Philadelphia 132
Puebla, Mexico 94, 96, 97, 107, 111, 126, 137, 139, 164
Puros 141, 147, 150, 157, 162

Queretaro, Mexico 130, 133, 137, 141, 145, 149, 158–162, 165, 173, 198
Quitman, Maj. Gen. John A. (U.S.) 101, 102, 108, 115, 122, 139, 193

Randolph, Martha Jefferson (daughter of Thomas Jefferson) 6, 8, 10
Randolph, Thomas Jefferson (grandson of Thomas Jefferson) 6, 7, 190
Randolph, Thomas Mann (son-in-law of Thomas Jefferson) 6
Refugio, Texas 25
Remini, Robert V. (biographer of Jackson) 20
Rejon, Manuel C. (Mexican gen., for. min.) 83, 84, 119, 173
Republican, St. Louis 164
Resaca de la Palma, Battle of 75

Riley, Brig. Gen. Bennett (U.S.) 110, 111
Rincon, Gen. Manuel (Mexico) 111, 112, 141, 151
Rio Frio (mountains and pass, Mexico) 94, 99, 108, 169
Rio Grande River (El Norte) 18, 24–26, 36, 37–39, 55, 57, 59–68, 71–77, 79–81, 89, 117–120, 129, 131, 132, 146, 147, 151–155, 166, 176, 180, 183, 195, 197
Ritchie, Thomas (editor) 50
Rives, George Lockhart (historian) 193
Rosa, Luis de la (Mexican for. min.) 103, 140, 157, 160–163

Sabine River 17, 22, 83
Salas, Brig. Gen. Jose M. (Mexico) 83
Saligny, Count (French min. to Mexico) 34, 35
Saltillo, Mexico 21, 195
San Antonio, Mexico 110, 111, 113
San Antonio, Texas 21, 24, 25, 80
San Augustin, Mexico 110, 111, 113
San Diego, Calif. 78, 79, 155–157, 174, 181
San Francisco, Calif. 78, 79, 120, 171, 174
San Jacinto, Battle of 21, 23
San Juan de Ulua, fortress of 84
San Luis Potosi, Mexico 56, 198
San Pasqual, Calif. 79
Santa Anna, Antonio Lopez de (Mexican gen., president of Mexico) 2, 19, 22, 25, 32, 37, 70, 71, 81–84, 86, 87, 91–98, 100, 101, 103–106, 109, 110, 113–124, 126, 128, 130, 131, 133, 137, 138, 141, 164, 165, 184, 198
Santa Fe, New Mexico 24, 78, 79, 117, 152
Santa Fe Expedition 24, 25, 128
Santa Fe Trail 78, 152
Schroeder, John H. (historian) 53
Scott, Maj. Gen. Winfield (U.S.) 76, 80, 85, 87, 91, 92, 94, 96–98, 100–105, 108–114, 117, 118, 120–123, 125, 127, 128, 130, 138, 139, 143, 145, 146, 149, 158–162, 164–168, 187, 188, 190, 194, 197
Sellers, Charles (biographer of Polk) 37, 38, 47, 185
Seminole War 80

Sevier, Ambrose (U.S. senator, Arkansas, commissioner to Mexico) 168, 171, 173, 188
Shannon, Wilson (U.S. min. to Mexico) 32, 35
Sherman, Gen. Sidney (Texas) 36
Shields, Brig. Gen. James (U.S.) 101, 102, 111
Sierra Madre mountains 140, 194–196, 198
Slave trade 12–15
Slavery issues 20, 27, 32, 68, 86, 144, 185, 195, 196–199, 200
Slidell, John (appointed U.S. min. to Mexico) 47, 48, 52, 53, 55–57, 60, 61, 64, 65, 70–72, 75, 88, 183, 184, 185
Sloat, Commodore John D. (U.S.) 50, 53, 78, 79
Smith, Asbel (sec. of state of Texas) 28, 34
Smith, Justin (historian) 42, 68, 118, 178, 192
Smith, Brig. Gen. Persifor F. (U.S.) 97, 110, 111, 115, 140
Sonoma, Calif. 79
Sonora (Mexican state) 153, 195
Soto, Miguel E. (historian) 69
Spain 1, 11, 14, 17, 31, 70, 96, 143, 152
State Department, U.S. 8–10, 40, 41, 45, 96, 99, 182
Stockton, Commodore Robert F. (U.S.) 36, 79
Sun, Baltimore 127, 132, 164
Sun, New York 132

Tacubaya, Mexico 110, 114–116, 122
Tamaulipas (Mexican state) 195, 196
Tampico, Mexico 171
Taylor, Maj. Gen. Zachary (U.S.) 36, 40, 50, 54–56, 58–60, 62–69, 71–75, 79, 81, 84, 87, 100, 167, 183, 197
Tehuantepec, Isthmus of 86, 89, 103, 105, 179, 180
Texas 2, 6, 9, 17–22, 24, 27, 29, 32, 33, 50, 53, 56, 59–61, 72, 74, 78, 89, 117, 119, 120, 131, 151, 152, 170, 171, 176, 181, 183
Thompson, Waddy (U.S. min. to Mexico) 24, 26, 28, 34, 59

Thornton, Edward (British diplomat in Mexico) 95–99, 103–106, 109, 113, 118, 141, 142, 144–146, 149
Thornton, Capt. Seth (U.S.) 67, 73–75
Times, Boston 132
Toluca, Mexico 159
Tornel, Jose Maria (Mexican gen., min. of war) 69, 119
Trade issues 8, 9, 11, 26
Treaty of Guadalupe Hidalgo: description and evaluation 65, 174–181, 199; negotiation 113–121, 151–163; ratification 169–173, 188, 189
Trist, Eliza (grandmother of Nicholas P. Trist) 5, 6
Trist, Hore Browse (brother of Nicholas P. Trist) 6
Trist, Hore Browse (father of Nicholas P. Trist) 5, 6
Trist, Dr. Hore Browse (son of Nicholas P. Trist) 10, 15, 190
Trist, Martha Jefferson (daughter of Nicholas P. Trist) 7, 190
Trist, Mary Brown (mother of Nicholas P. Trist) 5, 6
Trist, Nicholas Philip (U.S. peace commissioner in Mexico): at Monticello with Jefferson 7–8; characteristics 15–16; chief clerk, U.S. State Department 40, 41, 53, 83, 87; clerk at State Department 8–10; commisioner, appointed to Mexico 89, 90; decides to ignore recall 133, 138, 139, 142–150, 166–168; efforts to "purchase a peace" 100–102, 164, 165; evaluation and assessment 189, 191–200; family and early life 5–7; feud with General Scott 91–94, 97, 118, 125, 126; first negotiations with Mexicans 113–121, 180, 185; in battles of August 19 and 20 122, 123; later life 187–191; negotiates peace treaty 151–153, 155, 159–161, 163, 178–180; opposes nullifiers 10, 11; Polk's reactions to his treaty 165–166, 172, 177, 184; recalled by Polk 125–131; seeks British assistance 94, 95, 99; temporary secretary to Pres. Jackson 9, 19; U.S. consul, Havana 11–15, 20
Trist, Thomas Jefferson (son of Nicholas P. Trist) 8, 121

Trist, Virginia Randolph (wife of Nicholas P. Trist) 6, 11, 12, 147, 157
Tubac, Arizona 153
Turnbull, Mr. (British merchant) 97, 106, 117
Tuscon, Arizona 152, 153
Twiggs, Brig. Gen. David E. (U.S.) 101, 102, 108, 110, 111, 165, 169
Tyler, John (U.S. president) 15, 24, 27, 32, 33, 99, 100

Union, Washington 125, 128, 138, 140, 142
United States Magazine and Democratic Review 135
University of Virgnia 7, 8
Upshur, Abel (U.S. sec. of state) 27–29
U.S. Army 68, 80

Valencia, Gen. Gabriel (Mexico) 105, 110, 111
Valley of Mexico 94, 105, 107, 108, 122, 123, 149
Van Buren, Major Abraham (U.S.) 116
Van Buren, Martin (U.S. sec. of state, president) 5, 8, 12, 13, 15, 23, 24, 30, 31, 195
Van Deusen, Glyndon (biographer of Jackson) 192
Vega, Brig. Gen. Romulo Diaz de la (Mexico) 44, 45, 65
Vera Cruz, Mexico 64, 82–85, 88, 89, 91, 93, 94, 102, 107, 119, 126, 137, 149, 165, 166, 169, 184, 185, 195
Victoria, Mexico 195
Vomito (Yellow Fever) 195, 197

Walker, Robert J. (U.S. sec. of the treasury) 43, 87, 127, 165, 168, 179, 182, 195
War with Mexico: causes 67, 68, 73, 75, 76; U.S. objectives 77, 80, 85, 127, 134, 138, 142, 167, 183
Webster, Daniel (U.S. senator, Massachusetts; sec. of state) 7, 10, 15, 27, 99, 171, 195
West Point 6–8, 17, 108, 143
Whigs 15, 49, 54, 55, 70, 74, 80, 82, 85, 87, 118, 126, 131, 139, 164–167, 171, 172, 182, 183, 189, 193, 199
Whistler, Colonel William (U.S.) 66
Wickliffe, Charles A. (U.S. agent in Texas) 36, 37
Wilcox, Cadmus (aide to Quitman) 108
Wilmont, David (U.S. rep., Pennsylvania) 82
Wilmont Proviso 82, 86, 144
Wright, Dr. (naval surgeon) 37
Wright, Silas (governor of New York) 89, 93
Woll, Gen. Adrian (Mexico) 25
Wool, Brig. Gen. John E. (U.S.) 79
Worth, Brig. Gen. William J. (U.S.) 62, 63, 65, 66, 94, 96, 108, 111, 122, 123, 138, 139, 165, 167

Yell, Archibald (U.S. conf. agent in Texas) 36

Zacatecas, Mexico 198